体育英语专业系列教材

总主编 田 慧

英语听说教程

ENGLISH LISTENING AND SPEAKING COURSE

（第二册）

主　　编：王秋雨
副 主 编：孙曙光　袁　哲
编　　委（以姓氏笔画为序）：
　　　　　王卓君　王秋雨　孙曙光　袁　哲　崔珣丽
审　　校：田　慧　Vera Lee

北京大学出版社
PEKING UNIVERSITY PRESS

图书在版编目(CIP)数据

英语听说教程. 2 / 田慧总主编. —北京：北京大学出版社，2009.3
(体育英语专业系列教材)
ISBN 978-7-301-14493-0

Ⅰ. 英… Ⅱ. 田… Ⅲ. 体育—英语—听说教学—高等学校—教材　Ⅳ. H319.9

中国版本图书馆 CIP 数据核字 (2009) 第 019201 号

书　　　名：	英语听说教程（第二册）
著作责任者：	田　慧　总主编
责 任 编 辑：	徐万丽
标 准 书 号：	ISBN 978-7-301-14493-0/H·2130
出 版 发 行：	北京大学出版社
地　　　址：	北京市海淀区成府路 205 号　100871
网　　　址：	http://www.pup.cn
电　　　话：	邮购部 62752015　发行部 62750672　编辑部 62765014　出版部 62754962
电 子 邮 箱：	xuwanli50@yahoo.com.cn
印 刷 者：	北京宏伟双华印刷有限公司
经 销 者：	新华书店
	787毫米×1092毫米　16 开本　18.5 印张　423 千字
	2009 年 3 月第 1 版　2020 年 9 月第 2 次印刷
定　　　价：	39.00 元（配有光盘）

未经许可，不得以任何方式复制或抄袭本书之部分或全部内容。
版权所有，侵权必究　举报电话：010-62752024
电子邮箱：fd@pup.pku.edu.cn

前言

从2002年开始,国内的体育院校纷纷开设了体育英语专业,培养在体育领域从事对外交流工作的国际体育人才。经过五年多的发展,体育英语专业既显示出强大的生机和活力,又面临着诸多困难,首要的问题就是教材问题。目前,体育英语专业大多在技能类课程,特别是基础阶段课程中沿用了全国统编英语专业教材。这些教材选材精当、设计合理,对夯实学生语言基本功起到了巨大作用。但是体育英语专业有其专业的特色,因此,从2004年开始,我们就着手策划编写一套供体育英语专业学生使用的系列教材,并于2007年获得北京市高等教育精品教材立项。此系列教材包括基础阶段的《综合英语教程》、《英语听说教程》、《英语阅读教程》和高级阶段的《体育英语阅读》等,首批推出的是基础阶段的《综合英语教程》和《英语听说教程》。

经教育部批准的《高等学校英语专业英语教学大纲》指出:英语专业学生应具有扎实的语言基本功、宽广的知识面、一定的相关专业知识、较强的能力和较高素质。基础阶段的各教程正是按照这一培养目标编写的,立足于加强学生语言基本功,在培养语言基本功的同时渗透体育元素、人文精神,以提高学生的体育知识水平和人文素养,并在设计中力图培养学生的跨文化交际能力和独立思维能力。同时,本系列教材的一个突出特点是将各门课程的同一单元统一于一个话题,学生在"综合英语"、"英语阅读"、"英语听说"课程中同步围绕一个话题进行不同的技能训练,也使得他们能从不同角度认识同一问题。

《英语听说教程》共4册,本书为第二册,内有12个单元。每单元的主题与《综合英语教程》的主题相同,但内容的取材原则体现不同的重点。每单元分为听说两大模块,听力部分计划用5个学时完成,口语部分计划用两个学时完成。本教程听说一体,学习者在接受了大量的相关话题的信息输入后,可以对此话题进行讨论。

听力材料的选择以短小精悍、难度适中的国外原版材料为主,兼顾材料的多样性、信息性、知识性和趣味性及语言的真实性与实用性,避免枯燥,每次课都有新的内容,有效地避免了各门课程脱节。

本教程强调多种目的听说训练,以便学习者适应不同内容、不同形式的英语。整册书中编排有英语对话、访谈、故事、文章、报告、讲座以及演讲等内容。为了提高学生的新闻英语听力的能力,每单元有3条新闻听力,并配有练习。与第一册相比,第二册适当增加了体育题材和体育新闻英语的比重,力求在为学生打下扎实的英语听力基本技能基础的同时,渗透体育专业英语,为学生以后的专业发展打下基础。

编纂过程中,北京体育大学外语系的外籍专家 Vera Lee 和 Maggie Carey 先后改写并审校了课文与练习,并且提出了宝贵意见,在此谨表谢忱。教程选材过程中,我们参阅了大量英美国家的报纸杂志、教科书,以及部分网络资源,对一些文章进行了选编,特此向原作者们致以诚挚的谢意。

北京体育大学外语系承担了本教程的编写工作。由于经验和水平有限,书中疏漏及不妥之处在所难免,敬请使用本教程的师生批评指正。

编者

2008 年 11 月

目 录

Unit 1　Family 1

Listening
Part I　　Dialogue 2
Part II　　Remember, We're Raising Children, Not Flowers! 3
Part III　　Stay-at-Home Dads 5
Part IV　　A Moving Story About FAMILY 7
Part V　　News 8

Speaking
Part I　　Pronunciation Practice 9
Part II　　Speaking Activities 10
Part III　　Situational Dialogue: Making Invitations 13

Unit 2　Jobs 17

Listening
Part I　　Dialogue 18
Part II　　Job Interviews—Selling Yourself 19
Part III　　Sports Manager 22
Part IV　　The Commencement Address at Stanford 24
Part V　　News 25

Speaking
Part I　　Pronunciation Practice 26
Part II　　Speaking Activities 27
Part III　　Situational Dialogue: Job Interviews 29

Unit 3   Business   33

Listening

Part I	Dialogue	34
Part II	Students Carve Out Early Careers in Business	35
Part III	Seven Principles of Admirable Business Ethics	37
Part IV	Listening for Numbers	39
Part V	News	41

Speaking

Part I	Pronunciation Practice	43
Part II	Speaking Activities	44
Part III	Situational Dialogue: Making Offers	45

Unit 4   Music   49

Listening

Part I	Dialogue	50
Part II	Fighting Music Piracy on College Campuses	51
Part III	Music at Sporting Events	54
Part IV	The Symphony: A Microcosm of Life	56
Part V	News	57

Speaking

Part I	Pronunciation Practice	58
Part II	Speaking Activities	59
Part III	Situational Dialogue: Likes and Dislikes	61

Unit 5   Disasters   65

Listening

Part I	Dialogue	66
Part II	Tsunami Wounds Still Fresh in Indonesia One Year Later	68
Part III	The Nature of Disasters	70
Part IV	Chinese Find Strength and Hope in Earthquake Rubble	72
Part V	News	74

Speaking

Part I	Pronunciation Practice	76
Part II	Speaking Activities	77
Part III	Situational Dialogue: Disappointment and Encouragement	79

Unit 6   Legends and Myths 83

Listening

Part I	Dialogue	84
Part II	Noah and Nü Wa	85
Part III	Great American Myths	87
Part IV	Athena, Arachne, and the Weaving Contest	88
Part V	News	90

Speaking

Part I	Pronunciation Practice	92
Part II	Speaking Activities	93
Part III	Situational Dialogue: Possibility and Impossibility	96

Unit 7   Shopping 99

Listening

Part I	Dialogue	100
Part II	Ten Steps to Smarter Food Shopping	101
Part III	Online Shopping—An Increasing Trend	104
Part IV	Listening for Signal Words	106
Part V	News	107

Speaking

Part I	Pronunciation Practice	109
Part II	Speaking Activities	110
Part III	Situational Dialogue: Shopping	111

Unit 8   Women Around the World 115

Listening

Part I	Dialogue	116
Part II	Meet the Power Sisters	117
Part III	Women Struggle for Their Rights	120
Part IV	All Women Are Born for Loving	122
Part V	News	123

Speaking

Part I	Pronunciation Practice	125
Part II	Speaking Activities	125
Part III	Situational Dialogue: Making Comparisons	128

Unit 9   Travel 131

Listening
Part I	Dialogue	132
Part II	Travel Smart: Dollars and Sense	133
Part III	The Experience of Travelling and Learning	135
Part IV	Life Is a Journey	137
Part V	News	139

Speaking
Part I	Pronunciation Practice	140
Part II	Speaking Activities	141
Part III	Situational Dialogue: Buying Tickets	143

Unit 10   Famous People 147

Listening
Part I	Dialogue	148
Part II	The Greatest Individual Athletic Achievements	150
Part III	A Great Scientist	152
Part IV	Guessing Vocabulary from Context	154
Part V	News	156

Speaking
Part I	Pronunciation Practice	157
Part II	Speaking Activities	158
Part III	Situational Dialogue: Getting Information	160

Unit 11   Health 165

Listening
Part I	Dialogue	166
Part II	Vitamin D	167
Part III	Health Issues for College Students	169
Part IV	Color Affects Your Moods and Health	172
Part V	News	173

Speaking
Part I	Pronunciation Practice	174
Part II	Speaking Activities	175
Part III	Situational Dialogue: Describing Moods and Feelings	177

Unit 12   Memories 181

Listening
Part I   Dialogue 182
Part II   Sporting Memory—Jordan Hits "The Shot" 184
Part III   Five Ways to Improve Your Memory 187
Part IV   How to Improve News Listening 188
Part V   News 190

Speaking
Part I   Pronunciation Practice 191
Part II   Speaking Activities 192
Part III   Situational Dialogue: Interrupting 195

Keys 198

Transcript 229

Unit 1 Family

Overview

- **Listening**
    - Part I   Dialogue
    - Part II   Remember, We're Raising Children, Not Flowers!
    - Part III Stay-at-Home Dads
    - Part IV   A Moving Story About FAMILY
    - Part V   News

- **Speaking**
    - Part I   Pronunciation Practice
    - Part II   Speaking Activities
    - Part III Situational Dialogue: Making Invitations

- **Skills**
    Talking About the Changing Roles of Families
    Learning Expressions Used in Making Invitations

- **Language Focus**
    Participle Clauses

Listening

Part I Dialogue

Word List

collectivism	individualism	go out of one's way	self-reliance
meddle in	let go	rewarding	make it on one's own
doom	Confucius		

A *You are going to hear a dialogue about the differences between Chinese and American way of life. Before listening, discuss the questions below.*

1. What are some differences between Chinese and American family structures?
2. How are their concepts about family different?

B *Now listen to the dialogue and fill in the chart below.*

	China	America
Society based on		
Families in general	close	
Parents' role		
When children become adults		
Parents are proud of	/	

C *Listen to the dialogue again and write T (true), F (false) or NG (not given) beside the following statements.*

(   ) 1. There aren't many kids in America who will let their parents tell them what to do.

(   ) 2. Most American parents don't really care about their kids and they just let them go their own way.

(   ) 3. Chinese children prefer their parents interfere with their personal affairs.

(   ) 4. American parents express their love of family in a different way from Chinese parents.

(   ) 5. Chinese culture and American culture are so different that sometimes there is culture shock when people from the two countries meet.

Unit 1 Family

Part II Remember, We're Raising Children, Not Flowers!

Word List

mower	level	pane	shatter
destruction	slippery	veritable	give sb. a lecture
puddle	clean up	make a mess	restore
sponge	mop	renowned	remark

A *Listen to the first part of the passage and fill in the blanks.*

One day when David taught his seven-year-old son Kelly how to push the ___(1)___ around the yard, Kelly pushed it right through the ___(2)___ at the ___(3)___ of the lawn. David began to ___(4)___ when he saw what had happened since he had put a lot of ___(5)___ and ___(6)___ into making the flowers the ___(7)___ of the neighbours.

As he began to ___(8)___ to his son, his wife Jan reminded him how important it is as a parent to remember their ___(9)___. Kids and their ___(10)___ are more important than any physical object. The flowers are already dead. Parents should not add to the ___(11)___ by breaking a child's spirit and ___(12)___ his sense of ___(13)___.

B *Now listen to the second part of the passage and choose the best answer.*

1. The scientist was more creative than the average person because _____ when he was about two years old.
   A. his mom taught him how to do the experiment
   B. he learned an important lesson from his mom
   C. he learned how to do things effectively
   D. he showed his talent

2. When the scientist's mother saw the milk on the floor, she _____.
   A. yelled at him   B. gave him a lecture
   C. didn't lose her temper   D. punished him

3. Which of the following statements is NOT true?

   A. The little boy spilled the milk all over the kitchen floor.

   B. The little boy played in the milk for a few minutes.

   C. The little boy went to the back yard to play afterwards.

   D. The little boy could carry a big water bottle with two tiny hands.

4. The little boy chose _____ to clean up the spilled milk.

   A. a sponge   B. a towel

   C. a mop   D. tissue paper

5. The famous scientist learned the following EXCEPT _____.

   A. he didn't have to be afraid to make mistakes

   B. he should be very careful when doing any experiment

   C. mistakes were opportunities for learning something new

   D. even though an experiment is not successful, he can still learn something from it

 The passages you just heard are based on two parenting incidences. *With your group, discuss the following questions.*

> 1. *What does "We're raising children, not flowers" imply? Do you agree with the statement?*
> 2. *What was the most important lesson you learned from your parents?*
> 3. *What role does family education play in a child's upbringing? Use examples to support your view(s).*

 Language Focus: Participle Clauses

Participles can combine with other words into participle clauses. We often use participle clauses after nouns in order to define or identify the nouns. Past participle clauses are often very much like relative clauses with a passive verb. For example:

The window pane **shattered by a baseball**, a lamp **knocked over by a careless child**, or a plate **dropped in the kitchen** are already broken. (= The window pane which was shattered by a baseball, a lamp which was knocked over by a careless child, or a plate which was dropped in the kitchen, are already broken.)

We often use a present participle clause instead of a defining relative clause with an active verb. For example:

I saw a girl **standing at the gate**. (= I saw a girl who was standing at the gate.)

The books **lying on the table** are mine. (=The books that are lying on the table are mine.)

Rewrite the following sentences using the information in brackets to make participle clauses. The first one is already done for you.

1. I was woken up by a bell. (The bell was ringing.)
   <u>I was woken up by a bell ringing.</u>
2. We saw trees. (The trees were laden with fruits.)
3. The child is John. (He is sitting in that corner.)
4. Most of the people didn't turn up. (They were invited to the party.)
5. The road repairs might delay traffic. (They are carried out on the motorway.)
6. The decisions will affect all of us. (It was made at today's meeting.)
7. At the end of the street there is a path. (The path leads to the river.)

Part III Stay-at-Home Dads

Word List

prior to	vest	blow sth. out of the water	nurturing
court	passionate	better end of the deal	trade up
quadruple	parenting	practicality	bond
daycare	subcontract	juggle	compromise

 A **Dictation.** *Listen to the following short passage and write down what you hear.*

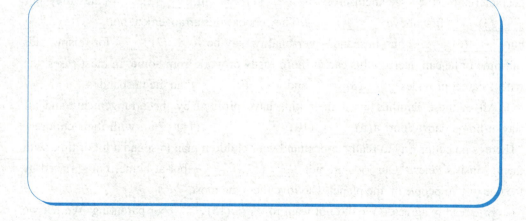

B *You are going to hear a passage about stay-at-home dads. Before listening, discuss the following questions with a partner.*

1. Quickly write down five words that relate to the word *mother*. Do the same for *father*.

Compare your word lists. How are they similar or different?

2. When you were a child, who looked after or took care of you? How often did you spend time with your father? What kinds of things did you do together?

3. How do you think being a father today differs from fatherhood twenty or thirty years ago?

C *Now listen to the first part of the passage and write T (true), F (false) or NG (not given) beside the following statements.*

(   ) 1. When Eric and Jody were studying in graduate school, they didn't discuss who would stay at home to take care of the kids in the future.

(   ) 2. Jody made more money than Eric, so it was an easy decision for Eric to stay at home.

(   ) 3. Eric and Jody have three boys in all.

(   ) 4. Eric loves being a stay-at-home dad since he didn't like his engineer job.

(   ) 5. Nowadays, the number of stay-at-home dads is four times that in 1986.

D *Listen to the second part of the passage and fill in the blanks.*

Based on survey results by researcher Bob Frank, these families share common characteristics: they see themselves as ____(1)____ in ____(2)____, and they put ____(3)____ first above ____(4)____. They choose this arrangement not ____(5)____, but ____(6)____: the husband's personality may be ____(7)____ for raising kids full-time or he can interrupt his career more easily or work from home. In most cases, the wife's career provides ____(8)____ and ____(9)____ than the husband's.

All of these families insist their kids have profited by the arrangement, and all stay-at-home dads report a(n) ____(10)____, ____(11)____ with their children. "There's no better way to really understand your children than to spend a lot of time with them," insists Peter. "Our kids are not ____(12)____ —but at home, being raised by the one or two people on the planet who love them the most."

Eric readily agrees. "We did not want to ____(13)____ our parenting. We felt we could only do ____(14)____ things well—her work, my work, or raising our children. Maybe others can ____(15)____ all three priorities. We couldn't, and we didn't want to ____(16)____ our kids."

Part IV A Moving Story About FAMILY

 Listen to the story and retell it to your partner.

A man came home from work late, tired and irritated (恼怒的), to find his 5-year-old son waiting for him at the door.

SON: "Daddy, may I ask you a question?"

DAD: "Yeah sure. What is it?"

SON: "Daddy, how much do you make an hour?"

DAD: "That's none of your business. Why do you ask such kind of things?"

SON: "I just want to know that, Daddy. Please tell me, how much do you make an hour?"

DAD: "Well, if you must know, I make $20 an hour."

"Oh," the little boy replied, with his head down. Looking up, he asked, "Daddy, may I please borrow $10?"

The father was furious (暴怒的). "If the only reason you asked that is so you can borrow some money to buy a silly toy or some other nonsense (无价值的东西), then you march yourself straight to your room and go to bed immediately. Think about why you are so selfish. I don't work hard every day to come home to such childish behaviour."

After hearing that, the little boy quietly went to his room and shut the door. The man sat down and started to get even angrier about the little boy's question. How dare he ask such a question only to get some money.

After about an hour or so, the man had calmed down and started to think. He never really asked for money before. Maybe there was something he really needed to buy with that $10.

The man went to the little boy's room and opened the door. "Are you asleep, son?" he asked. "No, Daddy, I'm awake," replied the boy.

"I've been thinking, maybe I was too hard on (对……刻薄) you earlier," said the man. "You know, it's been a long day and I took out my anger on (把怒气发泄在) you. Here's the $10 you asked for." The little boy sat straight up, smiling. "Oh, thank you, Daddy!" he yelled. Then, reaching under his pillow he pulled out some crumpled up (变皱了的) bills.

Seeing that the boy already had money, the man started to get angry again. The little boy slowly counted out his money, then looked up at his father. "Why do you want more money if you already have some?" the father grumbled (抱怨). "Because I didn't have enough, but now I do," the little boy replied. "Daddy, I have $20 now. Can I buy an hour of your time? Please come home early tomorrow, I would like to have dinner with you."

So what is the moral of the story? Don't work too hard but spend more time with your children. And remember, FAMILY means (F)ather (A)nd (M)other (I) (L)ove (Y)ou!

B What did you learn from the story? Have you read or heard of any other family stories? Share them with your partner.

Part V News

Word List

payout	hard-court	descending	slate	fling
margin	streak	in a row	supremacy	tremendous
seed	showcase	tenacity	triumph	dazzling
ranking	drift	wild card	blistering	thrash
Grand Slam				

A Listen to the news report and choose the best answer to the following questions.

1. How much was the singles champions' prize money worth in 2007?
   A. $1 million   B. $1.2 million
   C. $1.4 million   D. $1.5 million

2. Which of the following statements is NOT true?
   A. The total prize money at the U.S. Open this year is $1 million more than that in 2007.
   B. The increase of the total prize money this year is larger than that in the previous year.
   C. The Grand Slam tournament begins in August.
   D. Federer was the winner of the summer series and the U.S. Open last year.

B Listen to the news item. Complete the news summary and answer the questions you hear.

1. The news item is about
   _____

2. a. WHO?
   _____

   b. WHAT?

c. HOW MANY?

_____

d. HOW LONG?

_____

C *Listen to the news report and fill in the blanks.*

Zheng Jie yesterday became the first Chinese singles player to get through to the ____(1)____ of a major tennis competition.

She beat ____(2)____ Nicole Vaidisova 6-2, 5-7, 6-1. The match was a ____(3)____ for her attacking style and her ____(4)____.

This is the latest ____(5)____ in what is turning out to be a ____(6)____ tournament for the 24-year-old. Zheng won the 2006 Wimbledon doubles competition with Yan Zi, but a(n) ____(7)____ stopped her from playing for the whole of 2007. Her ranking drifted to ____(8)____ but she entered Wimbledon this year on a(n) ____(9)____.

Then she astonished the crowd on ____(10)____ by beating top seed Ana Ivanovic in two sets.

So there is now a chance she will play in the final, which happens to be on her birthday. But before that can happen, she'll have to ____(11)____ Serena Williams. Williams is ____(12)____ this year, thrashing Agnieszka Radwanska in the ____(13)____ 6-4, 6-0.

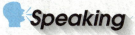

Speaking

Part I Pronunciation Practice

Listen to the following dialogue and imitate the recording. Pay attention to your pronunciation and intonation.

Tom and Maria bought a house last month. They don't have very much money. Maria is adding up all the money they spent on food and other things last week.

Maria: We spent £120 last week. £120! That's too much!
Tom: Er... that reminds me... did I tell you about the party?
Maria: Party? What party?

Tom: Well... er... you see, there's a tradition at the college. When a teacher there buys a house he has to... he has to...

Maria: "has to give a party"? Is that what you're going to say?

Tom: Yes, I'm afraid so. So we need some beer and wine and cheese for tomorrow evening.

Maria: What? Tomorrow evening! Why didn't you tell me this before?

Tom: Well... I suppose I forgot. I'm terribly sorry. I really am!

Maria: Oh, well, I suppose if we have to give a party, we have to. Anyway, we have some beer already.

Tom: Oh, how much?

Maria: At least a dozen bottles. Perhaps more than that.

Tom: How many? Only a dozen bottles? That's not enough.

Maria: What do you mean? How many people did you invite? Only three or four, I hope.

Tom: Er... more than that, actually. Now don't worry about the money.

Maria: What do you mean "Don't worry about the money?" Someone has to! You never worry about it! Now, how many teachers did you invite?

Tom: Well... naturally I had to invite all the teachers and not just some of them. I had to!

Maria: All the teachers? But how many teachers are there at the college?

Tom: Not many, really... only 35.

Maria: What? 35 teachers! Are you mad, Tom? It isn't just beer and cheese and wine we need! We need much more than that! Much more!

Tom: I don't understand, what do you mean?

Maria: We need a bigger house!

Part II Speaking Activities

 Key Sentence Patterns

Read aloud and memorize the following sentence patterns.

1. Family life is an important feature in nearly all societies.
2. In Britain, the basic social institution is the family unit. Certain aspects of home life in Britain differ from family customs in other countries.
3. I suppose family life has changed a lot in the last twenty years, hasn't it?
4. Families used to be much larger. My grandmother was one of fourteen children.
5. In the past, very few women took up careers outside of the home. They were too busy bringing up their families.

6. I think family life is much more pleasant today because it's freer and more informal.
7. Family life in the old days must have been very pleasant and secure.
8. Young people are given too much freedom and as a result, they've lost respect for their parents and the elderly.
9. My parents never interfered with my plans too much.
10. The living standard in one-child families is higher than in other families.

 Presentation and Discussion

1. Pair work. *Discuss the following questions with a partner.*
    (1) Describe the family in the photo above. How do you think the members are related?
    (2) How do you think the family unit has changed over the last twenty or fifty years? Do you think the changes have been positive or negative? Explain your answer.
    (3) How do you think the family unit will change in the future?
    (4) How many people are there in your family? If you have siblings, do you get along with them? Would you prefer to be an only child? If you are an only child, do you wish you had siblings? Why?
    (5) Do you think that only-child children tend to be lonely or more spoiled than those with siblings? Explain your answer.
    (6) Do most parents want to have sons or daughters? Why? Which do you prefer? Why?
    (7) What do you think of the one-child policy (or the birth control policy) in China?

2. Group discussion: Solving a Family Problem
    With your group, discuss and find solutions to the following problems and present them to the class.
Situation 1
    The woman's mother is a widow who lives alone in a large house she cannot afford to take care of. If she moves in with her daughter's family, her two granddaughters will have to share a room. The husband does not get along well with his mother-in-law. What can this

family do?

Situation 2

An eighteen-year-old daughter has decided to leave home. She wants to live in an apartment with a friend. Her parents do not want her to go. Their sixteen-year-old son wants to quit school and go to work and marry his girlfriend. The parents are really upset with their children. What can this family do?

Situation 3

A mother has returned to school to complete her education. She has a lot of studying to do, and she can't manage all the housework anymore. Her husband and her two teenaged children want her to be happy, but they don't like to do housework. What can they do?

Situation 4

A seventeen-year-old son has a twelve o'clock curfew. His parents want him home early at night. He thinks this is unreasonable because most of his friends do not have any curfew at all. His bedroom is always very messy. He seems to like it that way. What can they do?

C **Talk.** *Prepare a 2-minute talk on one of the following topics. You can jot down some ideas before speaking.*

1. Things I learned from my parents.
2. The effects of television on family life.
3. Children should/ shouldn't have limited freedom in the choice of friends, hobbies and careers.

D **Reflection.** *While television and other media have made it a practice to choose well-known celebrities as positive role models for kids, the majority of people still believe that parents should be the foremost role models for their children.*

Why should parents be the foremost role models for their children instead of celebrities?

What advice can you give parents who want to become better role models for their kids?

Unit 1 Family

Part III Situational Dialogue: Making Invitations

 Listen to the following dialogues and read after the recording.

Dialogue 1

(A knock at the door)

Gretchen: Good morning, Dr. Hampton. May I come in?

Dr. Hampton: Good morning, Gretchen. Of course. How can I be of help?

Gretchen: Well, it's not about school, Dr. Hampton. It's just that Alan and I wanted to have a few people over for a dinner party to celebrate me finishing my dissertation. We'd like to invite you especially since you're the chairman, and of course your wife as well. Would you be able to come the weekend after next, on Saturday?

Dr. Hampton: I'd be delighted to, Gretchen. Saturday, did you say?

Gretchen: If that's all right for you and Mrs. Hampton.

Dr. Hampton: I'll have to check with Elizabeth, but I'm pretty sure it'll be all right.

Gretchen: Good. If you could come around six-thirty or seven o'clock, that would give us time to chat a while over a glass of wine before dinner.

Dr. Hampton: That sounds fine. We'll be there around seven.

Gretchen: That would be great! I'm so pleased that you and Mrs. Hampton will be able to make it!

Dr. Hampton: Well, it should be fun. And you deserve it after all that hard work. But, say, Gretchen, will I have to start calling you *Doctor* Williams now?

Gretchen: Of course not, Dr. Hampton!

Dr. Hampton: Well, you can call me Henry then.

Gretchen: Of course, Dr... I mean, *Henry*—but it'll take some getting used to.

Dialogue 2

Susan: Hi! How are things going?

Troy: Fine, thanks. How about you?

Susan: Just fine. My husband and I are planning to go mountain climbing. You think you and your husband can come along? It'd be nice if you could.

Troy: Sounds great! What's the date?

Susan: Saturday morning, April third.

Troy: Oh, that's too bad. I'm busy then.

Susan: I'm so sorry. I wish you could come.

Troy: Can I take a rain check?

Susan: Sure. Let's plan to do something together another time.
Troy: OK. Thanks for the invitation though, Susan.

B *Practise the following expressions and sentence patterns used for making invitations and replying to them.*

Making an Invitation
- Want to come / pop over for... (dinner, a quick drink / snack...)?
- How about... (beer, coffee, dinner...)?
- We're going to... (a concert, a movie...). Do you fancy coming along?
- We're planning... (a dinner, a party...). It'll be nice to have you over.
- Are you free on...? Would you like / care to... ?
- We're going to have a few friends over on..., and we'd be very happy if you came.
- I was wondering if you'd like to..
- I'd like to invite you to... (dinner, a party...) next Friday.
- We would be very pleased / delighted if you could... (e.g. come and have dinner with us this evening)

Accepting an Invitation
- Sure. What time?
- Why not. When do you want me to be there?
- Sure. When should I be there?
- I'd like / love to. I'll bring... (e.g. dessert)
- Oh, certainly! Thank you.
- Thank you! I'd like / love to. Would you like me to bring anything?
- Thank you very much! I'd be delighted to. What time should I be there?
- That would be very nice / great.
- That sounds like a good idea.
- I'd like nothing better.
- It would be my honour.
- That's really very / most kind of you.
- With (the greatest of) pleasure.

Declining an Invitation
- Sorry, I can't / I don't think I can. I have to work. (But thanks anyway).
- Tonight's no good. I have an appointment.
- I'm busy tonight. Can I take a rain check on that?

- I'd love to, but... (e.g. I'm afraid I'm busy / I already have plans...) tonight.
- That's very kind of you, but...
- Thank you (very much) for asking me, but...
- I wish I could, but...
- As much as I would like to, I'm afraid I'm already booked up for that day.
- Much to my regret, ...
- Unfortunately, I ... (However, thank you for thinking of me.)

 Complete the following dialogues with the sentences provided.

▶ OK. Want me to bring something?
▶ Sure. Do I need to bring anything?
▶ Can I take a rain check?
▶ No, but thanks for asking.
▶ Oh, thank you! I'd be delighted to.
▶ No. Just bring yourself.
▶ Sure, why not.
▶ Tonight's no good.
▶ Want to pop over after work?
▶ My husband and I were just wondering if you would like to come over for dinner this evening.

Dialogue 1

Ann is inviting her colleague Jim over for a party.

Ann: Bob and I are having a little get-together at our place tonight. _____(1)_____
Jim: _____(2)_____ What time do you want me to be there?
Ann: Around 6:00.
Jim: _____(3)_____
Ann: _____(4)_____

Dialogue 2

Sam is inviting his friend Tom for dinner.

Sam: Want to come over for a quick meal tonight?
Tom: _____(5)_____ I have a date. _____(6)_____
Sam: OK. No problem. Enjoy your evening!
Tom: You too.

Dialogue 3

Jan is inviting her son's teacher, Mr. Brown, for dinner.

Jan: Hello Mr. Brown. _____(7)_____
Brown: _____(8)_____
Jan: Great! Could you come over at around 6:00?
Brown: _____(9)_____
Jan: _____(10)_____
Brown: OK. See you this evening then.

 A and B are both students in the same English class, but from different countries. They don't know each other very well, but A hopes that by inviting B out for dinner, they can become better acquainted.

A: [greets and invites B]
B: [accepts invitation]
A: [gives time and location]
B: [disagrees with the time, suggests alternate time]
A: [agrees, confirms exact location]
B: [expresses appreciation]
A: [anticipates meeting B later]

Unit 2 Jobs

Overview

- **Listening**
  - Part I   Dialogue
  - Part II   Job Interviews—Selling Yourself
  - Part III   Sports Manager
  - Part IV   The Commencement Address at Stanford
  - Part V   News

- **Speaking**
  - Part I   Pronunciation Practice
  - Part II   Speaking Activities
  - Part III   Situational Dialogue: Job Interviews

- **Skills**
  - Talking About Part-time Jobs
  - Getting Familiar with Job Interview Tips
  - Learning Expressions Used in Job Interviews

- **Language Focus**
  - Parody

Listening

Part I Dialogue

Word List

get accustomed to	housing office	distribute	leaflet
glamorous	intern	do sb. good	enrich
give it a shot			

A You are going to hear a dialogue about students' part-time jobs. Listen to the dialogue and fill in the table below.

Name	Work Place	Job Description	Working Hours/Pay
Dan			
Indian student			
John			/

B Listen to the dialogue again and answer the following questions with key words.

1. Who is Feifei?

2. What kind of jobs do British students usually do?

3. Why do students want to find part-time jobs in London?

Unit 2 Jobs

4. What can mass media majors do at a radio or TV station?
   _____

 In groups, discuss the following questions, giving examples where possible.

1. Have you had any part-time jobs? If so, what did you gain from them besides money?
2. If you want to work part-time, what do you want to do? Why?
3. Why do college students take on part-time jobs?
4. What jobs are suitable for English majors? Provide some ideas or suggestions.
5. Do you think that doing part-time jobs will interfere with your studies? Why or why not? How would you balance study and part-time jobs?

Part II   Job Interviews—Selling Yourself

Word List

outsider	cardinal	prospective	demeanor
stifle	refreshing	make the difference	applicant
pad	duck	figure out	go the extra mile
dress rehearsal	give sb. a shot		

 You are going to hear a passage about rules in job interviews. Listen to the passage and choose the best answer to complete each sentence.

1. In your job performance, you can _____ by selling yourself.
   A. earn a promotion   B. make yourself attractive
   C. enhance your earning power

2. In a job interview you should tell your future boss _____ .
   A. your educational background   B. your working experience
   C. your advantages over others
3. _____ can make the applicant outstanding if he/she displays it.
   A. Enthusiasm   B. Openness   C. Manners
4. It is extremely effective to _____ before the interview.
   A. write down your strong points on a yellow pad
   B. reflect on your past working experiences
   C. put yourself through a dress rehearsal of the interview
5. In a job interview, you'll have the best opportunity to _____ .
   A. learn more about the company or the boss
   B. show your intelligence
   C. display your initiative

B *Listen to the passage again. As you listen, fill in the missing information of the outline below.*

Introduction: Importance of selling yourself
Body: Four cardinal rules:
(1) Show what you can do for _____ .
    You should talk about your knowledge and skills—the _____ and _____ you have developed in your field and the abilities you have developed _____ .
(2) _____ .
    If you want to be successful, you need to show the quality of _____ .
    This is a _____ that employers don't always find in job interviews.
(3) _____ .
    Go over the _____ you want to make about yourself.
    Even _____ on a yellow pad and _____ them several times before the interview
(4) _____ .
    This shows you have two of the most _____ qualities:
    _____ , and _____ .

Listen again and decide what you should or should not do in a job interview. Put the letter(s) in the table below.

Dos	Don'ts

a. ask what your employer can do for you
b. tell them how you can do the job better than others
c. rehearse the interview with someone
d. avoid answering hard questions
e. show your enthusiasm for the job
f. what you can do for your employer
g. sell your features
h. tell the interviewers what's on your resume
i. ask questions about the company
j. prepare possible answers for interview questions
k. try to be business-like in your behaviors
l. sell your advantages

 In groups, discuss the following questions, giving examples where possible.

1. Of all the four rules mentioned in the passage, which one do you think is the most important? Why?
2. Have you ever experienced going through an interview? If so, what suggestions can you provide for others besides what were given in the recording? For example, how can one overcome nervousness?

 Language Focus: Parody

A parody in contemporary usage is a work created to mock, comment on, or poke fun at an original work, its subject, or author by means of humorous or satiric imitation. As a method of criticism, parody has been a very popular means for authors, entertainers and advertisers to communicate a particular message or point of view to the public.

For example, "Ask not what your employer can do for you, but what you can do for your employer" is a parody mocking President Kennedy's famous saying "Ask not what your country can do for you—ask what you can do for your country".

Another popular sentence that is often poked fun at is Shakespeare's "To be or not to be, that is the question". It can be paraphrased into different situations such as "To leave or not to leave", "To study or to play", "To eat or to do exercise", etc.

Now it's your turn to practice parodies. Translate the following sentences with the hints provided in the brackets (English to Chinese or Chinese to English).

1. Clearly, when it comes to marriage, practice beforehand doesn't make perfect. (Practice makes perfect.)
2. To do or not to do? The answer is a click away. (To be or not to be, that is the question.)
3. 在经济学方面,条条道路通向社会主义。(All roads lead to Rome.)
4. 并非所有的车都是生来平等的。(All men are created equal.)
5. 有遗嘱必有官司。(Where there's a will, there's a way.)

Part III Sports Manager

Word List

coordinate	away games	off-season	delicate
alienate	ritual	draft	scout
feasible	keep an eye on	factor into	give away
complimentary	slide into	streak	downfall
relocate	lateral	ownership	advancement

A **Dictation.** *Listen to the following short passage and write down what you hear.*

B *You are going to hear a passage about sports managers. Listen to the first part of the passage and choose the best answer to complete each sentence.*

1. As a sports manager, the most delicate aspect of the job is _____.
   A. to determine the most talented and economically feasible players
   B. to make deals that satisfy owners without alienating players
   C. to be subjected to both compliments and criticisms from the media

2. It is _____ who determine the player positions that the team needs.
   A. the sports managers   B. the coaches
   C. the sports managers, coaches and scouts
3. In the team's budget, _____ might lead to additional costs.
   A. attending press conferences
   B. buying equipment and uniforms
   C. the possible team success
4. For sports managers, they must be able to ignore _____.
   A. complimentary and critical press reports
   B. their intentions for the future
   C. a respected player's leaving
5. To work as a sports manager is a _____ job.
   A. highly paid   B. highly stressful
   C. highly satisfying

C *Listen to the first part of the passage again, and summarise the job responsibilities of sports managers. Write down the key words to finish the table below and then explain with details.*

Responsibilities of Sports Managers	1. 2. 3. ...

D *Now listen to the second part of the passage. Choose the status of sports managers at different stages by placing the letters in the right column under the appropriate stage in the left column.*

	a. high satisfaction
1. Two years out: _____	b. lateral moves
	c. partial ownership of the club
2. Five years out: _____	d. favourite pastimes
	e. new challenges
3. Ten years out: _____	f. financial rewards
	g. trust of the team owners and coaches
	h. presidency of the club
	i. involvement with the sport

Part IV The Commencement Address at Stanford

 A *Listen to the speech for appreciation.*

You've Got to Find What You Love
By Steve Jobs

This was delivered by the CEO of Apple Computer and of Pixar Animation Studios on June 12, 2005.

I am honored to be here at your commencement (毕业典礼). I never graduated from college. Truth be told, this is the closest I've gotten to a college graduation.

I found what I loved to do early in life. Woz and I started Apple in my parents' garage when I was 20. In 10 years, Apple had grown into a $2 billion company with over 4000 employees. We had just released our finest creation—the Macintosh—a year earlier, and then, I got fired. How can you get fired from a company you started? Well, as Apple grew we hired someone to run the company with me, and for the first year things went well. But then ideas began to diverge (分歧) and the Board of Directors sided with him. So at 30, the focus of my entire adult life was gone. It was devastating (毁灭性的).

It was a public failure. I didn't know what to do and even thought about running away from the valley. But then something began to dawn on me: the turn of events at Apple had not changed the fact that I still loved what I did. Though I had been rejected, I was still in love, and so I decided to start over.

During the next five years, I started a company named NeXT, and another company named Pixar. Pixar created the first computer animated (动画的) feature film, Toy Story, and is now the most successful animation studio in the world. In a remarkable turn of events, Apple bought NeXT, I returned to Apple, and the technology we developed at

NeXT is at the heart of Apple's current renaissance (新生).

This all wouldn't have happened if I hadn't been fired from Apple. Sometimes life hits you in the head with a brick. Don't lose faith. The one thing that kept me going was that I loved what I did. You've got to find what you love. The only way to be truly satisfied is to love what you do. If you haven't found it yet, keep looking, don't settle.

B *What do you think are some of the important factors in carving out one's career? What do you need to do to prepare before graduation?*

Part V News

Word List

gasoline	fancy	executive-branch	unprecedented
windfall	opt to	recruitment	bonus point
start-up	congestion	in a bid to	stagger
be exempt from			

A *Listen to the news report and fill in the blanks to the following statements.*

1. The aim of working four days per week is to _____.
2. "TGIT" means _____.
3. Government employees will work _____ per day. They will have the _____ as before.
4. The 4-day workweek will not involve people such as police officers, _____ _____ or _____ or Utah's _____.

B *Listen to the news and answer the following questions.*

1. Why do graduates this year face unprecedented pressure?

2. How many students have signed up to work in the countryside?

3. What are the favorable policies for students working in western and rural areas?

4. For students who start their own business, what is the government's policy?

_____

_____

C *Listen to the news report and choose the best answer to complete each sentence.*

1. From July 20th 2008, working hours in Beijing will be an hour later than normal to _____ .
   A. ease traffic jams and reduce pollution
   B. stagger office openings
   C. encourage people to work flexibly
   D. give people more time to relax

2. The following will have their working hours changed EXCEPT _____ .
   A. shopping malls   B. companies
   C. public institutions   D. Beijing Bus Corporation

3. Public institutions started work at _____ before July 20th.
   A. 9:00 a.m.   B. 8:30 a.m.
   C. 9:30 a.m.   D. 8:00 a.m.

4. Starting July 20, there will be many changes. For example, _____ .
   A. schools and administrative bodies will start working an hour later
   B. people will have flexible working hours and they can work from home
   C. cars with odd number plates will only be allowed on odd number dates
   D. factories and companies will be relocated to decrease air pollution

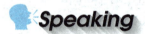Speaking

Part I Pronunciation Practice

Listen to the following story and imitate the recording. Pay attention to your pronunciation and intonation.

No Letter

A gentleman put an advertisement in a newspaper for a boy to work in his office. Out of the nearly fifty men who came to apply, the man selected one and dismissed the others.

"I should like to know," said a friend, "the reason you preferred that boy, who brought not a single letter—not a recommendation."

"You are wrong," said the gentleman. "He had a great many. He wiped his feet at the door and closed the door after him, indicating that he was careful. He gave his seat immediately to that old man, showing that he was kind and thoughtful. He took off his cap when he came in and answered my questions quickly, showing that he was polite and gentlemanly."

"All the rest stepped over the book which I had purposely put on the floor. He picked it up and placed it on the table; and he waited quietly for his run instead of pushing and crowding. As I talked to him, I noticed his tidy clothing, his neatly brushed hair and his clean fingernails. Can't you see that these things are excellent recommendations? I consider them more significant than letters."

Part II Speaking Activities

 Key Sentence Patterns

Read aloud and memorize the following sentences.

1. In my opinion, work is an essential part of life for all human beings.
2. People work for different reasons.
3. Some work for money; others work for love. Some work for self-fulfillment; others work for the contribution to the society.
4. The bottom line is that almost everyone works for money.
5. The ultimate goal of choosing a career is to find something that will make you happy.
6. If you're doing a job that you like, work itself can give you a feeling of satisfaction.
7. Interest is the best guide and the source of success.
8. Landing a well-paid job is what all job seekers dream of.
9. Frequent job change can maintain one's passion.
10. The top reason people leave their jobs is the inability to work with their manager.
11. I will quit the highly-paid job if it is against my personality.
12. I won't quit a job with a good salary. I have to support the family.

 Presentation and Discussion

1. In groups, discuss the reasons why people need to work. What can they get from their jobs? To earn money? To realize their dreams? Or to gain respect? Add them to the list below, and then choose the most important one to explain to the class.

No.	Reasons Why People Need to Work
1	Earn money
2	Support family
3	Gain respect
4	Realize dreams
5	
6	
7	
8	
9	
10	

2. What do you think will be tomorrow's most promising jobs? Add them to the list below and choose one you want to do in the future.

No.	Tomorrow's Most Promising Jobs
1	Medical technologists and technicians
2	Psychologists
3	Educators, university professors
4	
5	
6	
7	
8	
9	
10	

C Talk. *Prepare a 2-minute talk describing your* **working experience.** *You can share your part-time job story with your classmates. If you don't have any working experience, you can also make a plan for your* **work in the future.** *Jot down some ideas before speaking.*

Reflection. Presently there is an increasing pressure for college students to find a job. On the other hand, many young employees called "job hoppers" frequently change their jobs. Some of them might change 3 times a year. What do you think are the reasons for them to change jobs? Do you think it is a wise decision? In which cases or circumstances (situations) would you quit your job?

Part III   Situational Dialogue: Job Interviews

 Listen to the following dialogue and read after the recording.

Blake: Let's discuss your educational background, Miss Kelly. You were an English major, weren't you?
Kelly: Yes. That's right. It was my best subject at college.
Blake: Fine. And could you tell me what kind of work experience you've had?
Kelly: My last position was with Loomis and Martin. That's a law firm in Sacramento.
Blake: And when was that exactly?
Kelly: From 2000 to 2003.
Blake: Uh huh.
Kelly: Before that I worked for Bishop and Baldwin. That was from 1998 to 2000. And I've been freelancing for the last few months.
Blake: Well, Ms. Kelly, your qualifications for the job are excellent. Could you tell me what kind of salary you are expecting?
Kelly: Well, in my last job I was making $1500 a month. I understand that this position has a starting salary of around $1600 a month.
Blake: That's right.
Kelly: That would be fine with me.
Blake: And is there anything you'd like to ask about the job?
Kelly: Yes, I'd like to know if the company provides opportunities for further education.
Blake: Yes, our employees are allowed to take up to six hours a week with full pay to attend college courses.
Kelly: That's very generous.
Blake: Is there anything else you'd like to know?
Kelly: No, not at this time.
Blake: Well, I've enjoyed meeting and talking with you. We'll call you within this week.
Kelly: Thank you. I appreciate the time you've given me.

B Practise the following expressions and sentence patterns used for job interviews.

For Interviewers
- Why do you want to work for our company?
- What are your strengths? Your weaknesses?
- What do you know about our company?
- Have you received any sort of vocational training?
- What makes you qualified for this job?
- Do you have any licenses or other qualifications?
- Have you got any special skills?
- How much salary do you expect?
- Can you give me a reason to hire you?

For Interviewees
- I am here to apply for a job of...
- I graduated from... My speciality is...
- I've got a Bachelor / Master / Doctor degree in...
- I've got... years of (training, experience)...
- I've got some special experiences in...
- I'm good at...
- I'm quite familiar with...
- I believe I'm quite fit for the job.
- I'm sure I can do it well.
- How many hours will I work in one day?
- What type of training is available?

C Miss Lee (B) is applying for a job as an insurance salesperson. The interviewer (A) is now asking her some questions. Complete the following dialogue with the expressions provided.

- ▶ change the condition pretty soon
- ▶ help people through this job
- ▶ Thank you for your time
- ▶ starting your life all over again
- ▶ you're full of passion
- ▶ compensate for lack of experience
- ▶ thanks to those experiences
- ▶ apply for the position as a salesperson

Unit 2 Jobs

A: Miss Lee, may I know what made you decide to _____(1)_____? As I know, your working experiences could even make you a manager.

B: Right. I indeed benefited from those jobs, but _____(2)_____ I finally found what I wanted from now on, I'm positively sure that I'd like to _____(3)_____.

A: Miss Lee, I understand that _____(4)_____, but being an insurance salesperson is more than that.

B: Sure, but I am confident of my enthusiasm, diligence and ability that could _____(5)_____ in this field.

A: You really don't mind _____(6)_____, including the low salary at the beginning, do you?

B: No. And I know my efforts would _____(7)_____.

A: Sounds like you've got a strong determination. Okay, we'll inform you of the result within a week.

B: _____(8)_____.

 Work in pairs to do a mock job interview with the following information for reference. Change the role of the interviewer and interviewee after you practise once.

Interviewer	Interviewee
1. something about yourself	character, hobbies, suitability for the job...
2. something interests you most about this job	opportunity, challenge, future, working environment...
3. strengths you can bring to this company	skills, abilities, projects, working experiences...
4. weaknesses	a mild weakness (actually kind of a strength)...
5. qualifications for the job	educational background and experience, good personality, hard-working attitude...
6. reason to hire you	excellent skills, good personality, degree...

Unit 3 Business

Overview

- **Listening**
    - Part I   Dialogue
    - Part II   Students Carve Out Early Careers in Business
    - Part III   Seven Principles of Admirable Business Ethics
    - Part IV   Listening for Numbers
    - Part V   News

- **Speaking**
    - Part I   Pronunciation Practice
    - Part II   Speaking Activities
    - Part III   Situational Dialogue: Making Offers

- **Skills**
    - Talking About Youngsters Starting Business
    - Learning Some Principles of Business Ethics
    - Making Offers to People Who Need Help

- **Language Focus**
    - Gerund -ing

Listening

Part I Dialogue

Word List

discreet	portray	overwhelming	negative
shot	commercial charter flight		demilitarize
headline	straight away	stronghold	rumor
prevail	motivate	incentive	joint-venture
profitably	capitalism	market economy	
DPRK (the Democratic People's Republic of Korea)			
South Korea	Pyongyang		

A Listen to the interview and choose the best answer to the following questions.

1. What attracts the press' attention most about the DPRK?
   A. Business done in the DPRK.
   B. Commercial charter flights between South Korea and North Korea.
   C. Gunshots across the demilitarized zone.

2. Which of the following statements best describes why people know so little about business in the DPRK?
   A. Businessmen's discreet quality.
   B. Normal business that doesn't make the news.
   C. People's negative impression of the DPRK.

3. What do foreign firms expect from their current businesses?
   A. Economic profits.   B. Stronghold.   C. Foreign currency.

4. What does the phrase "View the cup half empty" mean?
   A. Have a negative view on somebody or something.

Unit 3   Business

  B. Think somebody is not competent.
  C. Think something is half done.
5. What is NOT considered a feature of the market in the DPRK?
   A. Developing.   B. Withering.   C. Surprising.

 Listen to the interview again and answer the following questions.

1. What are the reasons why corporations don't want to be known that they are doing business in the DPRK?
   _____
   _____
   _____

2. Give an example of negative media with the DPRK.
   _____

3. Why did Roger Barett say the DPRK is a real market?
   _____

 In groups, discuss the following questions, giving examples where possible.

1. As mentioned in the interview, what are the qualities of businessmen?
2. According to the interview, the media portrays a negative impression of the DPRK. What are the possible reasons for this?
3. What does it mean when companies have to give a little, spend a little and gain a little in a new developing market?
4. Do you care about the economy when reading newspapers or watching television? Why or why not?

Part II   Students Carve Out Early Careers in Business

Word List

carve out	trigger	entrepreneurship	transform
substantial	pocket money	backpack	sewing
snowball into	flourishing	enterprise	home schooled
manufacturer	expand	sheet	bazaar
headband	nail polish	entrepreneur	hand-picked
enroll in	medication		

35

A *Survey. If you were to start a business, what would you start with? Fill in the form below.*

Age to start business	Field of Business	Scale	☐ Small ☐ Medium ☐ Large	Form	☐ Individual ☐ With partners ☐ For companies
Source of Funding	☐ Loan from banks ☐ Family ☐ Acquaintances ☐ Part-time jobs ☐ Sponsors		Location of Business		☐ No fixed place ☐ Residence as office ☐ Houses ☐ Building offices of a certain scale Others _____
Plan of business expansion and possibility evaluation					

B *You are going to hear a passage about youngsters starting their own businesses. As you listen to the passage, fill in the missing information in the table below.*

Name	Age	Gender	Products	Company/Brand Name	Business Expansion	Business Record
Kim					☐ Yes ☐ No	
Alexis				/	☐ Yes ☐ No	
Marisol					☐ Yes ☐ No	
Melissa				/	☐ Yes ☐ No	/

Unit 3 Business

 Listen to the passage and match the youngsters' names in the left column with corresponding descriptions in the right column.

1. Kim	A. is influenced by his/her parents in doing business
2. Alexis	B. started business by tending to animals/pets
	C. runs a company with his/her twin brother
3. Marisol	D. plans more than one way of sales channel
4. Melissa	E. mother gave a helping hand more than economically

 In groups, discuss the following questions, giving examples where possible.

1. The four students started business at an early age either with the assistance and support from their parents or on their own. Do you think it is wise to encourage the young to step into the world of business? What would they learn from their experience and what would they lose in return? Should they limit themselves to doing business on a small scale only?
2. In the process of doing business, one may run into difficulties. What obstacles might youngsters face when they start their own business? Have you any suggestions to help them overcome certain difficulties?

Part III Seven Principles of Admirable Business Ethics

Word List

admirable	ethics	attribute	distinguishing
outperform	pay off	strive for	integrity
obligation	regardless of	awry	reclaim
brochure	hands-on	dubious	promptly
utmost	title	courtesy	instill

A *Dictation. Listen to the following short passage and write down what you hear.*

B *You are going to hear a passage about business ethics. Listen to the passage and fill in the blanks to finish the outline.*

1. Be Trustful: Trust, to a certain extent, is _____ on the character, ability, strength, and truth of a business.
2. _____.
3. Meet Obligations: Go all out to gain past customers' and clients' trust. Honor all _____ _____.
4. Make sure all print materials are _____.
5. Stay involved in _____.
6. _____: It allows you to end any dubious activities promptly.
7. Show _____. Treat others professionally, regardless of _____ _____.

C *Listen to the passage again, and answer the following questions based on your understanding.*

1. What can the leader of a company do for the company's continuous development?
2. How can a company be sure its printed materials are made clear?
3. What is the beginning of achieving the desired goals of a company?
4. How can a small business become evident among customers?

D *The passage deals with the principles of business ethics which are vital for a company's survival in the competitive business world. With your group, discuss the following question.*

What would be the result if a company had little or no business ethics?

E Language Focus: Gerund -*ing*

When **-ing** is added to an English verb, the new verb becomes either a **participle** or a **verbal noun/ gerund**.

As a gerund, the **-ing** word is used in the same way that a noun might be used.

Beating does more harm than good. (subject of *does*)

I hate *writing* letters. (object of *hate*)

One of my bad habits is *biting* my nails. (subject complement)

I am not used to *driving* on the left. (object of *be used to*)

Gerunds and **infinitives** are sometimes confusing. Some verbs can be followed by either a word ending in **-ing** form or an infinitive, usually with a difference of meaning. The most frequent or common cases include words such as *advise, attempt, begin, like, love, prefer, regret, remember, stop,* etc. This is also the case with certain adjectives, such as *accustomed, afraid, sure, used,* and so on.

Correct the following sentences, if they have any mistakes.

1. You should stop to smoke—it's bad for you.
2. I don't regret telling her what I thought, even if it upset her.
3. Don't forget writing to Aunt Mary. She misses you very much.
4. I don't remember to have said that I would never speak to Marsha.
5. I was interested to read in the paper that scientists have found out how the universe began.

Part IV Listening for Numbers

A *Listen to the following passage on how to listen for numbers and fill in the blanks.*

Numbers entail telephone numbers, dates, time, _____(1)_____, prices, ages, street and house numbers and so on. English listening exercises in this aspect _____(2)_____: direct listening and comprehension with calculation. The direct listening exercises refer to the exercises answered by finding out the numbers in question, such as telephone numbers, street numbers, house numbers, etc. The comprehension with calculation exercises are _____(3)_____. The correct answers for the questions are worked out through correct calculation based upon the right original number or numbers in question. In doing exercises of this category, listeners are expected to master the relationship between numbers and their calculations.

The first step towards mastering the skill of number comprehension is to _____(4)_____. For example, we need to understand the difference between fifteen and fifty, from the length of the vowels in the two words and from the positions of stress. In addition, numbers with several digits need special attention. English numbers are divided every three digits from the right, for example, thirteen thousand six hundred is written as 13,600, with _____(5)_____. When you listen, put down numbers like this to help you collect all necessary information. Furthermore, years are read every two digits. Therefore, 1984 is read nineteen eighty-four. But 2008 is read two thousand and eight and 570 B.C. is read five hundred and seventy B.C., with an "and" between the digits of hundred and ten.

Another sort of numbers is time. As we all know, the time before half an hour is the minutes past the hour, whereas that after the half an hour is expressed as _____(6)_____ to the next hour. Also, we need to pay attention to words like quarter, a.m., p.m. and so on. Last but not least, we need to know the words for _____(7)_____. The most frequently used units are dollars ($), pounds (£) and euros (€). $17.35 and £17.35 are read seventeen dollars and thirty-five cents or seventeen dollars thirty-five, and seventeen pounds and thirty-five pence or seventeen pounds thirty-five _____(8)_____.

In calculation, pay more attention to the words like *more, less, late, early, fast, slow* and *before* for _____(9)_____, *time, twice, triple, double, pair, percent, quarter* and *one-third* for _____(10)_____.

B **1. You are going to hear a short passage about people watching soap operas. As you listen, pay attention to the numbers, and then fill in the blanks with the correct numbers.**

(1) People aged between _____ formed the largest group who watched soap operas. The number totaled _____.

(2) The number of viewers aged below 20 was _____. The percentage was _____.

(3) The 31-35 age-group accounted for _____ percent of the total, which means the total number was _____.

(4) There were _____ viewers over age 40 watching soap operas, making up _____ percent of the total number of _____.

2. Listen to some basic information about Beijing's economy in 2007. Then finish the table below by filling in the correct numbers and increasing rates.

Beijing's nominal GDP	( ) RMB	( ) %
GDP per capita	( ) RMB	8.9%
Primary industry	10.13 billion RMB	/
Secondary industry	( ) RMB	/
Tertiary industry	( ) RMB	/
Urban disposable income per capita	( ) RMB	11.2%
Pure income of rural residents per capita	9,559 RMB	( ) %
Disposable income of the 20% low-income residents per capita	/	( ) %
The growth rate of the 20% high-income residents	/	( ) %

Part V News

Word List

hand over	intergovernmental	barrel	top	resort
seal off	bloc	crunch	alleviate	G-77
Antigua	Barbuda	Slovenia	Hokkaido	Toyako
the Organization of Petroleum Exporting Countries (OPEC)				

A Listen to the news report and answer the following questions with key words.

1. What was the ceremony about?
   _____
   _____

2. When was the G-77 established? What are its functions?
   _____
   _____

3. When and where was the declaration issued? What is it called?
   _____
   _____

B *Listen to the news and choose the best answer to complete each sentence.*

1. The price of oil now is _____ per barrel.
   A. £140   B. £114
   C. $140   D. $114
2. A summit between producers and consumers was held in _____.
   A. Brussels, Belgium   B. Jerusalem, Israel
   C. Ljubljana, Slovenia   D. Jeddah, Saudi Arabia
3. The increase in oil output will be _____ barrels per day.
   A. 2 thousand   B. 20 thousand
   C. 200 thousand   D. 2 million

C *Listen to the news report and fill in the blanks.*

Rising food and fuel prices are topping the agenda for leaders of the world's major industrialised nations as they start a three-day summit in Japan.

The G8 summit opened at a resort on the northern island of Hokkaido.

Leaders from member nations—Britain, Canada, France, Germany, Italy, Japan, Russia and the United States—will be joined by _____(1)_____ from some 15 other countries, including eight African states.

_____(2)_____ has spent a record sum of money and _____(3)_____ police to seal off the remote lakeside town of Toyako for the three-day talks.

As the summit began, the UN secretary general urged donor nations to keep their promises, to help poorer countries achieve the _____(4)_____.

Mr. Ban also told reporters that urgent action was needed to guarantee _____(5)_____.

The impact on the global economy of _____(6)_____ and other shocks, such as the _____(7)_____, have eclipsed other concerns, correspondents say.

The G8 may call for the creation of a panel of international experts to advise on how to _____(8)_____ another crisis like this.

The EU has already been spelling out plans to _____(9)_____.

Speaking

Part I Pronunciation Practice

Listen to the following story and imitate the recording. Pay attention to your pronunciation and intonation.

Old Mule in Well

A farmer owned an old mule. One day, the mule fell into the farmer's well. The mule brayed loudly and caught the attention of the farmer. Upon assessing the situation, the farmer ruled out any possibility of a rescue as it was simply too much trouble to lift the mule out of the well. Out of sympathy for the animal, he decided to get his neighbors to help haul dirt into the well to put the mule out of his misery.

The old mule was hysterical upon learning that his life would end. However, as the farmer and the neighbors shoveled the dirt into the well, a thought struck the old mule. He realized that if he could shake off every piece of dirt that landed on his back, the dirt would hit the floor and he could step on the dirt.

Shovel after shovel, he continued relentlessly to shake the dirt off and step on top of it. He fought the sense of panic and distress and just went on shaking off the dirt and climbing higher up the well.

With much determination and perseverance, the old mule eventually stepped out of the well, battered and exhausted, but otherwise triumphant that he had survived the ordeal. He faced the situation of adversity; the very act of burying him in fact saved his life.

There is a solution to every problem. Never give up. Adversity creates opportunity.

Part II Speaking Activities

A Key Sentence Patterns

Read aloud and memorize the following sentences.

1. A successful businessman should have a clear vision for his company.
2. The most important quality for a businessman is his insight of the market.
3. To give up college education for business is not a good option.
4. Good grades and a good job are easy to get. But a good education is a different story.
5. Dropping out of school to start a company is a good opportunity for students to be independent and know more about the society.
6. Practice is more important than knowledge in the books.
7. Business ethics can mean the difference between success and failure for a company.
8. Ethical behaviour in business life pays off in financial returns.
9. When it comes to profiting from disaster, most people think of price gouging or profiteering.
10. Price gouging is not only immoral and unethical, it's a criminal act in which you're taking advantage of people who have no choice but to pay.

B Presentation and Discussion

In groups, discuss qualities or qualifications that help make a businessperson successful. Add them to the list below, and then choose the most important one to explain.

No.	Qualities / Qualifications That Make a Successful Businessperson
1	knowledge
2	experience
3	determination
4	ambition
5	
6	
7	
8	
9	
10	

Unit 3 Business

Many young people start their own businesses from selling goods online to establishing their own company. In groups, discuss what youngsters can gain from carving out their own careers.

No.	Things Gained from Carving Out Careers
1	
2	
3	
4	
5	

C **Talk.** *Prepare a 2-minute talk stating your opinion of* **students giving up college education for business**. *You can start by naming some examples such as Bill Gates and Steve Jobs. You may want to jot down some advantages and disadvantages before speaking.*

D **Reflection.** *From the information you have just learned about business ethics, how important do you think they are for a company or businessperson? Some companies or people will put profit as priority and will try to make money through all possible channels, even if it means taking advantage of others' misery in poverty- or disaster-stricken areas. Do you think this is part of doing business?*

Part III Situational Dialogue: Making Offers

A *Listen to the following dialogue and read after the recording.*

At the airport, Sammy looked very upset because she couldn't find her bag. Addison, the airport porter noticed this and offered to help.

Addison: You look quite upset, ma'am. Do you need some help?
Sammy: Yes. I've just come off the last flight and my bag isn't on the baggage carousel.
Addison: I see. Can you describe the bag please?
Sammy: Yes. It's a holdall, a green holdall about this big. It's got a zipper across the top and yellow handles.
Addison: I see. Well, I'd better make a note of that. Have you got your baggage claim form filled out?
Sammy: Yes, it's right here.
Addison: Well, I think we need to go to the lost baggage office for a check.
Sammy: Ok. But I don't know where the office is. And I can't speak the local language.
Addison: I will show you the way. Follow me. I can explain your trouble to my colleagues.
Sammy: Thanks! It's very kind of you to be of such great help!

B *Practise the following expressions and sentence patterns used for offering help.*

- Do you need a hand?
- Can I help out?
- Do you need some help?
- May / Can I help you?
- What can I do for you?
- Is there anything I can do to help?
- Would you like any help?
- May I be of any assistance?
- Shall I...?
- I'll...
- Let me know if I can be of any help.

C *Sam (A) and Mariella (B) are talking about solving computer problems. Complete the following dialogue with the expressions provided.*

- ▶ began searching for some papers and articles
- ▶ I'll help you out with this problem.
- ▶ cannot log on to Windows.
- ▶ Did you use an anti-virus software to kill them?
- ▶ you will have to reinstall Windows.
- ▶ Is there anything I can do to help?
- ▶ What did you do after you turned on your computer?
- ▶ ran into a problem with my computer.

Unit 3 Business

A: Hi Mariella! Looks like you are quite busy doing something. _____(1)_____

B: Yes, Sam. I just _____(2)_____ It's down.

A: Why don't you restart it?

B: I have restarted it three times. But I still _____(3)_____

A: _____(4)_____

B: After I turned it on, I _____(5)_____ that might help with my economics essay. Suddenly it was infected with viruses, and then it just crashed.

A: _____(6)_____

B: Yes, but Kaspersky couldn't kill all the viruses.

A: Well, I'm afraid _____(7)_____

B: But I know so little about computers, not to mention installing an operating system.

A: _____(8)_____ Please give me the installation CD.

B: Thank you, Sam! Here you are!

D *In groups, make conversations based on the following situations. Use the expressions of offering help that you have just learned.*

1. You see an old lady trying to cross the street. She is stuck in the middle.

2. Mr. and Mrs. Johnson are moving to a new neighbourhood. The moving van is backing into their driveway. Their neighbours, Larry and Sarah offer some help.

3. You are going through customs. The man in front of you in the queue cannot speak English well. He's trying to explain to the customs officer that he has lost his passport. Your English is better than his.

Unit 4 Music

Overview

- **Listening**
    - Part I   Dialogue
    - Part II   Fighting Music Piracy on College Campuses
    - Part III   Music at Sporting Events
    - Part IV   The Symphony: A Microcosm of Life
    - Part V   News

- **Speaking**
    - Part I   Pronunciation Practice
    - Part II   Speaking Activities
    - Part III   Situational Dialogue: Likes and Dislikes

- **Skills**
    - Note-Taking While Listening
    - Understanding Words from Context
    - Talking About Music
    - Raising Awareness About Piracy
    - Expressing Likes and Dislikes

- **Language Focus**
    - Word Formation: Blends

Listening

Part I Dialogue

Word List

pounding	rhythm & blues (R&B)	hip-hop	rap
travesty	over-commercialization	weird	cute
rock'n'roll	legend	rocker	awesome
all-round	punk	hairdo	plaid
baggy	gang	Hall of Fame	New Orleans
Nashville	Cleveland, Ohio		

A *Janice is listening to Jay Chou's music on her stereo while her father is reading. Listen to the dialogue between Janice and her father and answer the following questions.*

1. What type of music does Jay Chou sing?
   _____
2. What are the characteristics of that type of music?
   _____
3. Where did it originate?
   _____
4. What does most modern music have in common?
   _____
5. What kind of music does Janice's father like?
   _____

B *A Chinese student and his American friend are talking about music in America. Listen to the dialogue and match.*

1. Singers and their accomplishments

Elvis Presley	a very famous guitar player	called "the King"
Jimi Hendrix	helped the rock music industry take off	called "the Boss"
Bruce Springsteen	an all-round rock singer and songwriter	

2. **Types of music and their fashion**

rock	cowboy hats, plaid shirts, jeans and boots
punk	baggy pants and loose clothes
country	jeans and T's
rap	tight clothing, weird hairdos and make-up

3. **Types of music and their origins**

jazz	Nashville, Southern U.S.
country	Cleveland, Ohio
rock'n'roll	New Orleans

C *Listen to the second dialogue again and fill in the blanks.*

1. Well, frankly I think much of today's music in America is a _____(1)_____ of real music. MTV has destroyed the quality of music with _____(2)_____. Now any sexy, pretty face or anyone with a weird _____(3)_____ can be a star. Today's musicians are not as _____(4)_____ as before. Many of them sound the same and act the same. _____(5)_____, today's young people haven't experienced early rock music so they don't know how pitiful today's musicians are by _____(6)_____.

2. Elvis is "the King" of rock'n'roll. He was _____(1)_____, _____(2)_____, and had _____(3)_____. His music was full of _____(4)_____ and young girls went _____(5)_____ him. He helped the rock music industry take off, but his influence _____(6)_____ music. He has become an _____(7)_____.

3. When it _____(1)_____ playing the electric guitar, Jimi Hendrix is considered one of the _____(2)_____ and maybe the greatest ever.

4. Bruce Springsteen, "the Boss", is the greatest _____(1)_____ of all time. He has a great voice, writes _____(2)_____ lyrics, is a great guitar player, and is an _____(3)_____ nice person.

5. Jazz _____(1)_____ in New Orleans. Country music _____(2)_____ in the south, centered in Nashville, and rock'n'roll _____(3)_____ in Cleveland, Ohio.

D *Discussion.* *Do you like music? What types of music do you like? Why?*

Part II Fighting Music Piracy on College Campuses

Word List

vinyl	hit	launch	pirate	piracy	violate
copyright	reproduction	commercial	Congress	House of Representatives	
federal	invest	Senate	fine		

A *Do you often listen to music? Think about your own music listening behaviour and answer the following questions. Then compare your answers with your partner's.*

1. What do you use when you listen to music? Check the item(s) you use.
   tape recorder   MP4 player
   CD player   mobile phone
   MP3 player   iPod

2. How do you get the music you like? Check the way(s) you use.
   buying tapes/CDs
   borrowing tapes/CDs from your friends
   copying your friends' MP3 music
   downloading music from commercial websites
   downloading music from peer-to-peer file-sharing networks

B *When we listen, we can guess the meaning of a word/phrase from its context. Listen to the passage and choose the best definition for the following words/phrases.*

1. the latest **hits**
   A. the most recent successful songs
   B. the most recent attacks
   C. the newest Internet search results

2. music **pirates**
   A. people who rob other boats on the seas
   B. people who copy or sell music illegally
   C. people who privately write music

3. civil **actions**
   A. things done politely
   B. activities done by ordinary people
   C. legal processes concerning the private affairs of citizens

4. **settlement**
   A. payment
   B. an official agreement
   C. a group of houses

5. a higher education **bill**
   A. money to be paid for higher education
   B. a written proposal for a new law on higher education
   C. a printed advertisement for a college or university

C Music piracy on college campuses has become an issue of growing concern in America. Listen to the passage again and note down what these organizations think and do (or have done/are doing) about the issue. Write down the key words as you listen and then put them into sentences orally.

	Opinions	Actions
the R.I.A.A. (the industry group)		
Educause		
the House of Representatives	/	
the Senate	/	
the schools		

D In groups, discuss the following questions.

1. What are the reasons why students pirate?
2. Do you think piracy is wrong? Why or why not?

E Language Focus: Word Formation: Blends

A **blend** is a word formed from parts of two other words (called source words) or a *word* plus a part of another *word* and combining their meanings. ***Educause*** is an example of blends. Another example is **Oxbridge**, which is formed by putting together the first part of *Oxford* and the last part of *Cambridge* to form a new inclusive term for both universities. *Try to figure out the source words of the following blends and match them with their meanings.*

motel   • a film or piece of writing that describes travel in a particular country, or a particular person's travels

smog   • a hotel for people who are travelling by car, where you can park your car outside your room

sitcom   • dirty air that looks like a mixture of smoke and fog which occurs in some busy industrial cities

brunch   • documentary written as entertainment, with variable amount of fiction concerning actual events

travelogue   • a funny television programme in which the same characters appear in different situations each week

docutainment   • breakfast taken nearly at lunchtime

Can you think of any other blends?

Part III Music at Sporting Events

Word List

resurgence	repetitive	announcer	fanfare	home team
major- or minor-league		inning	ballpark	organist
debut	supplement	subgenre	coincide	chart
in collaboration with		subset	novelty	album
public address system				

A   **Dictation.** *Listen to the following short passage and write down what you hear.*

Unit 4   Music

B You are going to hear a passage about music at sporting events. Listen to the passage and choose the best answer to the following questions.

1. What kind of music is played at NBA games?
   A. Drum music.   B. Organ music.
   C. Symphonic music.   D. Keyboard music.
2. Which of the following songs is NOT related to baseball?
   A. Take Me Out to the Ball Game.   B. Charge.
   C. Meet the Mets.   D. Let's Go Mets.
3. What is novelty football music?
   A. New football music.
   B. Popular football music.
   C. Football music with humorous lyrics.
   D. Football music with a strong beat.
4. In which sport does each competitor have a particular entry theme song?
   A. Professional boxing.   B. Professional wrestling.
   C. Professional fencing.   D. Professional judo.
5. What music is closest to popular music?
   A. Basketball music.   B. Baseball music.
   C. Volleyball music.   D. Football music.

C Listen to the passage again and write T (true), F (false) or NG (not given) beside the following statements.

(   ) 1. At NBA games, music is played only at the beginning and end of a game to accompany the teams entering and leaving the court.
(   ) 2. There is often a particular piece of music played or sung for each inning stretch of baseball games.
(   ) 3. Organ music, pop and rock music are played at baseball games.
(   ) 4. The Hockey Night in Canada theme song is like another national anthem to many Canadians.
(   ) 5. So far "ESPN Presents Stadium Anthems" has been the only sport music album released.

55

D Do you know any music or song which is related to a certain sport? Can you hum the tune or sing the song?

Part IV The Symphony: A Microcosm of Life

A Listen to the following passage and fill in the missing words.

  The auditorium is full of people conversing in the audience. On the stage the performers are shuffling their music and _____(1)_____ their instruments as they prepare for the performance. The conductor enters, takes a bow, and all is silent. He raises his baton(指挥棒) and the symphony(交响乐) begins to play. All of the instruments have different sounds, and the parts they play blend and _____(2)_____ with one another. The music would not be as exciting if every part were the same. The symphony is a symbol for life, especially in a community. Diversity and the coming together of each instrument is what gives the symphony its _____(3)_____ and special sound. This is also true in life and the world we live in. Individuals bring in their own input that influences others.

  A symphony orchestra (交响乐团) is composed of a variety of brass (铜管乐器), woodwind (木管乐器), percussion (打击乐) and stringed instruments (弦乐器). Each of these instruments has its own unique sound but when played together they _____(4)_____ each other. Like a symphony and its instruments, the world is _____(5)_____ of many races and cultures. They are uniquely different but can have an influence on each other.

  Individuality is an important part of the symphony. Each player has his or her own part to perform. These parts can be played _____(6)_____ but do not have the same effect as when they are combined with the other parts of the orchestra. They blend into a harmonious piece of music. In life, each person has a _____(7)_____ that they are particularly good at. When they work together with others, it accentuates (使更突出) their talent.

  Another _____(8)_____ between life and the symphony is that a performer may not always have the melody but will _____(9)_____ someone who does. Or in another case, a performer will not always have a solo (独唱, 独奏) and the chance to be in the spotlight (聚光灯). In life, everybody has their moments of _____(10)_____ although they may go unnoticed like the accompanist (伴奏者). This does not mean, however, that they are any less important than anyone else. The melody does not stay with one instrument for the whole song but moves throughout the orchestra. As in life, everyone _____(11)_____ has their moment to shine and their chance to be in the spotlight.

Unit 4 Music

The orchestra continues to play. It moves together as a group yet _____(12)_____, with each person contributing their own part. Each musician is an active member of the symphony. We move together in life, contributing what we have to offer from day to day as active members in our community.

There is a moment of silence that is broken by the applause of the audience.

B In what way is life compared to a symphony? List all the similarities between life and a symphony. Then choose the two paragraphs which you like best and recite them.

Part V News

Word List

transfer	playmaker	season	hike	staggering
AC Milan	FC Barcelona	Manchester City	Rossoneri	
Premier League	UEFA Cup	Champions League		San Siro
Nou Camp	Emirates Stadium		Barclays Premier League	
Arsenal -	Major League Soccer (MLS)			

A Listen to the news report and choose the best answer to the following questions.

1. For which club will Ronaldinho play in the year of 2010?
   A. AC Milan.   B. FC Barcelona.   C. Manchester City.
2. Approximately how much did Manchester City bid for the playmaker?
   A. 18.5 million euros.   B. 25 million euros.   C. 25 million pounds.
3. Ronaldinho was named FIFA World Player of the year in _____.
   A. 2004.   B. 2005.   C. Both A and B.

B Listen to the news report and write T (true) or F (false) beside the following statements.

(   ) 1. Arsenal's season tickets have increased 6.5% at the Emirates Stadium.
(   ) 2. Liverpool's season tickets do not include all cup and Champions League matches.
(   ) 3. There hasn't been any price increase at Arsenal for the last four years.

Listen to the news report and answer the following questions.

1. When will the Major League Soccer All-Stars play against English Premier League club West Ham United?
   _____

2. Who voted for the All-Star team?
   _____

3. How many of New England Revolution's players have been voted to be on the All-Star squad?
   _____

Part I Pronunciation Practice

Listen to the following poem and imitate the recording. Pay attention to your pronunciation and intonation.

The Sound of Music

The hills are alive with the sound of music
With songs they have sung for a thousand years
The hills fill my heart with the sound of music
My heart wants to sing every song it hears

My heart wants to beat like the wings of the birds
that rise from the lake to the trees
My heart wants to sigh like a chime that flies
from a church on a breeze
To laugh like a brook when it trips
and falls over stones on its way
To sing through the night like a lark
who is learning to pray

I go to the hills when my heart is lonely
I know I will hear what I've heard before
My heart will be blessed with the sound of music
And I'll sing once more

Part II Speaking Activities

A Key Sentence Patterns

Read aloud and memorize the following sentences.

1. How much time do you spend listening to music?
2. Have you ever been to a concert?
3. Have you ever taken part in a singing contest?
4. What is one of your favourite songs? Why do you like it? When did you first hear it? Who sings it?
5. Who is your favourite singer? What is your favourite band?
6. What makes you like a particular song, the lyrics of the song or the melody?
7. Can you play a musical instrument? If so, what do you play? How long have you been playing it?
8. If you could play any musical instrument, what would it be?
9. If you could invent a new instrument, what would it sound like?
10. If you could start a band, what type of music would you play? Why?
11. Is there any kind of music that you can't stand?
12. What was your favorite music five years ago? What about ten years ago? Do you think your favorite music twenty years from now will be the same as it is today?

B Presentation and Discussion

1. Interview at least three of your classmates about their music habits and preferences. Write down your own in the chart as well.

	Student A	Student B	Student C	Myself
Time spent listening to music (hours/day)				
Concert/singing competition				
Favourite song				
Favourite singer /band				
Musical instrument				
Type of music				
Changes in musical tastes				

2. *Have you heard of the "Mozart Effect"? Do you believe that "Mozart makes you smarter"? Categorise the following examples into three groups. You may discuss them with your classmates.*

   a. Exciting music can increase our heart rate, our breathing, and our blood pressure.
   b. Some athletes use music to help them train and perform better.
   c. Almost everyone has found themselves, at times, tapping their feet or wanting to get up and dance to their favourite song.
   d. Couples might use music to create a romantic evening.
   e. Organisers of sports events like football or basketball games use music to "pump up" the crowd and motivate the team.
   f. Calming music can relax our muscles and even lower our skin temperature.
   g. Some businesses use music to increase productivity and efficiency.

   Category 1: Music can affect us physiologically. _____
   Category 2: Music can affect us physically. _____
   Category 3: We often use music to help ourselves feel a certain way or do certain things. _____

> What other effects does music have? Can you give more examples?
> Now talk about the following questions in small groups. Then share your ideas with the whole class.
> 1. Can you concentrate on other things while you are listening to music?
> 2. Do you listen to music while doing your homework?
> 3. How does music make you feel?
> 4. Can you think of examples of music calming people or increasing their efficiency?
> 5. Do you think music can heal sick people?
> 6. Do you think that animals enjoy music? How do you know?

 Talk. *Make a 2-minute speech to your class about one of the following topics. You may do some research before you give the speech to make it more persuasive or interesting.*

Topic 1: Stop pirating
   You may have realized through the activities in Listening Part II that piracy eventually kills creativity and that we will all be losers in the long run if it continues. Prepare a speech to raise awareness about the harmful effects of piracy. Try to persuade your classmates to avoid pirating in the future.

Topic 2: Introduce a traditional Chinese musical instrument
   The origins of Chinese music can be dated back to antiquity. Traditionally the Chinese have believed that sound influences the harmony of the universe. They have left a

wealth of musical instruments, including the erhu, guzheng, guqin, suona, xun, pipa etc. If you're interested in any of the traditional Chinese musical instruments, introduce it to your classmates to arouse their interest in it.

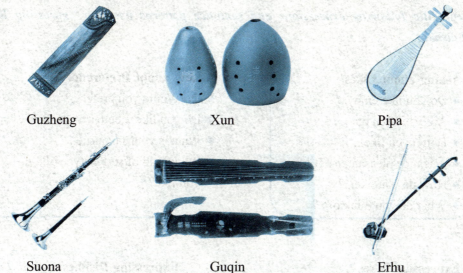

Guzheng Xun Pipa

Suona Guqin Erhu

D **Reflection.** *Can you imagine what the world would be like without music? What does music mean to you and to the whole of human society? Give your view on this topic.*

Part III Situational Dialogue: Likes and Dislikes

A *Listen to the following dialogue and repeat after the recording.*

Lucy and Dave are driving to a friend's house. They are talking in the car.

Lucy: Oh, hey, can you turn that up a little?
Dave: Sure. Do you like jazz?
Lucy: Oh, yes, I love it.
Dave: Really? So do I. What kind of jazz do you like?
Lucy: Oh, all kinds, but especially fusion.
Dave: How do you like dixieland?
Lucy: It's all right, but I'm not really crazy about it.
Dave: No, neither am I. I like a mellow sound. What's your favorite band?
Lucy: Well, I think I like Chuck Mangione best.
Dave: Me, too. I think he's terrific. Do you like going to concerts?

Lucy: Sure, but I like listening to CDs better. I can't stand mobs of pushy people.
Dave: Yeah, I know what you mean.

B *Practise the following expressions and sentence patterns used for expressing likes and dislikes.*

Asking about Likes
- Do you like/enjoy...
- Are you keen on...
- Don't you like...
- ... is nice/pleasant, isn't it?
- How do you like...?
- What do you think of...?

Asking about Preference
- Do/Would you prefer...?
- Do you like... better/more than...
- What's your favourite...?
- What kind of/sort of/type of... do you like?

Expressing Likes
- I love/like it.
- I'm crazy/mad about it.
- It's great/super/fantastic/terrific.
- I'm very keen on...
- I've always liked/loved...
- ... is wonderful/very enjoyable.
- There is nothing I like/enjoy more than...

Expressing Dislikes
- I'm afraid I don't like...
- I'm not very keen on...
- I (really) hate...
- I can't stand...
- I can't work up any enthusiasm for...

C *Pair work. Ask your partner if he/she likes the following things and people.*

1. jazz
2. rock'n'roll
3. Peking opera
4. rap
5. Jay Chou
6. going to concerts

Look at the list of things and people below. First mark your own likes and dislikes with a check (√). Then ask your partner and mark his/her likes and dislikes with a triangle(△).

	love/be crazy about	like	O.K.	not (like) very much	not (like) at all	hate/ can't stand
ping-pong						
dancing						
Liu Dehua						
Zhang Ziyi						
cartoons						
dogs						
the school dining-hall						
mathematics						
studying English						

Now work with another classmate. Ask him/her about some of his/her partner's likes and dislikes.

For example:
—Does he/she like ping-pong?
—Not very much.
—What about cartoons?
—He thinks it's OK.

Unit 5 Disasters

Overview

- **Listening**

    Part I   Dialogue
    Part II   Tsunami Wounds Still Fresh in Indonesia One Year Later
    Part III   The Nature of Disasters
    Part IV   Chinese Find Strength and Hope in Earthquake Rubble
    Part V   News

- **Speaking**

    Part I   Pronunciation Practice
    Part II   Speaking Activities
    Part III   Situational Dialogue: Disappointment and Encouragement

- **Skills**

    Talking About Disasters
    Expressing Disappointment and Encouragement

- **Language Focus**

    Words Functioning as More Than One Part of Speech

Listening

Part I Dialogue

Word List

massive	drought	migrate	relief supply	refugee camp
rubble	casualties	deputy	hurricane	port
spike	disrupt	oil stock	refinery	it turns out that...
implication	Iranian	EU (the European Union)		

 You are going to hear a dialogue about disasters. Listen to the dialogue and choose the best answer to the following sentences.

1. The cause of the forest fire in Australia is _____.
   A. from natural heat   B. from arson
   C. not known yet   D. from an accident

2. In Africa, a(n) _____ has caused starvation.
   A. fire   B. drought
   C. flood   D. earthquake

3. The international community is helping Africa in the following ways EXCEPT _____.
   A. Refugee camps have been set up.
   B. Several planes have been sent with relief supplies.
   C. Soldiers have been sent to hand out food and medical supplies.
   D. Money has been raised to help out millions of people.

4. Iran suffered from _____ yesterday.
   A. a few earthquakes   B. a serious earthquake
   C. an earthquake that was not serious D. diseases caused by earthquakes

Unit 5   Disasters

5. There were _____ people who were hospitalized in Iran.
   A. less than 20   B. over 20
   C. less than 100   D. over 100

B Listen to the dialogue again and fill in the table below.

Disaster	Place	Damage	Solutions
Forest fire	Australia	Covering _____ _____ ; destroying _____	
_____	Africa	Causing starvation; millions of people _____	1. EU: _____ _____ 2. Several countries: _____ _____ 3. Setting up _____ _____
Earthquake	Iran	Casualties: _____ _____ dead; _____ in hospital	1. Iranians dealing with it _____ 2. Purchasing some special equipment to _____ _____

C You are going to hear another dialogue about Hurricane Katrina. As you listen, fill in the blanks.

1. David Wessel is _____ of the Wall Street Journal.
2. The Gulf of Mexico is very important because it is
   (1) a centre of _____;
   (2) a port for _____ into the United States.
3. The reason why oil prices have spiked is that there are concerns _____ _____.
   Here the word "spike" means _____.
4. The President's possible solution is to _____ from the Strategic Petroleum Reserve which has _____ that need to be refined.
5. It is a very delicate moment because _____ come out from the ports affected by the hurricane. If it turns out that those ports are damaged, it'll _____ _____. The economic effects could _____.

6. _____ are a very important part of the economy in the affected region, and that could have _____.

Part II   Tsunami Wounds Still Fresh in Indonesia One Year Later

Word List

pledge	emergency aid	languish	devastated
forlorn-looking	an array of	rivalry	red tape
squalid	barrack	wash up	canvas
foundation	ring out	sanitation	coordinator

 You are going to hear a passage about tsunami damages in Indonesia. Listen to the passage and choose the best answer to the following sentences.

1. Which of the following is NOT true concerning the tsunami in 2004?
   A. 169,000 people were dead or missing.
   B. 500,000 people were left homeless.
   C. 300,000 people were in need of jobs.
   D. 70,000 people were living in tent camps.

2. Petria is a woman who _____.
   A. lost her husband and four children
   B. is grateful for the food aid and camp building
   C. is living in a tent camp along the east coast
   D. complains an aid agency is breaking promises

3. Since the reconstruction aid has been slow, many survivors have chosen to _____.
   A. reinforce the construction of the dirty tent camps and barracks
   B. move back to their damaged villages and build their own shelters
   C. build consolidated huts with wood, bricks, or concrete
   D. live under plastic or canvas above the foundations of their destroyed homes
4. The sign "It's better to stay here in our own village" shows people's _____.
   A. frustration   B. sadness
   C. anger   D. dissatisfaction
5. According to camp leader Dalman, the conditions in the camps are unbearable because _____.
   A. there's not enough food
   B. there's no protection for public health
   C. there's no electricity
   D. there's no communication
6. _____ will be most important to help people re-control their own destinies.
   A. Having their own homes
   B. Getting the economy to work again
   C. Having a cash wage and employment
   D. Taking matters into their own hands

B *Listen to the passage again and answer the following questions with key words.*

1. How much money has the international community promised in aid to Aceh? To provide survivors with new homes, how much is included in the budgets of aid agencies?

2. Describe the conditions in the tent camps.

3. What problems have slowed reconstruction in the tsunami-stricken area?

4. What impact did the tsunami have on Ulhee Lhee?

5. Who in particular needs to rebuild their homes and re-establish their lives?

6. Who is Bo Asplund? According to him, what is the priority in reconstruction?

C *In groups, discuss the following questions, giving examples where possible.*

1. What are some of the important issues that need to be addressed when a disaster happens? Which do you think is the most important one?
2. How can people rebuild their homes and re-construct their lives after a disaster? What can college students do to help people out in disaster-stricken areas?

Part III The Nature of Disasters

Word List

practitioner	assessment	atmospheric	discourse	emission
mitigate	tornado	spiral	torrential	surge
spawn	landslide	twisting	funnel-shaped	override
velocity	debris	interior	presidential	sewer
avalanche	unconsolidated	landfill	trailer	

A *Dictation. Listen to the following short passage and write down what you hear.*

B *Look at the pictures below and name each of the disasters. What are some of their characteristics or destructiveness?*

Unit 5   Disasters

C *You are going to hear a passage about natural disasters. Listen to the passage and choose the best answer to the following sentences.*

1. _____ are huge destructive ocean waves.
   A. Hurricanes   B. Tornadoes
   C. Cyclones   D. Tsunamis
2. Wind speeds of a tornado can reach _____ miles per hour.
   A. 74   B. 200
   C. 300   D. 400
3. _____ are the most common and widespread of all natural disasters.
   A. Floods   B. Fires
   C. Earthquakes D. Storms
4. The following statements are true EXCEPT _____.
   A. Earthquakes can cause tsunamis.
   B. Flooding can occur after melting snow.
   C. Sometimes tornadoes can bring forth hurricanes.
   D. Hurricanes can bring heavy rains when approaching land.
5. According to the passage, landslides can be triggered by _____.
   A. hurricanes and tornadoes   B. floods and tornadoes
   C. floods and earthquakes   D. hurricanes and earthquakes

D *Listen to the passage again and write T (true), F (false) or NG (not given) beside the following statements.*

(   ) 1. The center of a hurricane, which is also known as the "eye", is absolutely calm.
(   ) 2. Torrential rains generating floods and flash floods can also cause damage and loss of lives.
(   ) 3. Tornadoes are tropical storms with a funnel-shaped cloud created by thunderstorms.
(   ) 4. Tornadoes occur most often in the central part of the United States.
(   ) 5. The best protection during a tornado is an indoor basement.
(   ) 6. Over the past 40 years, half of all disasters are floods in the United States.

(   ) 7. Human factors as opposed to technological factors can cause flooding.
(   ) 8. Earthquakes are caused by the collision of tectonic plates.
(   ) 9. The most dangerous places to be in during an earthquake are buildings or trailers that are not tied to a reinforced foundation.
(   ) 10. Earthquakes can happen at any time of the year.

E *Fill in the table with key words to summarise the four natural disasters based on what you have just heard.*

Names	Definition	Characteristics	Damages/Causes	Places at Risk
Hurricanes				/
Tornadoes				
Floods	/	/		
Earthquakes		/		

Part IV Chinese Find Strength and Hope in Earthquake Rubble

A *Listen to the following passage and repeat it with the same emotion.*

On May 12, 2008, an earthquake of magnitude 8 struck Sichuan. Everyone in China was shocked and became heartbroken as reported deaths climbed from 10,000 to 32,000 to more than 62,000 people. The death toll kept rising and the number of injured and missing was many times more.

The Chinese people faced this disaster with compassion (爱心) and courage. I was touched by the teacher who died forming a bridge with his body between two desks, protecting four surviving students under him, by the trapped child who told the rescue workers to save others first, and by the dying mother who texted her baby, "My Treasure: If you survive, always remember I love you." She died using her own body to shield her 3-month-old from harm. But don't worry about this baby growing up without a family. Thousands of families in China have volunteered to adopt earthquake orphans.

The Chinese faced this disaster with resourcefulness (智慧) and tenacity (勇气). A brave executive took his weekend SUV (Sports Utility Vehicle 越野车), drove hundreds of miles, started digging, and saved several lives. A child used his hands to dig out two fellow students. His hands were severely injured, but his friends survived. Cab drivers turned their cars into ambulances and delivery trucks. More than 100,000 brave soldiers risked (and some gave) their lives to find survivors.

In the Internet Age, heroism need not be on location (身临现场). At Google China, where I work, one team worked all night and built a "lost loved one" search to accurately find information about missing people in Sichuan. Another team put together a satellite image map to help the rescue effort and to connect supply donors(捐赠者) with rescue areas in need. Finally, a team made sure that when a user searched for "earthquake donations" or similar words, he or she could complete a donation in as little as one minute. Almost $1 million was donated in one week.

These are the heroes among us, whether they use an SUV, a shovel, a phone or a keyboard. Their heroic deeds and selflessness inspired me so deeply that I can recall only one other such occasion. It was 9/11—I vividly remember the NYPD(New York Police Department 纽约警察局) police officers, the firefighters, and of course the passengers and crew on United Flight 93.

As a Chinese American, I hope that the Chinese and the Americans will see that they have so much in common—their compassion, courage, ingenuity (创造性), generosity and grace. Amid recent differences between China and America, I hope that people will see that these heroic commonalities are much stronger than any differences, and will bind the two great peoples together. And I hope that these heroes from 9/11 and 5/12 will inspire all of us to turn our anxiety into courage, our misery into tenacity, and our sorrow into love.

B *In the face of severe disasters, what do you think human beings are capable of doing? Express your understanding of the power of love vs. the impact of disasters.*

C *Language Focus: Words Functioning as More Than One Part of Speech*

There are thousands of words in any language, but not all words have the same function. For example, some words express "action" while other words express "things". When we want to build a sentence, we use different types of words, each with its own function. We can categorize English words into 8 basic classes called "parts of speech":

nouns, verbs, adjectives, adverbs, pronouns, conjunctions, prepositions and interjections.

Many words in English can have more than one function, or be more than one part of speech. For example, "trigger" can be a verb and a noun; "slow" can be an adjective and a verb; "near" can be an adverb, a preposition and a verb. In addition, many nouns can act as adjectives.

Note: In English, almost any noun can be made into a verb. This is known as anthimeria, where the use of a word that is normally one part of speech in a situation is required to be understood as a different part of speech.

For example:
1. You can even *office* while you're supposed to be on vacation in Tahiti.
   (To perform office-related tasks, such as photocopying and faxing.)
2. We can look for friends on the Internet, and *friend* them via MSN or ICQ.
   (On a social networking website, to add a person to one's list of acquaintances, and vice versa.)

Translate the following sentences (English to Chinese, Chinese to English) with the words provided. Pay attention to the words' functions.

1. The thunder would not *peace* at my bidding.
2. Wrongs must be *righted* when they are discovered.
3. You can *gift* him his favourite albums.
4. 妇女在各方面都有同等的发言权。(say)
5. 2007年中国电影国内票房达到33亿元。(total)

Part V   News

Word List

crew	epicenter	diminish	makeshift	army-ruled
toll	impoverished	hard-hit	delta	perish
spell	mountainous	amputation	frostbite	hinder
appeal for	Myanmar	the Irrawaddy Delta		Yangon
Herat	Badghis			

 Listen to the news and fill in the blanks.

1. Casualties: _____ people left homeless;
   _____ people confirmed dead.

Unit 5 Disasters

2. Foreign rescue crews started work near _____.
   It's the first time that China _____.
3. The number one priority: _____.
4. _____ days have passed after the earthquake.
   The chances of rescuing survivors are _____.
5. A major challenge for the government now: _____.

B *What do the following numbers represent? Listen to the news report and write down the details of the numbers in the table below.*

Numbers	Relevant Information
_____	Population of Myanmar
4000	
190	
46	
_____	The number of people missing within the Yangon and Irrawaddy divisions in a storm 3 days after Cyclone Nargis
2/5	
_____	Death toll from official reports
_____	The number of people who died within the Yangon and Irrawaddy divisions in a storm 3 days after Cyclone Nargis
41	

C *Listen to the news report and choose the best answer to complete each sentence.*

1. The severe cold in Afghanistan has caused the following EXCEPT _____.
   A. more than 715 people's deaths
   B. people to have amputation operations due to frostbite
   C. several families to sell their children due to lack of food
   D. the death of 230,000 cattle
2. Afghanistan is a country _____.
   A. with a lot of mountains   B. very poor in west Asia
   C. largely relying on industry D. with a high consumption level
3. Because of heavy snowfalls, _____.
   A. there is not enough food, water and medical care in Afghanistan
   B. many key roads have been blocked, making it hard to deliver supplies
   C. the United Nations World Food Program has distributed extra food
   D. 2.55 million Afghans will depend on aids from across the world until the next harvest in June

Speaking

Part I Pronunciation Practice

Listen to the following poem and imitate the recording. Pay attention to your pronunciation and intonation.

Natural Disaster

Darkened clouds, wind and rain.
Left alone with all this pain.
It's winter here without you.

Landslides always drag me down
Trapped for days, will I be found?
I pray for skies of blue.

Flooded plains within my head
Tornadoes draw near, leave me for dead.
I feel alone without you.

Drought from tears I know not for
I've cried for days, I cry no more.
I've made mistakes, it's true.

Hurricane waves pound on my shore
I'm drowning on my bedroom floor.
Will we never be together?

This natural bridge from heart to heart
Collapsed in shreds, fallen apart
These seasons last forever.

Unit 5 Disasters

Part II Speaking Activities

A Key Sentence Patterns

Read aloud and memorize the following sentences.

1. A natural disaster results when a natural hazard affects humans.
2. Man-made disasters are disasters caused by human action, negligence, or error, and involve the failure of a system.
3. Natural disasters (such as hurricanes) can have far-reaching negative effects on the economic conditions in the affected countries.
4. Global warming increases the temperatures of the earth's oceans and atmosphere, leading to more intense storms of all types, including hurricanes.
5. Scientists believe that the increase in disasters is due to a combination of natural and man-made factors.
6. Rapid and unplanned urbanization increases the likelihood that towns and villages will be affected by disasters such as floods.
7. Sometimes there will be epidemics following disasters such as earthquakes or floods.
8. Earthquakes can disrupt gas, electric and phone services. Roads are sometimes blocked, thus hindering delivery of supplies.
9. People throughout the world have been inspired by the courage and resilience of the Chinese people—their discipline, calm and selfless heroism in the face of appalling catastrophe.
10. There are many disruptive effects of flooding on human beings. However, flooding can bring benefits, such as making soil more fertile by providing more nutrients.

B Presentation and Discussion

1. *Disasters can be classified into natural disasters and man-made disasters. In groups, discuss different kinds of both types. Add them to the list below. Then select some that you are familiar with and explain their possible causes.*

No.	Natural Disasters
1	Earthquakes
2	Volcano eruptions
3	Floods
4	
5	
6	
7	
8	

No.	Man-made Disasters
1	War
2	Riots
3	Terrorism
4	
5	
6	
7	
8	

2. *Discuss the positive and negative impacts of disasters on human beings, societies, and / or the environment.*

Disasters	Positive Effects	Negative Effects
Earthquake	E.g. Make people realize the importance of…	

Unit 5 Disasters

C **Talk.** *Prepare a 2-minute talk on the consequences of a disaster. You can start by talking about the people's or government's reactions and solutions to assist those in danger. You may also choose to focus on what students can do to help. You can jot down some ideas before speaking.*

D **Reflection.** *In recent decades, natural disasters have become more frequent and severe, and this upward trend is set to continue. Growing urbanization and the rise in global surface temperatures appear to have increased the frequency and intensity of adverse weather events such as hurricanes, floods, and droughts. Are natural disasters totally natural? Should human beings be blamed for the damages? What can we do to protect ourselves since the earth seems like a more active and dangerous place to live?*

Part III   Situational Dialogue: Disappointment and Encouragement

A *Listen to the following dialogue and read after the recording.*

Molly Hughes has recently finished college. She is deciding on her career and is talking to her uncle, Mike, about her plans for the future.

Mike:	What are you going to do now, Molly?
Molly:	I don't know. I have to give up my hope of being a mathematician. My college days are over and I have to be realistic about myself.
Mike:	Why is that? Why do you have to give it up?
Molly:	I am so disappointed at my grades in math. They've been so bad. I couldn't live up to the goals my parents set for me.
Mike:	Come on! You did well in college. I don't think you let your parents down.

Molly: Perhaps. It's really a shame. I wish they could tell me face to face how they really feel.
Mike: You are doing fine, Molly. Even if you can't be a mathematician, you can still try finding a good job. Why don't you tell them what you'd like to be?
Molly: Perhaps I will. I used to want to be a teacher. I think my parents would like that.
Mike: Then tell them! It's important for you and your parents to understand each other.
Molly: Yes, you are right.
Mike: Molly, don't worry! I'm sure you'll be a good teacher.
Molly: Thanks for your encouragement, Uncle Mike. It means a lot to me.

B *Practise the following expressions and sentence patterns used for expressing disappointment and encouragement.*

Showing Disappointment
- Oh, no!
- That's too bad.
- I'm sorry to hear (about)...
- What a pity / disappointment!
- That's very disappointing, (I must say).
- (Oh / I have to say) I'm (rather / very) disappointed (about / at)...
- It's a real shame / pity...
- ... is a great pity / disappointment.
- That's a real shame / pity / let-down.
- I must say I had hoped (for)...
- (Oh, dear,) I was hoping (for)... / I'd been hoping...
- ...comes as a great disappointment.

Encouraging People
- Well done!
- You can do it!
- Come on!
- Stick to it!
- Keep it up!
- Keep at it!
- Don't give up!
- Great! / Terrific! / Lovely!
- I'm right behind you!
- You have our whole-hearted support!
- You're doing fine / very well!
- That's fine / good / lovely / all right.

 Complete the following dialogues with the phrases or expressions provided.

▶ You're halfway there.
▶ You always do a very good job!
▶ Finding a job is another headache for me.
▶ I'm so disappointed.
▶ I was supposed to have finished my thesis today.
▶ spend at least one more day revising the format
▶ You have my moral support.
▶ There's no reason to feel discouraged.
▶ There are still lots of mistakes.

A: _____(1)_____

B: Why is that?

A: Well, _____(2)_____ But when I saw my tutor's comment, I felt so discouraged.

B: Are there any serious problems with your thesis?

A: No. But I have to _____(3)_____

B: That's not a big deal. _____(4)_____

A: But I've revised the format five times. _____(5)_____ I am so stupid!

B: No. _____(6)_____ You are just occupied, hunting for a job.

A: Right. _____(7)_____

B: Cheer up! _____(8)_____ At least you've already got an offer.

A: I'm still waiting for a better one. Anyway, I need to revise the paper now.

B: _____(9)_____

 Work in Pairs. *Take turns to make dialogues to show disappointment or to encourage people in the following situations. Use the patterns in the above dialogues.*

1. Peter Coles couldn't make it to your birthday party.
2. You are watching your friend compete in a race. You are encouraging him/her to win.
3. You are going to have an exam. You are quite nervous and feel rushed for time.
4. You are teaching your friend, Paul, how to swim/ski/dance, etc. He is having trouble and he wants to quit.

Unit 6 Legends and Myths

Overview

- **Listening**
  - Part I   Dialogue
  - Part II   Noah and Nü Wa
  - Part III Great American Myths
  - Part IV   Athena, Arachne, and the Weaving Contest
  - Part V   News

- **Speaking**
  - Part I   Pronunciation Practice
  - Part II   Speaking Activities
  - Part III Situational Dialogue: Possibility and Impossibility

- **Skills**
  - Learning Some Legends and Myths
  - Talking About Cultural Stereotypes
  - Expressing Possibility and Impossibility

- **Language Focus**
  - Present Participles as Adjoining Adverbial Modifiers

Listening

Part I Dialogue

Word List

word of mouth	unverifiable	knight	atmosphere
strained	demanding	low-key	entertain
in store for	ingredient	magical	

A Listen to the dialogue and fill in the chart below.

	Definition	Examples
Fairy Tale		/
Folktale		/
Legend		
Myth		

  You are going to hear an interview with the legendary figure skater Alexei Yagudin. Listen to the interview and choose the best answer to the following questions.

1. Which of the following statements is NOT true?
   A. Yagudin won the World Championships four times.
   B. Yagudin won the European Championships three times.
   C. Yagudin won the Winter Olympics twice.
   D. Yagudin won the Grand Prix of Figure Skating once.

2. According to Yagudin, what is the atmosphere NOT like before a competition?
   A. Relationships between skaters become strained since everybody wants to win.
   B. They are nervous to a high extent, trying to give their best performance.
   C. The atmosphere is very tense since the competition is really important.
   D. They are all focused on the competition.

3. What does Yagudin think is the toughest part about competing?
   A. The nervousness before competitions.
   B. Trying his best every time.
   C. Waiting for his turn.
   D. The overwhelming timetable.

4. How did Yagudin celebrate his Olympic win?
   A. He went out to the clubs with his friends.
   B. He celebrated it with his coaches and family members.
   C. He had a home dinner party with those closest to him.
   D. He celebrated it with his coaches and a few close friends by going out for dinner.
5. Which of the following best describes Yagudin's prospect for the 2006 Olympics?
   A. He believes he can defend his Olympic title.
   B. He has no idea about what the future holds for him.
   C. He has no intention to compete in the 2006 Olympics.
   D. He plans to retire after the 2006 Olympics.
6. According to Yagudin, which of the following is NOT mentioned as a key factor that contributes to becoming an Olympic champion?
   A. Love of sport.   B. Self-confidence.
   C. Hard-working.   D. Others' support.

 In this part, we have learnt something about legends and a famous legendary sports figure.

In groups, discuss the following questions, giving examples where possible.

1. Of all the bedtime stories your grandparents or parents told you when you were a little child, which one was the most attractive? What kind of Chinese legends and myths do you like? Why?
2. China is a country rich in fables, including such stories as "Three at Dusk and Four at Dawn" (朝三暮四) and "The Finishing Touch"(画龙点睛). Can you tell one of these famous fables to your group members?
3. Who is your favorite Olympic champion? Why do you like him/her? What makes him/her a sports legend?
4. Do you like Yao Ming and Liu Xiang? They are both outstanding athletes who have a great reputation in the world. What kind of modern athletic legend do they make? Why are they so popular both at home and abroad?

Part II   Noah and Nü Wa

Word List

saga	stir up	survive	biblical	righteous	ark	ride out
raven	altar	sacrifice	covenant	mythology	populate	recount
rammed	slay	Genesis	Mesopotamia		Turkey	

A Look at the following picture. Who is the old man? What is he doing?

B You are going to hear a passage about legendary figures. Listen to the first part and choose the best answer to the questions below.

1. Which of the following statements is NOT mentioned?
   A. Noah was chosen by God to survive "The Great Flood".
   B. According to Genesis, God decided to destroy the world due to the wickedness of the people in it.
   C. God selected Noah because he was the only righteous man in his generation.
   D. God felt regret that He created human beings because they often offended Him.
2. According to the passage, Noah needed to take into the ark all of the following EXCEPT _____.
   A. his family	B. animals	C. tools	D. plants and seeds
3. Noah sent out _____ to find dry land.
   A. a dove and an eagle	B. a raven and an eagle
   C. a dove and a raven	D. a dove
4. The dove brought back an olive branch, indicating _____.
   A. peace in the world	B. new life appeared
   C. dry land had finally appeared	D. a forest had been found
5. Which of the following statements is NOT true?
   A. Noah worshipped God by building an altar.
   B. God promised to destroy the earth again if humans continue to be wicked.
   C. God set a rainbow in the sky as a reminder for His agreement with Noah.
   D. God will never destroy the earth even though humans become evil.

C Now listen to the second part of the passage and fill in the blank below with no more than three words.

Nü Wa is the goddess of _____ in Chinese _____. According to legend, she _____ before there were any people. Because of _____, she made copies of herself from mud _____. After a while, Nü Wa realized that it would take _____ fill the earth with people if she made them in this way. So she _____ a rope into the mud and flung the drops _____. Those people made _____ were rich and powerful, while those made by the rope were _____.

Another popular story _____ how Nü Wa saved the world from _____. The water god had tried to _____ the fire god but _____. Then he _____ Imperfect Mountain which _____ the heavens, _____ in the sky and causing the ends of the earth to _____. Nü Wa _____ of the universe by selecting stones and shaping them to repair the hole in the sky. She also _____ a giant _____ and used its legs to support the heavens.

Part III Great American Myths

Word List

omnipresent	inaccurate	stereotype	ethnic
descent	Caucasian	minority	family tie
nursing home	both ends of the spectrum		adequately
contrast	poverty	mobile home	personality
reserved	taboo	unflattering	immigrant
descendant			

A Dictation. *Listen to the following short passage and write down what you hear.*

B *You are going to hear a passage about some American myths. Listen to the passage and write T (true), F (false) or NG (not given) beside the following statements.*

(   ) 1. The myth that Americans have blond hair and blue eyes may be regarded as the number one misleading American stereotype.

(   ) 2. Seventy percent of Caucasian Americans have blond hair and blue eyes.
(   ) 3. Nursing homes are the best choice because they can provide great facilities and a good environment.
(   ) 4. Some people cannot provide enough care for their parents who live at home.
(   ) 5. Fourteen percent of American children live in poverty.
(   ) 6. Sixty-eight percent of Americans have big yards.
(   ) 7. Suburban American homes have bigger yards than the typical Asian home.
(   ) 8. Despite the cultural factor, people as individuals generally vary greatly in personality.
(   ) 9. Chinese people are open about their marital status.
(   ) 10. Americans like to make flattering comments about people's appearance.

C *Listen again and note down the four great American myths, then answer the following questions with your own words.*

Great American Myths

Myth 1: _____
Myth 2: _____
Myth 3: _____
Myth 4: _____

1. Why is the U.S. regarded as one of the most diverse nations in the world?
   _____

2. When you meet people coming from unfamiliar nations, how can you judge them objectively?
   _____

3. What have you learned from the passage besides breaking cultural stereotypes?
   _____

Part IV Athena, Arachne, and the Weaving Contest

 Listen to the following story and retell it to your partner.

In a small town of Ledia there once lived a beautiful maiden with the name Arachne. Arachne was famous in town for being a very skillful weaver and spinner and every day many girls and Nereids would stop by to see her weave.

Arachne was very vain (自负的) and couldn't stop boasting about her talent, claiming that she had learned the skill all by herself and that there was no one else in the world who could weave as delicately as her; she even felt she could compete against Athena, the goddess of the skills, and win her with ease.

When Athena heard these words, she was disappointed and decided to disguise (伪装) herself as an old lady and appear in front of Arachne. "My dear," she told Arachne, "I am old and have much experience from life, so let me give you one advice: don't ever mess with a goddess; no mortal can compete against Athena. Take back your words and kindly ask for forgiveness."

Arachne was furious and threw the thread against the old woman, telling her, "I don't need your advice. I know best what I can do. If Athena really dares, then she should come here and compete against me."

At that moment, the old woman transformed herself into the radiant (发光的) goddess Athena. At the first sight of her, everybody in the room kneeled down in awe, except for Arachne who couldn't wait to compete against her.

So the competition started and both contestants were doing really well. Athena was weaving the Parthenon and her contest with Poseidon; Arachne, on the other hand, was making fun of the gods by weaving scenes of gods full of weaknesses and fears.

Arachne's work seemed to be perfect technically, yet was not beautiful because it was showing disregard (漠视) for the gods. Athena was very offended and told Arachne, "You may be foolish and stubborn, but you love your skill. So why don't you go ahead and spin forever!"

Then Athena sprinkled (喷洒) her with the juice of magical herbs (药草) and the body of Arachne transformed into a small and ugly insect, which nowadays is known as the spider. From that moment on, Arachne was cursed to be trapped inside her own web, weaving constantly and endlessly.

B *Myths give human emotions and qualities to the super-natural beings who are the heroes and heroines of their stories. Greek myths such as Jason and the Golden Fleece, Pandora's Box, and the Trojan War are very famous in world literature.*

Do you know of any other famous Greek or Roman myths? If so, share them with your classmates. If not, do some research and share what you have found with your partner.

C **Language Focus: Present Participles as Adjoining Adverbial Modifiers**

The present participle in English is active. It is formed by adding the suffix *-ing* to the base form of the verb: *base form + -ing = present participle*. It can be used like an adjective to describe a noun, e.g. *She opened the door quietly so as not to disturb the* *sleeping child*. Here, *sleeping* describes the state of the child. The present participle can also be used as an adjoining adverbial modifier, indicating an action or state taking place simultaneously as the action in the main clause. For example,

1. God made an agreement with Noah, *promising* never again to destroy the earth. The adverbial modifier *promising* tells the content of the agreement, and suggests that the action *promising* and *making an agreement* are happening at the same time.
2. The mountain crumbled, *tearing* a hole in the sky and *causing* the ends of the earth to give way. The adverbial modifiers *tearing* and *causing* give the attendant circumstance.
3. Arachne was very vain, *claiming* that she had learned the skill all by herself. The adverbial modifier *claiming* answers the question why Arachne was very vain.

Now, it's your turn to practice present participles as adjoining adverbial modifiers.

Fill in the blanks with the words given below. Change the form where necessary.
discuss   approach   huddle   request   want

It was the last day of final examinations in a large Southern university. On the steps of one building, a group of engineering seniors _____, _____ the exam due to begin in a few minutes. The _____ exam, they knew, would be a snap. The professor had said they could bring any books and notes they _____, _____ only that they did not talk to each other during the test.

Part V   News

Word List

reconstructive	fracture	reputation	a narrow victory
grimacing	wryly	adrenaline	ebb away
lick	heed	defend	bogey-free
birdie	front-nine	back-nine	gala
head up	vibe	amateur	vie
slot	karate	roller sports	rugby seven
British Open	PGA Tour		

Unit 6 Legends and Myths

A *Listen to the news report and write T (true) or F (false) beside the following statements.*

(　) 1. Tiger Woods will not attend the rest of the 2008 season due to the injury to his right knee.
(　) 2. Woods is the luckiest golfer of all time, because he battled to a narrow victory in the US Open.
(　) 3. Woods was so excited and focused on the competition that he ignored the advice from doctors.

B *Listen to the news report and choose the best answer to the following questions.*

1. Angela Stanford won the Safeway International by _____.
   A. 52 shots on Tuesday over Ochoa
   B. 52 shots on Thursday over Ochoa
   C. 62 shots on Tuesday over Ochoa
   D. 62 shots on Thursday over Ochoa
2. How did she feel after winning the game?
   A. She was still under the weather.
   B. She was so happy that she could not find her own way.
   C. It all happened too quickly for her to realize that she actually won.
   D. She was in a thick fog.
3. Ochoa won _____ title(s) in 2007.
   A. one　　　B. seven　　　C. eight　　　D. nine

C *Listen to the news report and choose the best answer to the following questions.*

1. Which of the following statements best describes the main topic of the press conference?
   A. Efforts to place golf in the 2016 Olympics were revealed to the public.
   B. The British Open at Royal Birkdale was declared open.
   C. Many of golf's biggest players founded a union.
   D. The game "globality" was invented.
2. Who will negotiate with the IOC?
   A. PGA
   B. International Golf Federation
   C. International Association of Golf Tours
   D. United States' Golf Association

3. Which two sports are part of the 2008 Olympics and candidates for the 2016 Games?
   ① golf   ② baseball   ③ softball   ④ karate   ⑤ roller sports   ⑥ squash
   A. ②④   B. ③⑥   C. ②③   D. ①⑤

Speaking

Part I   Pronunciation Practice

Listen to the following conversation and imitate the recording. Pay attention to your pronunciation and intonation.

Bar attendant: And here's your change, sir.
Jim: Thank you.
Julia: Can we sit down somewhere, Jim? I don't like standing here.
Jim: All right. Look! There's a table over there. Come on.
Julia: (sitting down) This is much more comfortable. I think women look terrible standing at the bar.
Jim: Really? I don't think so. Anyway, cheers!
Julia: Cheers!
Jim: Would you like a cigarette?
Julia: No thanks. I've decided to give up smoking.
Jim: Really? Why?
Julia: Well... it's just that I think if you don't enjoy doing something anymore you should stop doing it.
Jim: I see. You mean you don't enjoy smoking anymore?
Julia: That's right. You should give it up, too. It's bad for your health.
Jim: Stop talking like my mother. That's what she keeps saying.
Julia: But it's true. It's a nasty habit. I can't think of why I ever started. Anyway, it's obviously got you in its grip!
Jim: What do you mean? What are you talking about?
Julia: I mean you couldn't give it up!
Jim: Who? Me? Couldn't give up smoking? Nonsense! Of course I could! I know I could!
Julia: How do you know?
Jim: Because I've already proved it. Smoking is the easiest thing in the world to give up. I've done it hundreds of times!

Unit 6 Legends and Myths

Part II Speaking Activities

A Key Sentence Patterns

Read aloud and memorize the following sentences.

1. Mythical stories are entwined with history.
2. Ancient heroes and leaders are both historical figures according to legend and important characters in mythical stories.
3. Myths and legends sing the praises of labor and creation, perseverance and self-sacrifice, rebellion against oppression, and the yearning for true love.
4. Myths and legends also encourage good deeds and warn against sin.
5. Mythical creatures are basic elements that repeatedly appear in myths.
6. The Chinese dragon is a mythical creature in East Asian culture. It is depicted as a long, scaled, snake-like creature with five claws.
7. The dragon was historically the symbol of the emperor in China.
8. Many Chinese people often use the term "Descendants of the Dragon" as a way of expressing their ethnic identity.
9. Culture shock describes the anxiety and feelings felt when people have to operate within an entirely different cultural or social environment, such as in a foreign country.
10. A stereotype can be a conventional and oversimplified concept, opinion, or image, based on the assumption that there are attributes that members of the other group hold in common.
11. Stereotypes are sometimes formed by a previous illusory correlation. They may be positive or negative in tone.
12. To be communicative is to be open, responsive and non-judgmental.
13. Reduce ethnocentrism and learn to appreciate others' point of view and life orientation.

B Presentation and Discussion

1. *Look at the following pictures. Match them with the right name of the corresponding gods and goddesses and guess their identity and symbols.*

No. 1

No. 2

No. 3　　　　　　　　　　　No. 4

No. of Picture	Roman Name	Identity	Symbols
No._____	Venus	Goddess of _____	_____
No._____	Mars	God of _____	_____; spear; _____
No._____	Apollo	God of _____; son of Zeus	_____; lighted torch
No._____	Diana	Goddess of hunting; Goddess of _____	forest; _____; _____

2. Choose one of the following idioms that originate in Greek mythology and do some research to find their origins and meanings. Tell the stories in class and be prepared to answer questions about the details from your classmates. Then try to make appropriate sentences with each of these idioms.

　　(1) Pandora's box

　　(2) under the rose

　　(3) Penelope's web

　　(4) an apple of discord

　　(5) Helen of Troy

　　(6) Achilles' heel

　　(7) swan song

3. *Journey to the West* (西游记) is one of the four great masterpieces in Chinese literature, and it is also a great myth in China.

　　In groups, discuss the following questions, giving examples where possible.

　　(1) Which legendary figures do you like best, Tripitaker, Monkey King, Pigsy, or Sandy? Explain the reason.

(2) Summarize the typical personalities of each legendary figure.

(3) Retell a story from their journey if you can.

(4) What are the features of Chinese mythology presented in these stories?

(5) What are the differences between Chinese legendary figures and western legendary figures, such as Apollo and Achilles?

(6) Modern stories such as *Harry Potter* and *The Lord of the Rings* have become very popular recently. What is it about these stories that make them so popular?

(7) How are personalities of legendary figures presented? What themes often appear in mythical stories?

4. In Great American Myths, we have learned some stereotypes of Americans.

In groups, discuss the following questions about stereotypes, giving examples where possible.

(1) Do you have any friends who have experienced culture shock? If so, what were their experiences?

(2) What are the reasons for stereotypes between peoples from different countries? What are the main sources of stereotypes?

(3) How can we adjust ourselves more easily and express more effectively in cross-culture communication?

C **Talk.** *Prepare a 2-minute talk about* **my favorite mythical creature/ legendary figure.** *You can describe the image of the mythical creature first and then talk about its cultural implications. Jot down some ideas before speaking.*

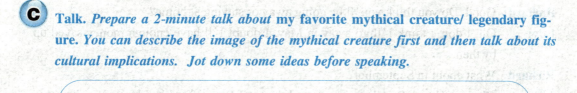

D **Reflection.** *Myths have the function of moral education. What is implied through myths is usually the truth in life.*

   In groups, discuss the following moral ideas that are usually presented in myths, and give examples to support your ideas.

(1) Virtue will be rewarded.

(1) A good heart is more important than appearance.

(2) Nothing can be gained without any effort or hardship.

(3) A person's strength, skills and judgments are the guarantee of success.

(4) The most precious gift in the world is to hold the present happiness.

Part III Situational Dialogue: Possibility and Impossibility

 Listen to the following dialogue and read after the recording.

Richard: Hi Lily! How are you?

Lily: Hello, Richard! I'm alright. You?

Richard: Fine, thanks.

Lily: Good!

Richard: I'm a bit fed up with this weather though.

Lily: Ah, yes, yes.

Richard: You taking a holiday this year?

Lily: Yes, I'm hoping to take three weeks off in May and then another three weeks later on this year—September, possibly.

Richard: Good. Do you think you'll be going away or staying at home?

Lily: Oh, I don't think I'll go away in May. I doubt I'll have enough money saved up by then.

Richard: What about in September?

Lily: Oh, yes, I'm definitely going abroad then—if I can afford it. I haven't quite made up my mind where though. Greece, maybe. Or Spain, Italy... Bound to be hot and sunny somewhere over there.

Richard: Yes. Suppose you couldn't afford it?

Lily: Oh, I expect I'd stay at home and just spend days out at the coast or in the country, you know.

Richard: Supposing you had all the money in the world, where would you go?

Lily: I think I'd go to Canada. Yes, I've always wanted to go there.

Richard: Marvellous!

Lily: Well, how about you? Do you think you'll go abroad this year?

Richard: Yes. Booked it already. We're going to Norway in August.

Lily: Really? Oh, what's the weather like out there at that time of year?

Richard: Oh, you never know with Norway. I wouldn't be surprised if it rained!

Practise the following expressions and sentence patterns used for possibility and impossibility.

Possibility
- It's (quite) possible/probable/likely...
- Maybe/Perhaps/Probably...
- ...is/looks/seems (quite) possible/likely/probably...
- It looks like/looks as if...
- I wouldn't be surprised if...
- You can be sure...
- I reckon/bet/assume/believe/predict...
- There's a good chance of ...
- I think there is every possibility that...
- It's reasonable to believe/assume/expect...
- One can't rule out/exclude the possibility of ...
- There's always/certainly the possibility...
- It's more than likely/probable...
- ...is bound to...

Impossibility
- That's out of the question.
- Impossible!
- It's extremely unlikely, in my opinion.
- That just can't be done.
- Not much chance of that.
- It's very doubtful...
- I cannot believe...
- It would not be sensible/wise to assume...
- There's no way...
- Surely not.
- Not a chance.
- No way.
- Perhaps not.
- I think there's very little chance/likelihood/probability...

 Complete the following dialogue with the expressions provided.

> ▶ I thought that we might go hiking in the hills.
> ▶ It's going to rain, isn't it?
> ▶ It might rain in the afternoon.
> ▶ Maybe we'll meet some of the artists too.
> ▶ I could play but I may be seeing Jill tomorrow.
> ▶ I heard it may rain.

Dialogue 1

Lihua: Do you think the weather will be good this weekend?
Paul: _____(1)_____
Lihua: Oh. That's a pity. _____(2)_____
Paul: Mmm... Well we could go to that new art gallery instead.
Lihua: Yes, that might be a better idea.
Paul: _____(3)_____
Lihua: Ok. Let's do that then!

Dialogue 2

A: You ready for the soccer game tomorrow?
B: _____(4)_____
A: No. _____(5)_____
B: The weatherman said it will rain. And it'll snow as well.
A: I don't think you really want to play, do you?
B: _____(6)_____

 In groups of four, discuss what the weather is usually like in China in each season.

- In spring it's usually _____
- In summer it's usually _____
- In fall it's usually _____
- In winter it's usually _____

Look at the following pictures.

These people are coming to China for a holiday:

- a married couple with a six-year-old child
- a retired couple with their grandchildren
- a group on an adventure holiday
- a group of college students

Discuss the following questions in your group.
1. When should they visit?
2. Where should they go?
3. What kind of clothes/other items will they probably need to bring?
4. How might the weather affect their holiday plans/choices?

Compare your ideas with a student from a different group.

Unit 7 Shopping

Overview

- **Listening**
  - Part I   Dialogue
  - Part II Ten Steps to Smarter Food Shopping
  - Part III Online Shopping—An Increasing Trend
  - Part IV Listening for Signal Words
  - Part V   News

- **Speaking**
  - Part I   Pronunciation Practice
  - Part II Speaking Activities
  - Part III Situational Dialogue: Shopping

- **Skills**
  - Listening for the Main Idea
  - Taking Notes While Listening
  - Listening for Signal Words
  - Talking About One's Shopping Experience and Preference
  - Shopping in English

- **Language Focus**
  - Countable or Uncountable Nouns

Listening

Part I Dialogue

Word List

| count on | stressed | mall | shopaholic |
| electronics | Levi's | | |

A "Some women include shopping in their list of favourite activities. Men usually hate it." Do you think this is true? Do you like shopping? Talk about it with your classmates.

B Listen to the dialogue between Alice and Rosa, and choose the best answer to the following questions.

1. Where was Rosa before she met Alice?
    A. She was at home.   B. She was at the movies.
    C. She was downtown shopping. D. We don't know.
2. What day is it "today"?
    A. Sunday.   B. Saturday.
    C. Tuesday.   D. Thursday.
3. Who does Rosa usually go shopping with?
    A. She usually goes shopping with her friends.
    B. She usually goes shopping with her husband.
    C. She takes her kids with her every time she goes shopping.
    D. She usually goes shopping alone.
4. Which is NOT true about Simon, Alice's husband?
    A. He hates shopping.
    B. He is happy to accompany Alice when she asks him to go shopping with her.

C. He doesn't like to spend much time in the shopping mall.
D. He doesn't want to spend much money.
5. What is shopping to Rosa and Alice?
   A. It is a pleasure.   B. It is more than just buying things.
   C. It makes them forget their worries.   D. All of the above.
6. Which of the following does Ivan, Rosa's husband, enjoy doing?
   A. Shopping for clothes.
   B. Buying jeans for himself.
   C. Buying electronics from the TV shopping channels.
   D. Staying at home and taking care of the children.

 Listen to the dialogue again and answer the following questions.

1. When will Rosa and Alice go shopping together?

2. Why aren't they going on the weekend?

3. What is the term that Alice uses to describe herself and Rosa?

Part II Ten Steps to Smarter Food Shopping

Word List

unload	deli	fall back into	dietary	enticing
astray	stay on track	impulse	browse	perimeter
lean	venture	aisle	calorie	heap
serving	beware of	condiment	carbohydrate	cashier
captive	register			

A *You are going to hear a passage on how to shop for food wisely. Listen to the passage and fill in the blanks.*

Ten Steps to Smarter Food Shopping:
1. Make a _____.
2. _____ your trips.
3. Avoid shopping on an _____ stomach.
4. Follow the _____.
5. Pay attention to _____.
6. Ignore the _____.
7. _____ your grains.
8. Watch _____.
9. Add _____ to your life.
10. Keep your eye on _____.

B *The following is the introductory paragraph of the passage you have just heard. Fill in the blanks.*

You came, you _____(1)_____, you shopped. But then you got home from the supermarket and started _____(2)_____ fatty snack items and deli meats. What went wrong? You _____(3)_____ the habit of shopping like an average American rather than a person with a _____(4)_____ purpose. In an enticing palace of eating designed to _____(5)_____, here's how to stay on track.

C *Listen to the passage again and write T (true) or F (false) beside the following statements.*

( ) 1. We are advised to make a shopping list beforehand in order not to forget anything when shopping.
( ) 2. Fresh foods like fresh meat and fish are arranged along the walls of the store, while processed foods are in the aisles.
( ) 3. Whole-grain bread contains more fibre and is considered to be healthier.
( ) 4. Food labelled "no sugar added" contains no sugar at all.
( ) 5. Although many spices have little nutritious value, they're very useful for improving the flavour of the food.
( ) 6. You need to keep your eye on the cashier in case there's any mistake at the cash register.

Unit 7 Shopping

 D *Discuss the following questions with a partner.*

What kind of food do you usually buy from a supermarket? Are they healthful foods? Why do you buy them?

 E **Language Focus: Countable or Uncountable Nouns**

Read the two questions above again. Is food countable or uncountable?

Many English nouns have both a countable and an uncountable sense. Depending on the context, these nouns sometimes refer to a particular thing and at other times to a general idea. For example,

- ***Death*** (in general) is inevitable.
- She missed work because there was ***a death*** in her family.

However, many nouns are thought of as general more by custom than for any clear reason. Many food items fall into this category, e.g., *chicken, cheese,* and *fruit*.

Thus, we see ***a chicken*** on a farm, but we eat ***chicken***; we say that the tomato is a *fruit*, not a vegetable, but we like *fruit* on our cereal.

Other nouns that can be either countable or uncountable include substances that things can be made of, like paper or glass. When you write an essay on ***paper***, it becomes ***a paper***.

Here are some common examples with their respective uses and meanings illustrated. Make sure you know the difference between the uncountable and countable meaning.

cake
- —Would you like some of **my birthday cake**?
  —I'll have just **a small piece**, please.
- —Could you get **some cakes** for tea?
  —**How many** shall I get?
  —Well, there are six of us, so get **about a dozen**.

chocolate
- There were at least **ten chocolates** in this box last night and now there is only **one**. Who has eaten **them** all?
- —Here, have **some chocolate**.
  —That's **a huge bar**. I couldn't eat all of **it**. I'll just break off **two pieces**.

pepper
- For this dish you need **two red peppers, one green pepper** and **one yellow pepper**.
- Would you like **some black pepper** and some grated cheese on your pasta, sir?

paper
- —Have you got **any paper**? I've run out.
  —**How much** would you like?
  —Could I have **three sheets**, please?
- Could you get me **an evening paper** on your way back from work please?

glass
- There's **broken glass** all over the place. Be careful.

- —**A glass of wine**, Terry?
  —I've had **two glasses** already, Norman. I'm driving, so not a drop more!

experience
- For this job, you need the **experience** of working with animals. She doesn't have **this kind of experience.**
- Accompanying Dora on her visits last week was **a really useful experience**. It was a useful training opportunity.

Now fill in the blanks with the correct forms of the words given.

1. trade
   a. _____ with China has increased dramatically over the last five years.
   b. He's not clever enough for college so he's going to pursue _____ such as carpentry.

2. time
   a. We've still got (a lot of) _____. The train doesn't leave for another two hours.
   b. —Did you have (good) _____, Henry?
      —I had (wonderful) _____, Mary, thanks.

3. light
   a. There are two _____ in our bedroom.
   b. Close the curtain. There's too much _____!

4. noise
   a. Shhhhh! I thought I heard _____.
   b. It's difficult to work when there is too much _____.

5. hair
   a. She has long blonde _____.
   b. My father's getting a few grey _____ now.

Part III Online Shopping—An Increasing Trend

Word List

search engine	cosmetics	priority	high street
reliability	boom	turnover	run-up
lure	bank balance		

Unit 7 Shopping

A Dictation. *Listen to the following short passage and write down what you hear.*

B *You are going to hear a passage about online shopping in the UK. Listen to the passage and follow the directions.*

1. Tick the statement that best sums up the main idea.
    A. The advantages of shopping online.
    B. The growing popularity of online shopping and its impact on the high street.
    C. Women do more online shopping than men.
    D. People have security worries over online shopping.

2. Look at the table below and write the correct figures on the blanks according to the information you hear.

Average amount spent online by women this Christmas	(1) £_____
Average amount spent online by men this Christmas	(2) £_____
Average amount spent per person on the high street this Christmas	(3) £_____
Percentage of Internet users buying Christmas gifts online	(4) _____%
Percentage of Internet users worried about online security	(5) _____%
Percentage of store turnover from Christmas trading for some stores	(6) _____%

105

C Listen to the passage again and to answer the following questions with key words.

1. What are the advantages of shopping online?
   _____

2. What is the evidence that online shopping is getting more popular?
   _____

3. What's the high street's reaction to the popularity of online shopping?
   _____

D Do you have any online shopping experience? If yes, share your experience with your classmates. If not, do you think you would try it someday? Why or why not?

Part IV Listening for Signal Words

A Listen to the following passage and fill in the blanks.

Signal words, which are also called transitions, conjunctions, connectors, link-words, etc., are words or phrases that help listeners follow the ____(1)____ of the speaker's thoughts. They function like traffic lights or road signs, giving listeners the ____(2)____ of the content, thus helping them ____(3)____ the main idea and the supporting details.

A speaker has many ways to ____(4)____ that he or she is moving from one point to another, giving an example, repeating a point, or whatever the change may be. For a listener, these ____(5)____ words may be easily missed.

The speaker, for example, uses time signal words such as *first, later, next, finally, before, after, now,* ____(6)____, *last, then, when, immediately, formerly, subsequently, meanwhile, presently, initially,* ____(7)____, *etc.* to arrange ideas in the order in which they appear. These signals can help the listener answer the questions of when something is happening. When the speaker continues with the same idea by providing ____(8)____, words such as *also, in addition, and, further, another, etc.,* are used as a ____(9)____ that there are more ideas to come. Contrast signals such as *on the other hand, in contrast, however, but, in spite of, conversely, despite,* ____(10)____, *on the contrary, instead, rather, though, yet, regardless, although, unlike, even though* and *whereas*, are used when the speaker is switching to a different, opposite, or ____(11)____ idea than what was previously discussed. In order to show the connection between two or more things, for example, how one thing causes another or how something happens as a result of something else, the speaker will use ____(12)____ signals like *because, accordingly, for this reason, hence, resulting, as a result, so, then, thus, therefore, since* and *consequently*.

Basic transitional words and phrases are used to ____(13)____ the understanding of the organization of a talk, connections between ideas, and the importance of ideas. Therefore, it would be ____(14)____ for listeners to learn to listen for these signal words in order to better connect and comprehend the various parts of a speech.

Part V News

Word List

make a splash	drag	bonded seams	fabric
compress	claim	backdrop	adhere to
segment	freestyle	haul	medallist
fray	Omaha, Nebraska	Speedo	NASA
USA Swimming	Ian Thorpe	Michael Phelps	Splash Aquatic Center
Mark Spitz	Janet Evans	World Water Park Association	
Shane Gould	Murray Rose	Fiji Swims Championships	
Aussie	Allison Wagner	Neil Rogers	Melbourne
Montreal			

 Listen to the news report and choose the best answer to the following questions.

1. What is attracting more attention at the US Olympic swimming trials?
   A. The swimmers.
   B. The swimsuits.
   C. Speedo's new advertisements.
2. What is the advantage of the Laser Racer suit?
   A. It is cheaper than other swimsuits.
   B. It is comfortable to wear.
   C. It helps swimmers to swim faster.
3. Who was the first athlete to wear a similar swimsuit?
   A. Ian Thorpe.
   B. Michael Phelps.
   C. Mark Spitz.

B *Listen to the news report and answer the following questions.*

1. Who went to the Splash Aquatic Center on Thursday?
   _____
2. Why were they there?
   _____
3. Who asked them to do it?
   _____

C *Listen to the news report and choose the best answer to the following questions.*

1. Which sport competition will be held next week?
   A. The ninth FINA World Swimming Championships.
   B. The fifth Fiji Swims Championships.
   C. The 2008 Olympic Games.
2. Who won five solo medals in a single Olympiad?
   A. Shane Gould.
   B. Murray Rose.
   C. Allison Wagner.
3. Where was the 1956 Olympic Games held?
   A. Montreal.
   B. Rome.
   C. Melbourne.
4. Who will be participating in next week's competition for the third time?
   A. Murray Rose.
   B. Allison Wagner.
   C. Neil Rogers.

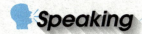 Speaking

Part I Pronunciation Practice

Listen to the following poem and imitate the recording. Pay attention to your pronunciation and intonation.

Shopping with a Friend
By Rita El Khoury

Shopping with a friend is cool
There's nothing forbidden, no rule
And no parents to say what's suitable
Or to tell you what's unaffordable,
Actually you don't need to be rich
To try on whatever your eyes wish.

Shopping with a friend is so nice
You might forget budget and price
And buy things you don't need
Just by habit, not by greed
Like get ten or eleven similar tops
From two or three different shops.

Shopping with a friend is funny
Even if you don't have money
You can try a formal blue shirt
With a long gypsy orange skirt
Pretend to buy them but act lost
Then don't, because they're low-cost.

Shopping with a friend is naughty
You can act humble or haughty
Change personalities between stores:
Be a girl who laughs and snores
Or an English tourist, elegant and neat
Who went walking on the street.

But shopping is more pleasant with a friend
Who has a thousand dollars to lend.

Part II Speaking Activities

A Key Sentence Patterns

Read aloud and memorize the following sentences.

1. Next time we can go shopping together since we are both shopaholics.
2. Women usually have a better fashion sense than men.
3. It's no accident that supermarkets pile their impulse items next to the registers.
4. Shopping online offers lots of benefits that you won't find shopping in a store or by mail.
5. Lots of people can do their shopping in the comfort of their own home with the help of the Internet.
6. Many companies are concerned that not enough shoppers are coming through their doors in the run-up to Christmas.
7. Bad news for the high street has become good news for the bank balances of UK shoppers this Christmas!
8. Shopping is a social event. It makes you feel normal. Most people find it cheers them up—even window shopping.
9. Clothes, furniture, all the things that we buy involve decisions and the use of our choice.

B Presentation and Discussion

1. Ask your partner the following questions and take notes of his / her answers. Tell your partner your answers as well. Then go to someone else and tell your new partner about your previous partner's shopping behaviour.

    1. How often do you go shopping?
    2. What do you usually shop for? What do you prefer shopping for?
    3. Do you always buy something when you shop? Do you go window shopping when you don't have money to buy things?
    4. Do you buy only what you need? Why or why not?
    5. Are you willing to pay more for clothing that has a designer label on it?
    6. Describe your favourite place to shop. Why is it your favourite?

2. Interview as many of your classmates as possible to find out what is important to them when they buy different things. Ask them to give reasons why they think it is important or unimportant. Summarize your findings to the class.

What is important to you when shopping?							
Items	Price	Comfort	Quality	Brand Name	Look	Function	Warranty
coat							
shoes							
school bag							
bicycle							
camera							
computer							
mobile phone							

C Talk. Make a 2-minute speech to the class, telling them which you prefer, shopping in supermarkets or grocery stores, big malls or boutiques. Elaborate on your reasons.

D Reflection. Read the following statements and decide whether you agree with them or not. Share your opinion with your classmates.

People have three stages as consumers or shoppers: Young people want "possession experience"; they want to buy a house and fill it with objects. Middle-aged people spend money on things like travel, education, and sports. Older adults want "being experiences"; they get the most happiness from simple pleasures and hanging out at the local market.

Part III Situational Dialogue: Shopping

A Listen to the following dialogues and repeat out loud after each sentence.

Dialogue 1

A tourist is shopping for some clothes in a department store.

Clerk: Have you been helped?
Tourist: I'm just looking right now, thank you...
(Five minutes later) May I see these ties?
Clerk: Yes, certainly. Here's a nice-looking one.

111

Tourist: Yes, it is attractive. But I think it's a little too loud. My friend's tastes are quite conservative. Let me see that grey and blue one.

Clerk: This one?

Tourist: Yes, that's the one...it's very nice. I'll take it.

Clerk: Fine. Will there be anything else?

Tourist: No, but could you tell me where the ladies' department is?

Clerk: Yes, it's on the next floor up. Will this be cash or charge?

Tourist: Charge...that is, if you accept American Express.

Clerk: Yes, that'll be fine.

(In the ladies' department)

Tourist: I'd like to try on this blouse, please.

Clerk: The fitting room is right over there.

Tourist: Excuse me...this is too large—do you have this same blouse in a size 10?

Clerk: Let me check for you...yes, we do, but only in yellow. Would you like to try it on anyway?

Tourist: Yes, please.

Dialogue 2

Anna is shopping in a supermarket.

Anna: Excuse me. Where are the eggs?

Clerk: They are in aisle D, next to the butter.

Anna: Thank you.

(Anna has chosen all the items she needs. She goes to a checkout counter.)

Clerk: I'm sorry. You're in the wrong lane. This is the express lane.

Anna: Sorry? I don't understand.

Clerk: This is the express lane. It's for 8 items or less. You have more than 8 items in your cart.

Anna: Oh, excuse me.

(Later, in a regular lane)

Clerk: Plastic or paper?

Anna: Paper, please.

Clerk: The total is 59 dollars.

Anna: Here's sixty dollars.

Clerk: Alright. Here's your receipt and one-dollar change. Thank you.

B *Practise the following expressions and sentence patterns used for shopping.*

- —Excuse me, miss. Where's the children's department?
  —Third floor, to the right of the escalator.

Unit 7 Shopping

- —Can I help you?
  —No. It's all right. Thank you. I'm just looking. / Yes, may I look at some sunglasses?

- —Is this what you're looking for? / What kind do you have in mind?
  —Well, actually I wanted something slightly smaller.

- —How much is it? / How much did you say it is?
  —It costs $100. / They're $5 each.

- —Do you have any cheaper ones? / Do you have something for less?

- —Will there be anything else?
  —No, not at the moment. Thank you.

- —What does it come to?
  —That comes to $40 with tax.

- —Cash or charge?
  —Do you take cheques/credit cards? / I'll pay cash.

 Pair work. *Match each sentence in column A to the correct response in column B. Then practise the mini-dialogues with your partner.*

A	B
1. Do you need some help?	a. I take a size 10C shoe.
2. What size shoes do you wear?	b. His waist is 28 inches.
3. I'd like to see a sweater.	c. It's $12.98 plus tax.
4. Where are the skirts for little girls?	d. Yes, I'm looking for ladies' raincoats.
5. I'm buying this as a gift for someone. If it doesn't fit, can I return it?	e. They're right opposite the elevators.
6. May I try this on?	f. In a small, medium, or large?
7. How much is this shirt?	g. Certainly. The dressing room is in the the rear.
8. What size jeans does he need?	h. Certainly, just be sure to hold onto your sales slip.

 Chinese New Year is coming and you are going shopping for gifts.

1. Think of three people you want to get something for, e.g. your parents, relatives or friends.

Write down their names first. Then discuss with your partner what presents would be good for them. Prepare a shopping list.

2. Exchange your shopping list with one of your classmates. Have a look at the things he / she is going to buy. Make believe you are the shop assistant. Help him / her choose the things he / she wants.

3. Change roles. Your partner is the shop assistant now and you are going to buy the items you have listed. Use the expressions you have learned above.

Unit 8 Women Around the World

Overview

- **Listening**
    - Part I   Dialogue
    - Part II   Meet the Power Sisters
    - Part III   Women Struggle for Their Rights
    - Part IV   All Women Are Born for Loving
    - Part V   News

- **Speaking**
    - Part I   Pronunciation Practice
    - Part II   Speaking Activities
    - Part III   Situational Dialogue: Making Comparisons

- **Skills**
    - Listening for Details
    - Making Comparisons

- **Language Focus**
    - Idioms

Listening

Part I Dialogue

Word List

eonomic restructuring	laid-off	state-owned company
basic livelihood	subsidized housing	re-employment rate
pilot project	micro-credit loan	preferential
tax waiver	respond to	on one's initiative
supervisory	All-China Women's Federation	

A You are going to hear an interview about women and their jobs. Listen to the first part of the interview and finish the outline below.

Women are laid-off due to _____.
The problems laid-off women face are: ① _____
② _____
③ _____
The current situation of women's re-employment is: _____.
   Supporting statistics:
   Women's re-employment rate is less than _____.
   Men's re-employment rate is almost _____.
To change the status quo of women's re-employment,
   (1) the All-China Women's Federation has been conducting _____:
      ① offering _____ for starting businesses
      ② giving _____, such as tax waivers, for companies _____
      _____
   (2) the laid-off women are:
      ① taking the initiative to _____
      ② not relying on _____

B Listen to the second part of the interview and choose the best answer to the following questions.

1. Which of the following statements is NOT true?
   A. Women's pay is equal in principle but lags behind men's in reality.
   B. The pay gap between women and men has widened during the last two decades.

Unit 8 Women Around the World

  C. China has adopted the policy of equal pay for equal work, which has been well implemented since 1990.
  D. Women earn less than men—30% less, to be precise.
2. The following are factors which may lead to women getting fewer promotions than men EXCEPT _____.
  A. women are discouraged from voicing their concerns
  B. women are expected to be quiet and hardworking
  C. women's suggestions are often ignored
  D. women are ignorant of office politics
3. Which of the following statements is NOT mentioned?
  A. Female supervisors get more pay than male supervisors.
  B. Supervisors pay more attention to men's suggestions.
  C. Women may get negative responses from their supervisors.
  D. Women are thought to be hardworking and not easily agitated.
4. According to the dialogue, what can women do when they face unequal pay?
  A. File a lawsuit against their workplace.
  B. Lodge a complaint to the All-China Women's Federation.
  C. Start their own business.
  D. Strive for promotion opportunities.

 During the interview, the topic "equal pay for equal work" is discussed.

In groups, discuss the following questions, giving examples where possible.
1. (a) What does "equal pay for equal work" mean? Does it exclusively refer to gender discrimination in employment? What other factors could be involved in this issue?
  (b) How can we help realize the decades-old promise of "equal pay for equal work"? Give your suggestions.
2. What are some traditional women's jobs and men's jobs? List at least three typical professions for each. Why do people make such a classification? Can men do well in women's jobs or vice versa?

Part II Meet the Power Sisters

Word List

organism	cut out	sustain	weight-lifting	pole vault
testosterone	goat roping	settle for	bust	chromosome
exceptional	softball	bodybuilding	groaning	buff

117

snatch	clean and jerk	hone	rodeo	contortion
heptathlete	daredevil	fascination	Victorian	NFL (National Football League)

A You are going to hear a passage about two sisters in the Olympics. Listen to the passage and tick (√) the right information to complete each sentence.

1. The first women's marathon in the Olympics was held in _____.
   ☐ 1896   ☐ 1948   ☐ 1984
2. Women's _____ events debuted in the Sydney Olympics.
   ☐ archery and softball   ☐ equestrian and baseball   ☐ weight-lifting and pole vault
3. Haworth is the world's best junior weight-lifter at the age of _____.
   ☐ 17   ☐ 16   ☐ 19
4. Haworth can run the _____ dash in an _____.
   ☐ 41-yd. / NFL-like 5 seconds
   ☐ 34-yd. / NBA-like 5 seconds
   ☐ 40-yd. / NFL-like 5 seconds
5. In weight-lifting, the _____ is when you lift the weight first to the chest, then overhead.
   ☐ snatch   ☐ clean and jerk
6. Dragila holds the world record of _____.
   ☐ 20 ft. $1\frac{3}{4}$ in.   ☐ 15 ft. $1\frac{3}{4}$ in.   ☐ 16 ft. $1\frac{3}{4}$ in.

B Listen to the first part of the passage again and write T (true), F (false) or NG (not given) beside the following statements.

(   ) 1. Women's organism is weak, so they can't sustain certain shocks.
(   ) 2. Men's weight-lifting and pole vault were two events in the Victorian Olympics.
(   ) 3. Haworth broke the gender barrier and became the world's best junior weight-lifter before she finished high school.
(   ) 4. Haworth was overweight so she couldn't play softball.

Unit 8 Women Around the World

(   ) 5. Haworth once dreamed of appearing in bodybuilding TV shows.
(   ) 6. Haworth used her speed and power to lift the bar easily.

C *Listen to the second part of the passage again and answer the following questions.*

1. What sports events did Stacey Dragila engage in before competing in pole vault?
   _____

2. What is Dragila's attitude towards women's pole vault?
   _____
   _____
   _____

3. Why did Dragila say she had men to thank for her success in her pole vault career?
   _____
   _____
   _____

4. What can female athletes learn from Haworth's and Dragila's stories?
   _____
   _____
   _____

D **Language Focus: Idioms**

An idiom is a group of words whose overall meaning is different from the meanings of the individual words it's made up of. In other words, it does not make sense by its literal translation, but has a completely different and metaphorical meaning. For example, "Haworth is an exceptional athlete in a body that screams couch potato". Here, *couch potato* is not a variation of potato, but a product of modern society, referring to a person who spends most of his or her free time sitting or lying on a couch, watching television.

We use idioms to express something that other words do not express as clearly or as effectively. For example, "*in a nutshell*" suggests the idea of having all the information contained within very few words. Idioms tend to be informal and are best used in spoken rather than written English.

Now, it's your turn to practice idioms.

Fill in the blanks with the idioms given below and translate the sentences into Chinese.

couch potato   mouse potato   hot potato   mall rat

1. My friend Joe is such a _____ ; all he does every day is watch TV and eat pizza.
2. Unemployment is a real _____ in this year's election.

3. A _____ spends an excessive amount of time in front of a computer monitor.
4. I used to be a _____ hanging around the shopping center watching the crowds, especially the girls, but now I joined the football club, and I have no time.

Part III Women Struggle for Their Rights

Word List

take steps	honor killing	sizeable	enforce	approve
convention	elimination	bill of rights	infect with	human trafficking
Liberia	Chile	Pakistan	Arab	Bahrain

A **Dictation.** *Listen to the following short passage and write down what you hear.*

B *You are going to hear a passage about women around the world struggling for their rights. Listen to the first part of the passage and fill in the chart below.*

Inequality	Country	Phenomena	
Domestic Violence	Russia	_____ women killed each year by _____	
	_____	hundreds of women murdered every year by their families	
Social Aspects	_____	_____	unwillingness
		Education	_____
		Family life	_____
Political Aspects	Arab nations	_____	
Financial Aspects	The United States	own property, but _____ than men and _____ health insurance	

Unit 8 Women Around the World

C *Listen to the second part of the passage and fill in the blanks with no more than three words.*

> To protect and _____ the rights of women, the United Nations approved the Convention on the _____ of All Forms of Discrimination Against Women in _____, regarding it as a _____ for women. So far, _____ nations have approved it. However, women in many of these countries are still treated as _____. The progress of women's struggle for rights and _____ is slow.
>
> _____ women die while having babies every year. A growing number of women and girls _____ H.I.V. and AIDS in the world. And violence against women, _____ labor and _____ of young females continue.

D *Listen to the whole passage again. Write T (true), F (false) or NG (not given) beside the following statements.*

(   ) 1. More women are killed in Pakistan than in Russia each year.
(   ) 2. "Honor killing" can partially explain the murder of women in Pakistan.
(   ) 3. Religion is the main reason why there are few women officers in Arab countries.
(   ) 4. Women's rights are well protected in every aspect in the U.S.A.
(   ) 5. Sexual attacks often make women and girls infected with H.I.V and AIDS.

E *In the recording, the problems women face in their struggle for equality are mentioned.*

> *In groups, discuss the following questions.*
> - Do you think the phenomena mentioned in the recording exist in China?
> - What are the most serious problems for Chinese women who struggle for their rights?
> - What changes have taken place in Chinese women's lives since 1949? Explain with examples.
> - Are women treated differently in rural and urban areas? Explain with examples.

Part IV All Women Are Born for Loving

 Listen to the following passage and fill in the blanks.

A little boy asked his mother, "Why are you crying?"

"Because I am a woman," she told him.

"I don't understand," he said.

His mom just hugged him and said, "And you never will."

Later the little boy asked his father, "Why does mother seem to cry for no reason?"

"_____(1)_____," was all his dad could say.

The little boy grew up and became a man, still wondering why women cry.

Finally he put in a call to God. When God got on the phone, he asked, "God, why do women cry so easily?"

God said, "When I made the woman, she had to be special. I made her shoulders strong enough to _____(2)_____, yet, gentle enough to give comfort.

"I gave her inner strength to endure childbirth, and the rejections that many times come from her children.

"I gave her hardness that allows her to keep going _____(3)_____, and take care of her family through sickness and fatigue (疲劳) without complaints.

"I gave her the sensitivity (感性) to love her children under any and all circum stances, even if her children have hurt her very badly.

"I gave her strength to carry her husband through his faults, and fashioned her from his rib (肋骨) to protect his heart.

"I gave her the ____(4)____ to know that a good husband never hurts his wife but sometimes tests her strength, and resolve (决心) to stand beside him unfalteringly (坚决地).

"And finally, I gave her ____(5)____. That is hers exclusively to use whenever it is needed.

"You see the beauty of a woman is not the clothes she wears, the figure she carries, or the way she combs her hair.

"The beauty of a woman must be seen in her eyes, because that is the doorway to her heart, the place where the love resides (居住)."

B Now do you understand the reason why the boy's mother was crying? Reflect on what God said to the man and flash back to your own childhood. Do you remember any moments when your mother cried? Could you understand her feelings? Knowing the great responsibility mothers shoulder, how should we help them out when they cry?

Part V News

Word List

auction	empirical	participant	resolution
empower	jurisprudence	articulate	institutional
pregnancy	maternal death	complication	calculate
live birth	emergency care	woefully	inadequate
abortion	U.S. Congress	Islamic	Caribbean
Oceania	sub-Saharan Africa	Scandinavia	

 Listen to the news report and choose the best answer to the following questions.

1. Which of the following statements is NOT true?
   A. Susan Athey from Harvard University is one of the most promising economists in the world.
   B. Susan Athey is thirty-six and the first woman to win the Clark Medal.
   C. Susan Athey won the Clark Medal mainly because she was the first woman to research empirical studies in economics.
   D. Susan Athey has worked in the area of government auctions and deals with economic problems in the real world.

2. The Clark Medal is/was NOT _____.
   A. awarded by the American Economics Association
   B. first awarded in 1969
   C. awarded every two years to an economist who is under the age of forty
   D. harder to win than a Nobel Prize in economics

3. Susan Athey was especially honored for _____.
   A. being the first woman Clark Medalist
   B. being the most promising economist

C. cross-domain economic research
D. empirical studies in economics

B *Listen to the news report and fill in the blanks below.*

1. The summer leadership program is sponsored to educate women about _____ _____, and _____, and enable Muslim women to _____.
2. The Islamic law provides the principles for freedom of _____, and the right to _____.
3. The focus of this training program includes traditional _____, and how women can deal with domestic _____ against women.

C *Listen to the news report and choose the best answer to the following questions.*

1. Pregnancy is getting safer in _____.
   A. Latin America, the Caribbean, and Oceania
   B. Latin America, North Africa and sub-Saharan Africa
   C. Oceania, North Africa and America
   D. Oceania, sub-Saharan Africa and America

2. The high number of maternal deaths in sub-Saharan Africa is due to _____.
   ① starvation   ② war
   ③ inadequate healthcare system ④ social and economic circumstances
   ⑤ the decrease of donor funding
   A. ①②③⑤   B. ②③④⑤
   C. ①②④⑤   D. ①③④⑤

3. How can we immediately resolve death from abortion?
   A. Teach women healthcare knowledge.
   B. Increase donor funding.
   C. Increase the value society places on women.
   D. Make abortions safe, legal and accessible.

Unit 8 Women Around the World

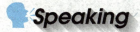Speaking

Part I Pronunciation Practice

Listen to the following poem and imitate the recording. Pay attention to your pronunciation and intonation.

> **Anyway**
> **By Mother Teresa**
>
> People are often unreasonable, illogical and self-centered;
> Forgive them anyway.
> If you are kind, people may accuse you of selfish, ulterior motives;
> Be kind anyway.
> If you are successful, you will win some false friends and some true enemies;
> Succeed anyway.
> If you are honest and frank, people may cheat you;
> Be honest and frank anyway.
> What you spend years building, someone could destroy overnight;
> Build anyway.
> If you find serenity and happiness, they may be jealous;
> Be happy anyway.
> The good you do today, people will often forget tomorrow;
> Do good anyway.
> Give the world the best you have, and it may never be enough;
> Give the world the best you've got anyway.

Part II Speaking Activities

 Key Sentence Patterns

Read aloud and memorize the following sentences.

1. For most women, work is not only a means of earning a living, but more importantly, it's the focus of their lives and the source of satisfaction.
2. Most women have no idea what is worth doing when they are out of work.

3. Withdrawal from employment to complete domesticity means the loss of a certain social status that women now enjoy after many years of struggle.
4. Men should take an equal share in housework so as to liberate women from the kitchen.
5. Prejudice against women violates the fundamental principle that all people are created equal.
6. Women should be given an equal chance at education in order to compete with men on an equal footing.
7. Women's participation in the Olympics is one aspect of their self-independence and self-reliance.
8. Unfair distribution of resources does exist between male and female athletes. Few female athletes and coaches are in leading posts or management positions, and there are many other social biases towards women taking part in sports.
9. A good education will benefit a woman throughout her life whether she is a career woman or a housewife.
10. Women hold up half the sky.

 Presentation and Discussion

1. There is a traditional belief that a woman's place is in the home and that a woman ought not to go out to work after marriage.

   In groups, list at least four more points under the pros and cons on the topic "**Should women return to the kitchen?**" Present your ideas with supporting examples, then discuss the questions that follow.

Pros	Cons
Jobs are scarce now and unemployment rates higher; if women returned to the kitchen, there would be more jobs available for men.	Deprived of work, most women will suffer unspeakable boredom and misery.

- Is it better to be a housewife than a career woman? Why or why not?
- What jobs do you think are good choices for women? Why?

- To be an excellent woman in business, what qualifications are needed?
- What advantages and disadvantages do women have at work? Explain with examples.
- If women want to be successful in their careers, what difficulties do they need to overcome?
- How can working women balance work and motherhood? Give three suggestions.

2. The passage Meet the Power Sisters tells about the outstanding talent and capability female athletes have in sports.

   In groups, discuss the following questions, giving examples where possible.
   (1) Do you know any other female athletes who have outstanding achievements in sports? Share their stories with your classmates.
   (2) Some people say that sports like judo and weight-lifting should be limited only to male athletes. What is your opinion? Do you think these events are not appropriate for women? Why or why not?
   (3) Are there any differences between women and men's participation in sports? If so, what are they?
   (4) Many women regard thinness as beauty. The thinner they are, the prettier they become. Is this perception a big obstacle for women promoting sports activities?
   (5) What are some ways to promote sports activities among women? Give two or three suggestions.

3. Women are generally more sensitive than men.

   In groups, discuss the following questions, giving examples where possible.
   - Do women really have a better sixth sense than men, or do men just not have it at all? Do you know any stories about women's or men's sixth sense?
   - Women are more romantic than men. Do you agree or disagree? Explain with examples.
   - Why do some women nowadays like to dress neutrally? Explain with examples.

C Talk. *Prepare a 2-minute talk about* **how to be a(n) attractive/confident/independent person.** *You can talk about the characteristics such kind of people have or what men/women find attractive/confident/independent in each other. Jot down some ideas before speaking.*

D **Reflection.** *From what you have just learned about the women's liberation movement, what can independent modern women do when they encounter trouble such as sexual harassment, sexual attacks, domestic violence, etc.? Should they keep silent owing to traditional moral requirements on women or bravely step forward to struggle for their own rights?*

Part III Situational Dialogue: Making Comparisons

A *Listen to the following dialogue and read after it.*

Sally: Well, Jack, it was great to get away, but it's good to be home again.

Jack: It really was a wonderful trip. So, which city did you like best: Paris, London, or Rome?

Sally: That's hard to say. There were good things and bad things about all three cities.

Jack: Wait a minute! What bad things?

Sally: Traffic, for one. The traffic in London was pretty bad, and the traffic in Paris was even worse! I was afraid to cross the street.

Jack: That's true... and how about Rome? I thought Rome was worse than Paris. Those drivers are crazy! And always honking their horns! It was really noisy there.

Sally: Paris was noisy too, a lot noisier than Rome.

Jack: You are right, Paris was noisy, but I still think Rome was noisier.

Sally: Well, all big cities have bad traffic and a lot of noise. Let's not think about the bad things. Think about all those art galleries we visited.

Jack: Yeah, the art galleries in Rome were fantastic, but I thought the Paris art galleries were better. Of course, I've always dreamed of going to the Louvre.

Sally: Me, too. I loved the galleries in London, but I liked the ones in Paris even more. The restaurants in Paris were better than those in London, too. I thought the food was more interesting. It had more flavor.

Jack: And the food in Rome was incredible! I liked the Italian restaurants better than the French ones. I thought they were more interesting. Before we went to Rome, I thought Italian food was all pizza and spaghetti!

Sally: Really? I'm sure I put on weight in Rome.

Jack: Maybe not. We did a lot of dancing at night. Those discos in Rome were great, but I think I liked the Paris nightlife better. It was more romantic.

Sally: You know where I had more fun in the evening? In London. Paris was good, but I thought the London nightlife was better.

Jack: Yeah, we saw a couple of great plays. Oh, I'll never decide which city I liked best.

Sally: Me, neither.

Practise the following expressions and sentence patterns used for making comparisons.

Comparison
- *Both* Mike *and* Jim have red hair.
- *Just like* Mr. Smith, Mr. Jones is a good teacher.
- *Like* most people, I'd prefer to have enough money not to work.
- She'll soon be *as* tall *as* her mother.
- Cars must stop at red traffic lights; *similarly*, bicycles should stop too.
- *Neither* my mother *nor* my father went to university.
- Just water these plants twice a week, and *likewise* the ones in the bedroom.
- When civilization is gone, men are *no better than* beasts.
- I would rather not accept *any* more charity *than* I have to.
- I had *no more than* 2 or 3 mistakes on my English assignment.
- There is *nothing* in the world that I *like so much as* music.
- He has *no less than* three daughters.

Contrast
- *Unlike* you, I'm not a great dancer.
- He *is not as* smart *as* she is.
- Their economy has expanded enormously, while ours, *in contrast*, has declined.
- She felt ill. She went to work, *however*, and tried to concentrate.
- *Although* he is poor, he is well contented.
- She is pretty, *but* her husband is ugly.
- He must be about sixty, *whereas* his wife looks about thirty.
- He is an able man, but *on the other hand* he demands much of people.

 Two students are talking about their apartment. Complete the following dialogue with the expressions provided.

▶ I could live in either one.
▶ I like the furniture in the modern one though.
▶ That wouldn't be so good if we're doing a lot of studying.
▶ Maybe I am more interested in luxury.
▶ The modern one's really nice, but the older one's a lot bigger.
▶ But the older apartment's cheaper.
▶ The modern one is nicer looking.

A: What do you think? Which apartment do you like better?

B: _____ (1) _____

A: Yeah. In the older one we could use the dining room for a study.

B: Mm-hm-m. _____ (2) _____ It's in really good shape.

A: _____ (3) _____

B: Well, not that much cheaper—only $10.00.

A: Hmm. That's true. And you're right. _____ (4) _____ Then again, modern apartments look nice, but sometimes the walls are so thin that you can hear every word your neighbors say.

B: Yeah. _____ (5) _____ On the other hand, though, the kitchen in the modern apartment is really nice. The refrigerator is huge and there's disposal and a dishwasher. It would save us a lot of time.

A: You seem to like the modern one more.

B: Hmm. I guess I do. But really, _____ (6) _____

A: Yeah, me too. I guess the question is—do we want roominess or luxury?

B: I don't know. _____ (7) _____

A: OK. Let's get the modern one.

B: You sure?

A: Really, I like them both.

B: OK. The modern one it is then.

 D *Two students, A and B are discussing which sports are more popular. Work in pairs and make conversations with the following information as reference.*

A	Golf	many people enjoy it but it's too expensive; plenty of golf courses; only a tiny number of people played in the past
	Extreme sports	a few people like them; the majority are afraid to try
	Rugby	plenty of rugby fans
	Football	more boys than girls; a few girls play really well
	Basketball	some people
	Tennis	more and more people
	Table tennis	fewer people play than before
B	Swimming	many people; fun, keep fit
	Extreme sports	only for a small minority of people, several enjoy most just watch
	Golf	no one
	Rugby	a great number of people follow

Unit 9 Travel

Overview

- **Listening**
    - Part I   Dialogue
    - Part II   Travel Smart: Dollars and Sense
    - Part III The Experience of Travelling and Learning
    - Part IV   Life Is a Journey
    - Part V   News

- **Speaking**
    - Part I   Pronunciation Practice
    - Part II   Speaking Activities
    - Part III Situational Dialogue: Buying Tickets

- **Skills**
    - Talking About Travelling
    - Learning Expressions Used in Buying Tickets

- **Language Focus**
    - Metaphors

Listening

Part I Dialogue

Word List

grind	head off	itinerary	megaphone	causeway
gondola	sleek	ebony-colored	criss-crossing	screeching
din	enormity	envision	quaint	expansive
strain one's neck		gigantic	roaming	porcelain
Kenya	Uganda	Venice	Marco Polo	Don Juan
Campanile				

A Have you ever been to or read anything about Venice? Look at the pictures below and give your impression of the city.

B You are going to hear a dialogue about travelling. Listen to the dialogue and write T (true), F (false) or NG (not given) beside the following statements.

(　　) 1. Most people love travelling because the work they do is torturing.

(　　) 2. Molly and Ronald plan to go to the Red Sea for their spring break.

(　　) 3. One reason why Molly doesn't like package tours is that she feels like a sheep being driven by tour leaders.

(　　) 4. The only way to get inside the city of Venice is by boat.

(　　) 5. Molly enjoyed different styles of architecture in Venice.

(　　) 6. There are no traffic lights, nor the sound of car horns in Venice.

(   ) 7. Before going to Venice, Molly thought it was a very small and delicate place.
(   ) 8. Campanile at Epcot Centre in Disney World is the same size as the one in Venice.
(   ) 9. Besides Venice, Milan is another highlight of Molly's trip to Italy.

C *Listen to the dialogue again and answer the following questions with key words.*

1. Why do most people want to take trips?

2. What is Molly's plan this spring? What is she expecting?

3. How can one decide whether to join a package tour or do an independent one?

4. Why does Molly like travelling independently?

5. What impressed Molly most when she arrived in Venice?

6. What is the main mode of transportation in Venice? How did Molly and her cousin travel there?

7. What did they see in Venice?

Part II   Travel Smart: Dollars and Sense

Word List

scarce	hop	catch	lodge
guest ranch	make up for	flyer	as opposed to
periodically	obsess	gratuity	notably
mandatory	wrangler	cruise ship	spelled out
insult			

A You are going to hear a passage about how to travel smart. As you listen, compare the prices below and put a tick beside the least expensive option. Fill in the blanks.

1. Travel in general:
   ☐ off-season ☐ peak season ☐ shoulder season
   It is because _____.

2. Summer airfares during peak season to:
   (1) ☐ popular mountain areas ☐ warm-weather destinations
   (2) ☐ Galapagos Islands ☐ the Caribbean ☐ Europe

3. Staying at resorts:
   (1) ☐ midweek ☐ weekends
   (2) for business travellers
       ☐ midweek ☐ weekends
       The best airfares often require a _____ unless it's a _____.
   (3) domestic airfares
       ☐ in the middle of the week ☐ at the beginning or at the end of the week
       ☐ working hours on weekdays ☐ off-hours on weekdays
       If you take off two days from work in order to get a midweek flight or book a midweek resort stay, you lose _____.

4. Shoulder season:
   (1) ☐ early in the season ☐ in the middle of the season ☐ late in the season
       You can still have the benefits of _____ and _____
       _____ available during peak season. But sometimes you cannot enjoy _____
       _____ as they are no longer available.
   (2) at guest ranches
       ☐ June and July ☐ July and August
       ☐ June and August ☐ June and September
       If you were counting on a children's program so you could get in _____
       time, the money you save by _____ may not make up for that loss.

B Now listen to the second part of the passage about bargaining skills at hotels. As you listen, write T (true), F (false) or NG (not given) beside the following statements.

( ) 1. You can only get a hotel bargain during the off-season.
( ) 2. The usual practice of hotels is to offer guests discounts.
( ) 3. People making reservations need to ask if there's a better deal.
( ) 4. Most hotels post their special deals or discounts in a newspaper.
( ) 5. For group members, there might be a better price.

Unit 9   Travel

( ) 6. To get the best price, people reserving a room should go to the hotel rather than make a phone call.
( ) 7. If a hotel doesn't offer you a deal, you can try another one.

 Listen to the third part of the passage about tipping. As you listen, choose the best answer to complete the following sentences.

1. For travellers, paying gratuities is usually _____.
   A. obligatory   B. voluntary   C. mandatory
2. The following statements are FALSE EXCEPT _____.
   A. most people's income is from their tips
   B. tips can help tour guides make a decent living
   C. you should tip whenever you travel with a guide
3. When travelling to ranches, _____.
   A. you have to tip the wranglers and other staff
   B. you need to give tips to waiters for good services
   C. what's exactly expected is not explained in the brochures
4. In foreign countries, _____.
   A. you can buy guidebooks to check whether to tip or not
   B. giving tips is always acceptable as good manners
   C. it's not necessary to give tips everywhere

D In groups, discuss the following questions.

1. Of all the tips mentioned in the passage, which one is most helpful to you when you prepare for a trip? Why?
2. For students, there are usually two long vacations every year. But the problem is, students don't have enough money to go on a trip. How can students enjoy a relaxing trip with their meager budget?
3. What is your understanding of the statement "When I have time, I have no money; when I have money, I have no time"? Explain with examples.

Part III   The Experience of Travelling and Learning

Word List

| immerse | hostel | blossom | barrier |
| erstwhile | glean | preconception | |

135

A **Dictation.** *Listen to the following short passage and write down what you hear.*

B *You are going to hear a passage about someone's experience of travelling and learning. Listen to the passage and choose the best answer to complete the following sentences.*

1. The best way to learn about a culture is to _____.
   A. read some books   B. observe the people
   C. be immersed in it
2. When a student first meets his host family, he usually feels _____.
   A. nervous   B. excited   C. surprised
3. _____ is the most effective way to learn about a culture.
   A. Staying in hotels and hostels
   B. Communicating with families of the culture
   C. Attending classes or lectures on culture
4. The following statements are TRUE EXCEPT that _____.
   A. the challenge of new experiences will make one learn how to deal with all of his/her personal hindrances
   B. one will realize that he/she can achieve or succeed at more than what he/she expected by coping with new situations
   C. learning about different cultures can teach one about one's own culture that he/she never appreciated or understood before
5. Some of the greatest joys of travel are obtained from _____.
   A. being able to show one's self-confidence
   B. knowing that one's preconceptions are wrong
   C. interacting with and learning from strangers

Unit 9 Travel

 Listen to the passage again and answer the following questions.

1. What do we expect from travelling in other countries?
   _____

2. What kind of questions might a student ask himself when first meeting the host family?
   _____
   _____

3. What is the feeling of the host family when first meeting a student?
   _____

4. What can a student gain from staying in another culture?
   _____
   _____
   _____
   _____

Part IV   Life Is a Journey

 Listen to the following passage for appreciation.

> Do not undermine your worth by comparing yourself with others.
> It is because we are different that each of us is special.
>
> Do not set your goals by what other people deem important.
> Only you know what is best for you.
>
> Do not take for granted the things closest to your heart.
> Cling to them as you would your life, for without them, life is meaningless.

Do not let your life slip through your fingers by living in the past nor for the future.
By living your life one day at a time, you live all of the days of your life.
Do not give up when you still have something to give.
Nothing is really over until the moment you stop trying.
It is a fragile thread that binds us to each other.

Do not be afraid to encounter risks.
It is by taking chances that we learn how to be brave.
Do not shut love out of your life by saying it is impossible to find.
The quickest way to receive love is to give love.
The fastest way to lose love is to hold it too tightly.
In addition, the best way to keep love is to give it wings.

Do not dismiss your dreams.
To be without dreams is to be without hope.
To be without hope is to be without purpose.
Do not run through life so fast that you forget not only where you have been, but also where you are going.

Life is not a race, but a journey to be savored (品味) each step of the way.

 Language Focus: Metaphors

A *metaphor* is an implied comparison between two unlike things that actually have something important in common. The comparisons are implied rather than introduced by *like* or *as* which is used in a simile.

Poets use metaphors in their poetry, and often an extended metaphor throughout. Fiction writers can improve their stories by using figurative language to create vivid images and to strengthen ideas. In his poem *The Fog*, Carl Sandburg wrote: "The fog comes on little cat feet". Here the fog is compared to a cat: the fog comes silently like a cat. The following are some other examples of metaphor:

1. Life is not a race, but a journey to be savored each step of the way.
2. Children flocked to the ice cream stand.
3. Juliet is the sun. (Shakespeare)
4. My heart is a lonely hunter that hunts on a lonely hill. (William Sharp)
5. Language is a road map of a culture. It tells you where its people come from and where they are going. (Rita Mae Brown)

Exercise: *Fill in the blanks with a creative metaphor.*

1. Time is _____.
2. Family and friends are _____.

3. Emily's parents love her deeply since she is _____.

4. He was courageous and fought furiously in the battle. He was _____
_____.

5. George has been working at the same automobile factory six days a week, ten hours a day, for the past twelve years. He is _____.

C As what we have learned, happiness is a journey; life is a symphony; life is a journey. Express your understanding of or reflection on different aspects of life with the use of metaphors. Then explain in what ways they are similar. The following is an example:

> Life ⟶ Journey
> People ⟶ ?
> Bad weather ⟶ ?
> ...

Part V News

Word List

exhibition games	crack	swelling	invisible
coverage	regular season	finale	postseason
fade	slide	home	pitcher
bullpen	MLB (Major League Baseball)	the All-Star break	
TBA (to be announced)		AL (American league)	

A Listen to the news report and fill in the blanks.

American Major League Baseball games are coming to China for the first time, with the Los Angeles Dodgers and San Diego Padres to _____(1)_____ on March 15 and 16 at _____(2)_____ for the 2008 Olympics.

Baseball—like soccer, American football and basketball—is eager to ___(3)___ in China, which has a population of 1.3 billion and _____(4)_____ keen to spend on foreign brands.

Unlike soccer and basketball, baseball and American football are ___(5)___ in China and _____(5)_____.

The two exhibitions and the Olympics in Beijing will give baseball a chance to _____(7)_____. The sport was _____(8)_____ but

139

looking to return in 2016.

Gene Orza, chief operating officer of the MLB Players Association, said his members seemed _____(9)_____ about making the long trip to China.

B Listen to the news report and answer the following questions.

1. Why is the Yankees' regular-season finale important?
_____.

2. Who will the Yankees' opponent be? When will the game begin?
_____.

3. Who will broadcast the game?
_____.

4. How much is a ticket for the game?
_____.

C Listen to the news report and write T (true), F (false) or NG (not given) beside the following statements.

( ) 1. Baseball's All-Star game lasted from Tuesday night to Wednesday night.
( ) 2. It was Justin Morneau's sacrifice fly that decided the game's result.
( ) 3. The American League has won 12 games consecutively.
( ) 4. The 4-hour-and-50-minute marathon made the stadium empty.
( ) 5. All pitchers from both teams had the chance of participating in the game.

Speaking

Part I Pronunciation Practice

Listen to the following dialogue and imitate the recording. Pay attention to your pronunciation and intonation.

Jenny: Why do you think people travel so much nowadays? What's this modern craze all about?

Jack: Well, you know, people travel for all sorts of reasons. Travelling for pleasure is only one of them. People travel for business, for work, for adventure, even for education. Travel is supposed to broaden the mind, you know. There's more leisure and money around, so travel has become available to more people.

Jenny: In the old days, people travelled very little because it was so slow and difficult. It used to take a fortnight to travel from London to Edinburgh by coach. Now you can travel many times around the world in that time!

Jack: And travel to the moon and back in a week!

Jenny: I know, it's amazing! And to think that the next generation will take it all for granted.

Jack: Think of what Columbus and his contemporaries would have thought. Crossing the Atlantic seemed miraculous to them. Distances have dwindled to nothing in this space age of ours. Travelling to far away places has become a common activity.

Jenny: Yes, but travelling on this planet is quite enough for me. You won't ever catch me travelling to the moon in one of those space-ships, thank you very much!

Part II Speaking Activities

A Key Sentence Patterns

Read aloud and memorize the following sentences.

1. When travelling in other countries, we can meet different people, see different sights and do different things.
2. Travelling not only teaches you about other cultures, but also teaches you more about yourself and your own culture.
3. Travel has a lasting impact on people's world view, self-confidence, and maturity.
4. Travel can make one's life rich and colorful.
5. People can get a taste of a different lifestyle when travelling to another place.
6. Travelling by air is the fastest yet most expensive way.
7. I prefer travelling by train because it evokes a spirit of nostalgia.
8. Travelling by bike or on foot is an ideal way for me as I can do some physical exercise and enjoy the beautiful scenery along the road at the same time.
9. Tourism is an industry that depends on the physical environment.
10. Tourism can boost a country's economy and provide more job opportunities.
11. Tourism has both negative and positive impacts on the natural environment.
12. The quality of the environment, both natural and man-made, is essential to tourism.
13. The negative impacts of tourism development can gradually destroy the environmental resources on which it depends.
14. Tourism development can put pressure on natural resources when it increases consumption in areas where resources are already scarce.

B Presentation and Discussion

1. (1) As Mark Twain once remarked, "Travel is fatal to prejudice, bigotry, and narrow-mindedness." A Chinese proverb also goes, "March thousands of miles and read thousands of books". People travel for different reasons. In groups, discuss the reasons why people travel. Add them to the list below, and then choose one to explain to the class.

No.	Why People Travel
1	Relaxation
2	
3	
4	
5	
6	
7	
8	
9	
10	

(2) Travelling is not always a pleasant experience. For example, people might be very exhausted after travelling with a package tour due to limited time; hence they cannot focus on their study or work afterwards because of their tiredness. In groups, discuss the negative effects of travelling and provide some of your suggestions.

2. There are many means of transportation that can be used while travelling. Discuss the different means and compare the advantages and disadvantages of each one. Then choose the one you prefer to use while travelling.

No.	Means of Transportation	Advantages	Disadvantages
1			
2			
3			
4			
5			

Unit 9   Travel

 Talk. *Prepare a 2-minute talk about your most memorable trip. You can consider the following questions while preparing: When and where did you go? Who did you meet? What did you do or see on the trip? You can jot down some ideas before speaking.*

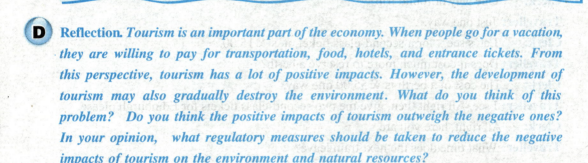

 Reflection. *Tourism is an important part of the economy. When people go for a vacation, they are willing to pay for transportation, food, hotels, and entrance tickets. From this perspective, tourism has a lot of positive impacts. However, the development of tourism may also gradually destroy the environment. What do you think of this problem? Do you think the positive impacts of tourism outweigh the negative ones? In your opinion, what regulatory measures should be taken to reduce the negative impacts of tourism on the environment and natural resources?*

Part III   Situational Dialogue: Buying Tickets

A *Listen to the following dialogues and read after the recording.*

Dialogue 1   Making Flight Reservations

　　Yasuro Mizuno and his wife are planning a trip to Honolulu. He is making flight reservations over the phone.

Agent:　　United Airlines. How may I help you?

Mizuno:　　Yes, I'd like to make reservations for flight number 220, departing for Honolulu on December 22nd at 7:30 in the evening.

Agent:　　Your name, please?

Mizuno:　　Mr. and Mrs. Yasuro Mizuno.

Agent:　　Do you want to fly first-class or economy?

Mizuno:　　Economy.

Agent:　　Yes, we still have room on that flight. Will this be a one-way trip?

Mizuno:　　No, round trip back to Chicago—on January 3rd. By the way, do you have any

143

direct flights coming back?

Agent: Yes, we do. Flight number 414, leaving Honolulu at 3:00 in the afternoon, flies non-stop back to Chicago.

Mizuno: That'll be perfect. What is the exact airfare?

Agent: Economy fare round trip from Chicago to Honolulu is $503 during peak season.

Mizuno: I see... then our tickets are confirmed?

Agent: Yes, your seats are confirmed on those two flights. Please be at the airport at least one hour before departure.

Dialogue 2　Buying Tickets at a Railway Station

Traveller: Can you tell me the price of two second-class tickets to Edinburgh?

Clerk: One way or round trip?

Traveller: Just one way.

Clerk: Let's see... for a second-class ticket, it's £15.00.

Traveller: Does it cost much more to reserve a berth?

Clerk: The cost of a berth is £55.00 one way.

Traveller: I see. All right then, give me two second-class tickets for Edinburgh please.

Clerk: All right, here you are.

Traveller: What time does the next train leave?

Clerk: At 8:32 from platform number 4.

Traveller: What time does it arrive in Edinburgh?

Clerk: At 6:00 in the morning.

Traveller: There must be a faster way. Is there an express leaving tonight?

Clerk: Yes, but it doesn't leave until 10:00. It arrives at 5:02.

Traveller: Well, I guess we might as well take the slower train then. Is there a dining car on that train?

Clerk: No, I don't believe there is, but you can buy sandwiches and cold or hot drinks on the platform at each stop.

Dialogue 3　Taking a Subway

Carl: Is this the right subway to the Rockefeller Center?

Judy: Yes, you take the F train on the downtown platform area, and go three stops.

Carl: How much is the fare?

Judy: Two dollars. Give me the money and I'll exchange it for a token for you.

Carl: What do I do with the token?

Judy: Put it in the slot at the turnstile and then push. That will get you into the platform area.

Carl: Oh, I see. By the way, how can I get out of the platform after I get off the train?

Judy: The exits are always open. After you get off, you can look at the map and choose

Unit 9 Travel

     the right exit.
Carl: Thank you very much!
Judy: You are welcome.

 Practise the following expressions and sentence patterns used for making flight reservations and buying train and subway tickets.

Making Flight Reservations
- I want to fly to... (destination) on... (date)
- I'd like to make a reservation / reservations to... (destination) for... (time)
- Could I make a reservation for flight... (number) to... (destination)?
- I'd like to travel at the cheapest rate.
- I want to fly economy class.
- I'd like to travel first-class, please.
- What flights do you have from... to...?
- How often is there a flight to...?
- How much is a one-way / round-trip ticket?
- Is it a non-stop flight?
- When does this flight depart?
- When should I be at the airport?

Buying Train Tickets
- I'd like to buy a hard seat / soft seat / hard sleeper / deluxe soft sleeper ticket to...
- Do you have a Pullman ticket to... for...?
- I want to buy a(n) local / express / special express train ticket to...
- What time does the train leave?
- How often is there an express from... to...?
- Do I have to make a connection at... (place)?
- From which platform should I catch the express to...?

Taking a Subway
- Which subway shall I take to...?
- Can you tell me which subway goes to...?
- Is this the right subway to...?
- How often does the subway run during rush hour?
- How much is the fare / a day pass?
- Must I have the exact change?
- Can you tell me how to use the token / card?
  (You deposit the token in the slot / swipe the card and the gate will open automatically.)
- Do I need a transfer?
- Is there any discount for seniors / youth / children?

C *Complete the following dialogues with the phrases or expressions provided.*

> ▶ We have a non-stop flight leaving Kennedy at 9:25.
> ▶ Thirty-two dollars for a hard sleeper.
> ▶ When should I get to the airport?
> ▶ The 18:05 express train.
> ▶ When is the next day's express to Los Angeles?
> ▶ What flights do you have from New York to London tomorrow?
> ▶ Do you want to fly first-class or economy?
> ▶ I'd like to have a Pullman ticket to Los Angele.

1

A: _____(1)_____
B: One moment please, and I'll find out what's available. _____(2)_____
A: I'd like to travel first-class.
B: Ok. _____(3)_____
A: _____(4)_____
B: Please be there by 8:45 at the latest.

2

A: _____(1)_____
B: What train do you want to take?
A: _____(2)_____
B: Sorry. There aren't any tickets available for the 18:05 express.
A: _____(3)_____
B: The next day's express will leave at 18:20.
A: Ok. I will take that one. How much is it?
B: _____(4)_____

D *Pair Work. Take turns to make dialogues about booking or buying tickets for the following situations. Use the patterns in the above dialogues.*

1. You want to book a flight to Dallas from Beijing.
2. Jasmine wants to go to Hamburg by train.
3. Feifei just arrived in London and needs to take the subway to her college.

Unit 10 Famous People

Overview

- **Listening**
  - Part I   Dialogue
  - Part II The Greatest Individual Athletic Achievements
  - Part III A Great Scientist
  - Part IV Guessing Vocabulary from Context
  - Part V   News

- **Speaking**
  - Part I   Pronunciation Practice
  - Part II Speaking Activities
  - Part III Situational Dialogue: Getting Information

- **Skills**
  - Listening for the Main Idea
  - Listening for Details
  - Guessing Vocabulary from Context
  - Talking About Famous People and Being Famous
  - Getting and Giving Information

- **Language Focus**
  - Reduced Adverb Clauses

Listening

Part I Dialogue

Word List

celebrated	sane	wear off	drag
creep	stalker	pathologically	soul mate
relentlessly	shed light on	stem cell	The Beatles
Henry Moore	Benjamin Britten	Bertrand Russell	Princess Diana
Nancy Reagan	Elton John		

A Two British people are talking about national figures. Listen to the dialogue and write T (true), F (false) or NG (not given) beside the following statements.

(   ) 1. The term "national figure" is hard to define and a bit confusing when used.

(   ) 2. A country may have hundreds of national figures because there are many outstanding people from all walks of life.

(   ) 3. Pop singers and film stars are usually not considered national figures because their contributions are less than scientists' and artists'.

(   ) 4. A person born into a rich and powerful family is more likely to become a national figure.

B Listen to the dialogue again and answer the following questions.

1. Does the term "a national figure" refer exclusively to someone who is alive?

2. How does David describe the term "a national figure"?

3. What possible effect can modern media have on the celebrity of national figures?

Unit 10 Famous People

 John, David, Lori and Amy are talking about whether they want to be famous. Listen to their conversation and fill in the blanks with key words.

Those who want to be famous:	
Those who do not want to be famous:	
Reasons why they want to be famous:	
Reasons why they don't want to be famous:	

 Listen to the conversation again and answer the questions below.

1. What did John, the second speaker, probably do when he was young?

2. According to John, how long does it take for the shininess of fame to wear off?

3. What would people pathologically addicted to attention like to be?

4. Do you think Lori would be interested in gossip news?

5. Who campaigns for the AIDS cause?

 The following are the "big names" mentioned in the two dialogues. Make sure you know who they are and what achievements they have made. You may do some research if necessary. Then choose one of them to describe to your classmates and let them guess who the person is.

The Beatles	Sir Isaac Newton
Henry Moore	Winston Churchill
Benjamin Britten	Princess Diana
Bertrand Russell	Nancy Reagan
William Shakespeare	Elton John

Part II The Greatest Individual Athletic Achievements

Word List

divert	sonata	homage	panel	diagnose
testicular	cyclist	gruelling	consecutive	mouthy
upstart	weigh-in	sting	pummel	strip
rope-a-dope	nickname	park	home run	tenacious
outrageous	defy	dunk	rack up	reign
cocky	brag	Forbes	Tour de France	
Big Ten Conference Championships			the Nation of Islam	
The Rumble in the Jungle			the American League	
Chicago Bulls			NHL	

A You are going to hear a passage about the greatest individual athletic achievements. Listen to the introduction to the passage and fill in the blanks.

At their best, sports are more than just about winning games and ____(1)____. They test ____(2)____ what the human body and spirit can achieve. A great athlete performing at the peak of his or her ability is as moving as a(n) ____(3)____ or a Bach sonata.

____(4)____ these extraordinary men and women, Forbes.com compiled a list of the ____(5)____ of the last 150 years. Here are seven of the top 20 voted by ____(6)____ experts, editors and readers.

B You will hear three athletic achievements.

1. Listen and match the athletes to their respective events and achievements.

Athletes	Events	Achievements
Lance Armstrong	track and field	three heavyweight titles
Jesse Owens	boxing	seven consecutive Tour de France victories
Muhammad Ali	cycling	four world records in 70 minutes

Unit 10 Famous People

2. Listen to the recording again and fill in the blanks.

(1) The Tour de France is a _____ race covering more than _____ kilometers (_____ miles). It is considered to be the most gruelling event in _____ sports. It takes place in France every _____.

(2) Jesse Owens broke three world records, namely in the _____, the _____ and the _____, and tied a fourth in the _____ in the year of _____. Owens won _____ gold medals at the 1936 Olympic Games in Berlin.

(3) Muhammad Ali won the Championship belt three times: respectively in _____, _____ and _____.

C You will hear another four athletic achievements.

1. Listen and match the athletes to their respective events and achievements.

Athletes	Events	Achievements
Babe Ruth	basketball	seven gold medals
Michael Jordan	baseball	2,857 career points
Wayne Gretzky	swimming	ten seasons at the top
Mark Spitz	hockey	60 home runs in a season

2. Listen to the recording again and fill in the blanks.

(1) Babe Ruth's _____ record of 60 home runs in just _____ represented _____ of all of the home runs hit in the _____ that year.

(2) Michael Jordan is a tenacious _____ and outrageous _____. His gravity-defying _____ earned him the nickname "Air" Jordan. He was the NBA's _____ five times, set the NBA record for most _____ games scoring in double digits (842), was a member of six _____ teams, and ended his career with a regular-season _____ of 30.12 points per game—the highest in NBA history.

(3) By the time he retired in 1999, Wayne Gretzky held or shared _____ records, including most career regular-season _____ (894), most career regular-season _____ (1,963), most _____ in a season (92) and most _____ (10).

(4) Mark Spitz won seven golds and broke _____ world records in the _____ Olympic Games.

Part III A Great Scientist

Word List

naturalization	renounce	chauvinistic	be devoid of
doctorate	equivalence	photon	extension
inertia	cosmology	pacifist	fascism
gravitation	electromagnetic	subatomic	reverence
comprehensible	mold	experimentation	draw on
predecessor	unerring	cosmic	intuition
Ulm, Germany	University of Zurich	Prague	Berlin
Academy of Science	Princeton, New Jersey		Milan
Jewish	Switzerland	Polytechnic Academy	

 A Dictation. *Listen to the following short passage and write down what you hear.*

 B *You will hear a passage about Albert Einstein. Listen to the passage and choose the best answer to the following questions.*

1. Which is NOT one of the three decisions Einstein told his father he had made?
   A. He would drop out of school.
   B. He would leave the Jewish community.
   C. He would give up his German nationality.
   D. He would study science instead of arts.

2. Which was NOT one of Einstein's achievements in 1905?
   A. He published four research papers.
   B. He received his doctorate in physics.
   C. He proposed the general theory of relativity.
   D. He proposed the photon theory of light.

3. The nuclear power plant is built on _____.
   A. the special theory of relativity
   B. the general theory of relativity
   C. the equivalence of mass and energy
   D. the theory of Brownian motion
4. When was Einstein awarded the Nobel Prize?
   A. In 1915.
   B. In 1919.
   C. In 1921.
   D. In 1933.
5. Einstein probably left Germany for America because _____.
   A. the Institute in Princeton offered him better research conditions and a higher salary
   B. the Institute in Princeton was the only place where he could pursue his research towards unifying the laws of physics
   C. he faced the danger of being persecuted by the Nazis in Germany
   D. all the rest of his family were moving to the U.S.A. and he wanted to be with them
6. What did Einstein mean by saying "The most incomprehensible thing about the world is that it is comprehensible"?
   A. There was a complex system in nature that was revealed to those who searched.
   B. There was nothing in the universe that he could not understand.
   C. He considered himself more a philosopher than a scientist.
   D. Only he and the Greek philosophers understood the laws of nature.
7. Einstein's achievements came mainly from _____.
   A. drawing on the insights of predecessors
   B. using the powerful analytical tools of mathematics
   C. working closely with his colleagues
   D. following his unerring cosmic intuition

C What other facts do you know about Albert Einstein? Share them with your group-mates.

D Language Focus: Reduced Adverb Clauses

Look at the following sentence in which "although" is followed by a noun phrase. This kind of structure is called a reduced adverb clause.

Although a committed pacifist, Einstein began to warn against the dangers of fascism as the Nazis denounced his work as Jewish science.

An adverb clause can be reduced only when the subject of the adverb clause and the subject of the main clause are the same:

1. Omit the subject of the clause and the BE form of the verb:
   While I was watching TV, I fell asleep.
   While watching TV, I fell asleep.
2. If there is no BE, omit the subject and change the verb to "-ing" form:
   After I signed the report, I gave it to the director.
   After signing the report, I gave it to the director.

   However, the adverb clause in the following sentence cannot be reduced, because the subjects are different:
   While the teacher was speaking, I fell asleep.

Reduce the adverb clauses in these sentences.

1. The customer paid for his groceries when he passed through the checkout stand.
2. Richard got a thorn in his finger when he was pruning the roses.
3. After they had heard the terrible noise, they ran for their lives.
4. He didn't see the dandelions (蒲公英) in the lawn until after he had watered it in the morning.
5. Will measured the board again before he made his final cut.
6. The necklace, even though it was staggeringly expensive, would match the dress perfectly.

Part IV Guessing Vocabulary from Context

A *Listen to a lecture on listening skills and fill in the missing words.*

Guessing meaning from context is an important listening skill. Even native speakers often hear ____(1)____ words in speech and must try to guess the meaning through context. Those who are successful at this skill use many ____(2)____ to help them in guessing the right meaning of the vocabulary. Here are three ____(3)____ that will help you make better guesses about the meanings of words you don't know.

1. Use the words and phrases surrounding the unknown word to make quick guesses about its ____(4)____ meaning. For example, when you hear:

Five years ago, the Recording Industry Association of America, the R.I.A.A., launched a major effort to catch music **pirates.** **Piracy** *violates copyright laws.*

You might not be familiar with the word *pirate* or *piracy*. However, because you know that the two words might be ____(5)____ with something that breaks the law, thus it might mean something ____(6)____. The exact definition usually doesn't matter; you only need a(n) ____(7)____ idea of its meaning. When you are listening, you need to make very fast guesses ____(8)____ the general meanings of words. If you stop to think about a word for too long, you will probably ____(9)____ your understanding of the speaker's next point. So be sure to make your guesses quickly and learn to be ____(10)____ with less than 100% certainty.

2. Recognize when the speaker offers a definition or a(n) ____(11)____ of an unknown word. For example,

A nightmare is a disturbing dream that causes the dreamer to wake up feeling anxious and frightened.

In this way, the speaker is directly telling us the ____(12)____ definition of a nightmare. Usually the speaker will use key words, or signal words to identify a definition so you don't need to look for them. The ____(13)____ key words are *is/are; means/mean; is/are called; what this means is; is/are known as; consist of; is/are defined as; refers/refer to; is/are described as and may be seen as...*

In addition, speakers sometimes define words or phrases using *appositives*. Here, an "appositive" is any word or phrase—a noun, pronoun, noun clause, ____(14)____ phrase, prepositional phrase, etc.—which stands after another word or phrase without a ____(15)____ link. For instance, when we hear:

Epic dreams or great dreams are so huge, so compelling, and so vivid that you cannot ignore them.

Here, the speaker ____(16)____ the phrase "epic dreams" using the appositive phrase "great dreams".

3. Finally, try to build your vocabulary as quickly and ____(17)____ as possible, since the more words you know, the easier it is to guess unknown words from context. As you complete this ____(18)____, keep a vocabulary log of the new words and idioms you encounter and learn, and review them frequently.

B Use context clues to guess the meaning of the words in bold print.

1. During the earthquake, bridges fell and cars were **crushed**.
2. Hail is a small round ball of **alternating** layers of snow and clear ice.
3. Hospitals now have large computers and machines that help doctors **diagnose** medical problems.
4. Some headaches cause **blurred** vision, and you can't read or drive.
5. A natural substance in the blood, **cholesterol** comes from the liver.

Part V News

Word List

reaffirm	dip	perfume	branch out
premiere	elegantly	spectacle	elated
a gaggle of	poised	pageant	trip
bejewelled	tumble	round out	Chanel
Warner Bros	Venezuela	Dominican Republic	Colombia

 A Listen to the news report and answer the following questions.

1. What title was Kaka holding at the time of the news report?

2. Had Kaka reached his peak?

3. What problem was Kaka facing? What did he think had caused the problems?

4. What is the maximum age limit of athletes in the Olympic soccer tournament?

5. Which country will hold the 2014 World Cup?

 B Listen to the news report and write T (true) or F (false) beside the following statements.

1. Emma Watson has signed a three-year contract with Chanel, a French fashion house.
2. Previously she had already signed a contract with Storm, a top modelling agency.
3. Warner Bros were unhappy about her deal with Chanel.

 C Listen to the news report and choose the best answer to the following questions.

1. Who won the title of Miss Universe 2008?
   A. Miss Colombia.
   B. Miss Dominican Republic.
   C. Miss Venezuela.
   D. Miss USA.

2. Who fell down during the 2008 Miss Universe evening gown competition?
   A. Dayana Mendoza.
   B. Riyo Mori.
   C. Crystle Stewart.
   D. Rachel Smith.
3. Who was NOT among the final five contestants?
   A. Miss Mexico.
   B. Miss Japan.
   C. Miss Colombia.
   D. Miss Russia.

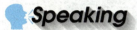

Speaking

Part I   Pronunciation Practice

Listen to the following poem and imitate the recording. Pay attention to your pronunciation and intonation.

Annabel Lee

By Edgar Allan Poe

It was many and many a year ago,
In a kingdom by the sea,
That a maiden there lived whom you may know
By the name of Annabel Lee;
And this maiden she lived with no other thought
Than to love and be loved by me.

I was a child and she was a child,
In this kingdom by the sea;
But we loved with a love that was more than love—
I and my Annabel Lee;
With a love that the winged seraphs of heaven
Coveted her and me.
And this was the reason that, long ago,
In this kingdom by the sea,
A wind blew out of a cloud, chilling

My beautiful Annabel Lee;
So that her highborn kinsman came
And bore her away from me,
To shut her up in a sepulcher
In this kingdom by the sea.
The angels, not half so happy in heaven,
Went envying her and me
Yes! that was the reason
(as all men know, In this kingdom by the sea)
That the wind came out of the cloud by night,
Chilling and killing my Annabel Lee.

But our love was stronger by far than the love
Of those who were older than we
Of many far wiser than we
And neither the angels in heaven above,
Nor the demons down under the sea,
Can ever dissever my soul from the soul
Of the beautiful Annabel Lee.
For the moon never beams without bringing me dreams
Of the beautiful Annabel Lee;
And the stars never rise but I feel the bright eyes
Of the beautiful Annabel Lee;
And so, all the night-tide, I lie down by the side
Of my darling, my darling, my life and my bride,
In the sepulcher there by the sea,
In her tomb by the sounding sea.

Part II Speaking Activities

A Key Sentence Patterns

Read aloud and memorize the following sentences.

1. When we talk about a national figure we mean a very famous person, a famous prime minister / an eminent poet / an honoured scholar, for example.
2. Who do you think has been the greatest writer in recent years / in the past?
3. What particular quality do you most admire in a statesman / novelist / poet?

4. Integrity / A good style / Imagination is what I most admire in a statesman / novelist / poet.
5. The Beatles are famous (as) pop singers. / Shakespeare is famous as a poet / is a famous poet.
6. Madame Curie was a woman of great distinction. / Mozart was a man of genius.
7. Confucius was extremely wise, wasn't he? / Napoleon was fantastically energetic, wasn't he?
8. You cannot be a great man or woman without possessing courage.

B **Presentation and Discussion**

1. Which Chinese people would you put in the following categories?

   a famous leader   a distinguished writer
   a celebrated artist   a popular athlete
   a war hero   an honoured scholar
   a well-known millionaire   an eminent statesman
   an eminent poet   an important philosopher
   a fine musician   a remarkable singer
   a great entertainer   a sought-after pop star
   a renowned film star

   Get together with two of your classmates and discuss your answers. Did you think of the same people? Do you consider them as national figures?

2. What qualities do you think a statesman should possess? How about an artist, a scientist, or a writer? Discuss these questions with your partner. The following are some words for your reference.

strength	courage	humanitarianism
moral courage	good looks	integrity
learning	piety	initiative
energy	talent	ambition

3. Read the following letter to The Times from a sociologist, and answer the question that follows.

   Sir, —I have great doubts about the merits of some so-called world celebrities.

   Nowadays, practically anyone who has achieved some degree of success in a particular field can become famous overnight as a result of a newspaper article or a television programme. We all know the impact of the cinema on the masses and above all how the press can blow up the importance of a person out of all proportion.

Before the invention of modern communication media people had to prove their worth the hard way before they received national recognition. The result was that only people of exceptional merit ever became world celebrities.

I suspect that the tendency today is for people to be less discriminating and for the masses to idolise figures that are not really worthy of much admiration.

Yours faithfully,

John Cunningham

Name three world celebrities and give your reasons for picking them.

(1) One that you consider a person of real talent.

(2) One that you do not consider to be worthy of the title "a world celebrity".

(3) One that you know was made famous through films, radio, the press or television.

C **Talk.** *Think of an international figure you would be most in awe of if you were to see him / her in person. Prepare a 2-minute speech about this person and explain why you respect him / her.*

Reflection. *What is the purpose of life? Which is most important to you, fame, money, power, faith or love?*

Part III Situational Dialogue: Getting Information

A *Listen to the following dialogues and read after the recording.*

Dialogue 1

(The telephone rings.)

Box office: Warner Theatre.

Jennifer: Yes, what are you showing this week?

Box office: Well, starting today we have *Batman* and *Journey to the Center of the Earth*.

Jennifer: *Batman and Journey to the Center of the Earth*? I've never heard of that movie. Who's in it?

Box office: I'm sorry, but you misunderstood. Those are two movies. *Batman* is the first one, and then *Journey to the Center of the Earth* is after that.

Jennifer: Oh, I didn't realize it was a double feature.

Box office: Yes, we always have a double feature during the week.

Jennifer: Could you tell me when the first one starts?

Box office: Seven-fifteen.

Jennifer:	OK, thanks a lot. Bye.
Box office:	You're welcome. Bye.

Dialogue 2

Stranger:	Excuse me.
Resident:	Yes?
Stranger:	I... I was wondering if you could help me.
Resident:	Well, I'll try.
Stranger:	I need to find out where the... er... town centre is. Now I see there's a sign up there that points to the left.
Resident:	Ah well, let me see... er... it all depends if you're on foot or going by car.
Stranger:	Ah no, I'm walking.
Resident:	Ah well, you turn to the right and then carry straight on.
Stranger:	Ah, right, thanks! Er... I wonder if you could tell me... um... if there's a good hotel... er... in town where I can stay.
Resident:	Oh, let me think a moment... um... yes, there are two hotels—they're in the High Street... er... one on each side of the road.
Stranger:	Right, well, I expect we'll manage to find one of those. Er, I wonder if you could tell me... er... anything about the... er... castle in town... er... where... where it is.
Resident:	Um, well, it's actually further on... er... down the High Street and then you cross over the bridge and it's on the other side of the river.
Stranger:	I see, I see. Could you tell me a bit more about it? Is it interesting? Is it old?
Resident:	I'm not really sure. I've never actually been there myself. It... yes, I think it's quite old, I think it's about... um... 500 years old—something like that.
Stranger:	Worth... worth visiting, you think?
Resident:	Well, it's one of the tourist attractions of the town... um...

 Practise the following expressions and sentence patterns used for asking for information and responding.

> **Asking for Information**
> - Any clue...?
> - (Got) any idea...?
> - Can you give me any information about...?
> - Sorry to bother you, but do you know...?
> - Excuse me, do you happen to know...?
> - I wonder if you could tell me...

- Would you mind telling me...?
- I hope you don't mind my asking, but I'd like to know...
- I was wondering if you could help me. I'd like to know...

Responding
- Well, let me see...
- Well now...
- Oh, let me think for a moment...
- I'm not sure. I'll just have to find out...
- That's a very interesting question...
- I'm really not sure.
- I'm terribly sorry, I really don't know.
- I've no idea, I'm afraid.
- I have to say I know very little about...
- I have to admit I don't know a great deal about...

C Complete the following dialogue with the sentences provided.

▶ I'm new in town.
▶ Could you tell me how to get to Carnegie Library from here?
▶ But I do know where Sears is.
▶ That's quite all right.
▶ On 10th?
▶ Let me get this straight...
▶ That's right.
▶ Let me see...
▶ You've been very helpful.

A: Excuse me, ma'am. _____ (1) _____
B: Of course. It's on 10th Street, just across from the Armory.
A: _____ (2) _____
B: That's right. You know where that is?
A: I'm afraid I don't. _____ (3) _____
B: Well, do you know where the old post office is?
A: No, I don't. _____ (4) _____
B: I'm not sure that's going to help us. _____ (5) _____ Why don't you follow this street, Paddington Way, until you get to the stoplight. Take a right there, that's Elm Street, and go up about two or three blocks until you get to 10th. Then turn left. The library is on your right about three blocks down.
A: _____ (6) _____ Go up to Elm, take a right, go three

blocks...

B: That's right, two or three.

A: ...turn left on 10th, and the library is on the right-hand side, three blocks down.

B: _____ (7) _____

A: Well, thank you very much, ma'am. _____ (8) _____

B: _____ (9) _____

 Pair work. *Look at each of the following situations carefully. Create dialogues with your partner using the appropriate words or expressions. Then get ready to perform the dialogue for the class.*

Situation 1

A is new in the country and is trying to find the consulate. A sees a police officer across the street.

A	Police Officer
1. Gets police officer's attention	1. Responds
2. Explains situation, asks where consulate is	2. Gives directions
3. Asks for clarification	3. Explains again
4. Repeats directions	4. Confirms directions
5. Thanks police officer	5. Replies to thanks

Situation 2

A calls the airport to make reservations to fly home to see his/her parents for two weeks. A wants to fly on Friday, but doesn't know when the planes leave or how much the round trip will cost.

A	Airline Representative
1. Calls the airport	1. Answers phone (_____ Airlines)
2. Wants information on flights	2. Offers to help with information
3. Asks for scheduled departures on Friday	3. Gives times of departure
4. Asks for fare information	4. Asks whether it is round-trip or one-way
5. Answers the question	5. Gives the fare, offers to make a reservation
6. Makes a reservation or Declines offer to make a reservation	6. Thanks customer for calling
7. Gives closing	7. Replies to closing

Unit 11 Health

Overview

- **Listening**
    - Part I   Dialogue
    - Part II   Vitamin D
    - Part III   Health Issues for College Students
    - Part IV   Color Affects Your Moods and Health
    - Part V   News

- **Speaking**
    - Part I   Pronunciation Practice
    - Part II   Speaking Activities
    - Part III   Situational Dialogue: Describing Moods and Feelings

- **Skills**
    - Learning to Summarize
    - Discussing Health Issues
    - Describing Moods and Feelings

- **Language Focus**
    - Negative Prefixes

Listening

Part I Dialogue

Word List

editor-in-chief	guideline	bottom line	circumstance
vigorous	cardio workout	make a dent in	intensity
low-impact	asthma	chlorine	appropriate
gasp for breath	tried-and-true	fluid	rule of thumb
urine	straw	amber	dehydrate
monitor	nutrient	supplement	allergy
breast cancer			

 A You are going to hear an interview on health rules. Listen to the interview and decide which health rules you should follow or break. Fill in the chart below by putting a tick (√) in the corresponding space and state the reason for your choice.

Health Rules	Follow	Break	Reason
A vigorous cardio workout is good for weight loss and for getting in better shape.			
A moderate workout is much more beneficial than a high-intensity workout.			
Swimming is an ideal low-impact exercise for all people.			
Cycling or walking is better for people with asthma.			
Drinking eight glasses of water a day is good for your health.			
All nutrients can be obtained from whole foods.			
Low blood pressure is better than high blood pressure.			

B Listen to the first part of the interview again and answer the following questions.

1. What indicates a moderate workout?

_____

166

Unit 11　Health

2. (1) According to the interview, who should not go swimming? Why?

_____

(2) For those people, what would a more appropriate, low-impact workout be?

_____

C *Listen to the second part of the interview and fill in the blanks below with no more than THREE words.*

> Most of us get all the _____ we need in _____, drinks and even _____. But there are also some people who _____ a lot of water. It depends on your _____ and body size. An easy _____ is to check the color of your _____, so that you can _____ your own intake. If you have a _____, or for some reason you are not drinking milk or _____, you may be low in vitamin B12 which is important for _____, and vitamin D which is important for _____. In this case, you must get your _____ from pills or _____.

D *During the interview, Liz mentioned several health rules that have been taken for granted but should in fact be broken.*

> *In groups, discuss the following questions, giving examples where possible.*
> 1. What health rules do you follow or have followed? Were the results satisfactory?
> 2. Besides the ones mentioned in the recording, do you know of any other health rules or housewives' tales which are not totally true?
> 3. From your own experience, what happened when you broke those so-called rules?
> 4. What does the saying "One size fits all" mean? Why does this saying not apply to health rules? Explain with examples.

Part II　Vitamin D

Word List

rickets	deformity	osteoporosis	ultraviolet
sunblock	salmon	tuna	mackerel
yolk	recommendation	rheumatic	exposure

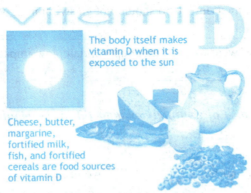

A Listen to a passage about vitamin D and write T (true), F (false) or NG (not given) beside the following statements.

( ) 1. Lighter skinned people produce more vitamin D than darker skinned people.
( ) 2. As people get older, they produce less amounts of vitamin D.
( ) 3. People living in northern areas can produce more vitamin D.
( ) 4. A lot of foods, especially milk and oily fish, naturally contain vitamin D.
( ) 5. Farmed salmon contains as much vitamin D as wild salmon.
( ) 6. Small amounts of vitamin D are found in beef liver, cheese, and egg yolks.
( ) 7. There is a tendency for doctors to test their patients' vitamin D levels.
( ) 8. An easy, direct and harmless way of getting vitamin D is exposure to the sun.
( ) 9. Higher levels of vitamin D can help prevent Parkinson's disease.

B Listen to the passage again and fill in the blanks with the missing information.

1. Vitamin D helps _____ grow strong and healthy, and it might also help _____.

2. Low levels of vitamin D can lead to _____ in children and _____ in older people, and may increase the risk of _____ in men and deaths from _____.

3. We can get vitamin D from _____, _____ and _____.

4. According to the passage, people who worry about _____ are afraid that they would get _____ and skin _____ from the sun, or that too much amount of vitamin D might act as _____. As a result, they _____, wear _____, or simply _____ the sun.

Unit 11 Health

Part III Health Issues for College Students

Word List

isolation	split	solitary	potential	transmit
undiagnosed	assault	acquaintance	rape	superficial
psychological	impair	abuse	distress	role modeling
at large	contraceptive	contribute to	inferiority	malnourished
disorder	bulimia	anorexia	access to	susceptible
STD (sexually transmitted disease)				

 A Dictation. *Listen to the following short passage and write down what you hear.*

B *You are going to hear a passage about health issues for college students. Listen to the passage and fill in the chart below.*

Health Issues	Subcategory
1. _____ health	1) sexually _____ diseases 2) unintended _____ 3) sexually _____ esp. acquaintance or date _____
2. Substance abuse	1) _____ abuse 2) _____ abuse 3) _____ abuse 4) food abuse

3. _____ health	_____ problems, esp. _____ and _____. For example, competitive academic environments can create feelings of _____, insecurity and emotional _____.	
4. Food and _____	1) malnourished 2) eating _____, such as bulimia and anorexia	
5. Health care	/	
6. Accidents and _____	_____ accidents and sports _____	

C Listen again and choose the best answer to the following questions.

1. Most American college students carry an STD. This statement is _____.
   A. true   B. false   C. not given

2. Issues related to peer acceptance are _____.
   A. substance abuse & mental health
   B. mental health & sexual health
   C. sexuality & substance abuse

3. Which of the following is often involved in sexual issues?
   A. drug abuse
   B. alcohol abuse
   C. emotional distress

4. Mental health may impair a student's _____.
   A. future intimate relationships
   B. sense of well-being and academic performance
   C. academic performance

5. Many students are highly concerned about their body size and shape because they want to _____.
   A. chase after love
   B. become healthier
   C. meet their image of social ideality

6. Many college students in the U.S. have limited access to health care because _____.
   A. their parents do not recognize this problem
   B. colleges do not provide all-inclusive services for them
   C. private health insurance is not necessary

D Language Focus: Negative Prefixes

A prefix is a letter or group of letters added to the beginning of a word to change its meaning. Many prefixes, such as *un-, in-, il-, dis-, non-*, etc. can be used to express negative meanings of the original words. There are no fixed rules for adding a negative prefix onto the beginning of adjectives, adverbs or verbs.

Now, it's your turn to practice negative prefixes. Use a dictionary if necessary.

1. *Fill in the blanks below by adding negative prefixes to the words in brackets.*
   (1) There is no doubt that cannabis will remain a(n) _____ drug in the foreseeable future. **(legal)**
   (2) It was _____ for us to drive all the way from Paris to Madrid in one day. **(possible)**
   (3) He made a(n) _____ attempt to climb the highest mountain in the range. **(successful)**
   (4) To take the boat out with four children and with no life jackets on board was quite _____ of him. **(responsible)**
   (5) The dress she was wearing was quite _____ for the occasion. **(appropriate)**
   (6) It was very _____ of him to insult his mother in front of his aunt. **(polite)**
   (7) They were a completely _____ family and I never thought that one day I would marry one of the daughters. **(religious)**
   (8) As a politician he was _____ so no one would trust him. **(honest)**
   (9) The goods were _____ and had to be returned to the store where we bought them from. **(perfect)**
   (10) She was _____ with her life and decided that things had to change. **(contented)**

2. *Collect as many negative prefixes as possible.*
   Draw 9 columns on a large piece of paper and insert a prefix heading in each column. Leave one or two columns empty for new prefix headings as they occur to you. Your piece of paper should look something like this:

un-	im-	in-	il-	dis-	ir-	mal-		

Now write as many adjectives with a negative meaning using these prefixes within 2 minutes.

Part IV Color Affects Your Moods and Health

A *Listen to the following passage and fill in the blanks.*

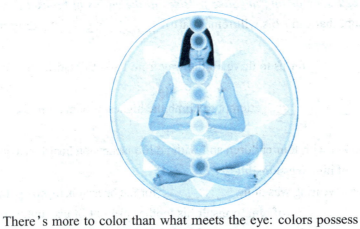

There's more to color than what meets the eye: colors possess _____(1)_____. Many ancient peoples believed in their powers; even today we _____(2)_____ a link between colors and the mind. And now scientists are discovering that certain colors indeed have a profound (深度的, 深远的) influence on our bodies, moods, thoughts and behaviors. Here are some "colorful" observations in everyday life.

Do you feel cool when you are dressed in blue? Would you rather wear red in winter than in summer? Does purple make you feel good, while yellow makes you _____(3)_____? Colors can really influence our moods and reflect, at least to some extent, our personalities. They can make us feel calm or excited, warm or cool. Colors may even affect how well we can _____(4)_____. Researchers have found that the so-called cool colors-blues and greens-can affect us this way. Being in a room painted blue or green makes people feel calm and relaxed. Blue and green surroundings can also lower one's blood pressure, pulse rate, and _____(5)_____. Both blues and greens also live up to their cool reputation by making people feel cooler than they might feel in warm-colored surroundings.

Not surprisingly, warm colors such as red, yellow, and orange affect us differently than cool colors do. Warm colors can actually make us feel warmer. They can also make us more excited. Warm colors _____(6)_____ the heartbeat, raise blood pressure, and quicken breathing. Yellow, a bright, sunny color, often makes people feel happier and more active. Yet, it can also make some people feel _____(7)_____. Red often makes some people feel energetic, but not everyone feels good wearing red. Color can affect our moods, and that's serious business as far as some people are concerned.

B *In groups, talk about your color preferences, and your perception on them. Then discuss how colors of rooms, walls and paper, etc. influence people's mood and health.*

Unit 11 Health

Part V News

Word List

opposition party	accomplish	electoral commission	run-off
rigged	outright	ominous	accreditation
nominate	secretary-general	candidate	veto
approval	endorse	stance	compatriot
Zimbabwe	President Mugabe	The Movement for Democratic Change (MDC)	
Security Council	U.N. Charter	General Assembly	

A Listen to the news report and choose the best answer to complete the sentences below.

1. President Mugabe will not negotiate with the opposition party. The statement is _____.
   A. true   B. false   C. not given
2. President Mugabe decided to hold the poll on _____.
   A. March 29th   B. June 27th   C. July 27th
3. The MDC withdrew from the presidential run-off because _____.
   A. there was a lack of support
   B. there was a withdrawal of observers
   C. there was too much violence involved
4. The forthcoming poll on Friday will have _____ observers.
   A. 38   B. 500   C. more than 9000

B Listen to the news report and choose the best answer to complete the sentences below.

1. Ban Ki-Moon topped _____ in the council and then was formally nominated to succeed Annan on _____.
   A. 5 informal polls; Monday
   B. 4 informal polls; December 31st
   C. 4 informal polls; Monday
   D. 5 informal polls; December 31st
2. There will be _____ name(s) on the ballot for secretary-general to be approved by the General Assembly.
   A. 1   B. 5   C. 6   D. 4

173

3. Ban is expected to be endorsed as the _____ secretary-general of the United Nations since 1946.

   A. sixth B. seventh C. eighth D. tenth

C Listen to the news report and fill in the blanks.

China _____ the election of a new leader for Taiwan's main opposition party who rules out _____ for the island. Ma Ying-jeou, formal Taipei _____ is now the new chairman of KMT. The Nationalist Party (KMT) favors _____ across the Taiwan Strait. "I _____ hope that the KMT and the CCP, together with _____ on both sides of the Taiwan Strait, will continue to promote the _____ development of cross-Strait relations, and _____ to create a bright future for the Chinese nation," Hu said in a message to Ma and the KMT.

Speaking

Part I Pronunciation Practice

Listen to the following story and imitate the recording. Pay attention to your pronunciation and intonation.

Give Yourself a Break

A patient came to see me about the stress in her life. I suggested she experiment by not making her bed for two weeks. She was appalled, probably thinking I'd been raised by wolves in a forest. However, she went along with my idea.

Two weeks later, she breezed into my office beaming. She had left her bed unmade for the first time in 42 years and nothing bad had happened. "You know what?" she said, "I don't dry my dishes any more either."

This woman had made two major breakthroughs. One was discovering that she had choices in her life that she had never seen before. The other was giving herself permission to be less than perfect. It was a watershed experience.

This story illustrates an important principle about managing time: No one can do it all. Each of us has to make choices and accept trade-offs.

The problem is, many people choose ways that put themselves and their health last. They take better care of their houses and cars than they do of themselves. They put everyone else's needs ahead of their own. That's fine if it's occasional. It would even be okay if there was a balance. But most people are wearing themselves out, feeling out of control. Fortunately, life doesn't have to be like that.

Part II Speaking Activities

 Key Sentence Patterns

Listen to the recording. Read aloud and memorize the following sentences.

1. Swimming is the best way to tone up your body.
2. Walking up and down the stairs would beat any exercise machine.
3. In the past decade, fitness has become a fad.
4. In the 21st century, more people are concerned about their physical health. When they are free, physical exercise is supposed to be their best choice.
5. Health is the best treasure a man can possess.
6. As long as a man has good health, he can enjoy the pleasures of life.
7. A healthy mind is in a healthy body.
8. A light heart lives long.
9. Bitter pills may have blessed effects.
10. Cheerfulness is the promoter of health.
11. Early to bed and early to rise, makes a man healthy, wealthy and wise.
12. Mischief comes by the pound and goes away by the ounce.
13. One cannot help being old, but one can resist being aged.
14. The love of beauty is an essential part of all healthy human nature.
15. Without health no pleasure can be tasted by man.

 Presentation and Discussion

1. *Health and living a modern lifestyle are hot topics these days. Good health conditions are closely related to habits formed in our lives.*

    In groups, list 5 or more good habits and bad habits in a modern lifestyle. Discuss the results of keeping good habits and the harm or problems bad habits bring to our lives.

No.	Good Habits in Life	Bad Habits in Life
1.	Early to bed and early to rise.	Staying up late.
2.	Doing physical exercises regularly.	Smoking a lot.
3.	Eating good healthy food.	Drinking alcohol.
4.		
5.		
6.		
7.		
8.		
9.		
10.		
	Benefits	Harm or Problems
	1.	1.
	2.	2.
	3.	3.
	4.	4.
	5.	5.

2. Among the habits discussed above, list the TOP 5 that best represent our modern lifestyles. Then discuss the following questions:

- What kind of lifestyle is considered healthy?
- Why do some people think that modern lifestyles are not healthy?
- Why do some people choose to lead unhealthy lives?
- What can be done to encourage people to live a healthier lifestyle?

3. Translate the following health proverbs, and discuss whether these sayings are true or not.

- 饭后百步走,活到九十九。
- 要想身体好,早餐要吃饱。
- 少吃荤腥多吃素,没有医生开药铺。
- A good laugh and a long sleep are the best cures in the doctor's book.
- An apple a day keeps the doctor away.

C Talk. *Prepare a 2-minute talk about health tips for* **losing weight** *or* **health being more valuable than wealth.** *You can start from your own experiences or your observations. Jot down some ideas before speaking.*

D Reflection. *When talking about health, more and more people have realized that mental health is as important as physical health. What are some symptoms of mental health problems? What are the reasons for mental health problems? What suggestions would you give someone to lead a mentally happy and healthy life?*

Part III Situational Dialogue: Describing Moods and Feelings

A Listen to the following dialogue and read after the recording.

A: What are you reading in the newspaper?

B: I was exhausted from studying, so I decided to read the newspaper to relax. Unfortunately, the news is so depressing. There has been another murder in the city center. I'm shocked that the police haven't caught the killer yet.

A: Yeah, I know. People are starting to get frightened by it. Everyone will be relieved when they finally catch the murderer.

B: You mean "if" they catch the murderer. I'm scared stiff about going into the city center at night.

A: There must have been some good news in the newspaper to uplift your spirits.

B: Well, there was one good piece of news. You remember the local girl who was dying of a rare blood disease?

A: Yes. Her parents were raising money to have her treated in the United States.

B: Well, they've got the money and she's going tomorrow for treatment.

A: That's great! I'm so happy for the family! They must be very relieved and excited about that.

B: I'm sure they are. Oh, and a local man won the lottery. I'm so jealous! I wish it were me! I buy a lottery ticket every week and I'm amazed that I haven't even won a small prize yet. It's so unfair!

A: Don't be so moody! I hope you're not tired, because we've been invited to a party this evening. I know how excited you get about parties.

 Practise the following expressions and sentence patterns used for describing moods and feelings.

For Moods
- He has an excellent temperament.
- What can I do to cheer her up?
- If I'm in the right mood, I'll head down to the beach for an evening stroll.
- Don't rely on your mood when making decisions.
- I'm in the mood for...
- When my grandpa is in a bad mood, he's grouchy with everyone.
- Stop being so moody. / Don't be moody.
- Why are you in such a good mood?

For Feelings

Expressing Anger
- What a nuisance! / Good grief! / That's typical!
- I've just about had enough of...
- Why the heck don't they...
- It makes me sick the way they...
- It makes my blood boil when this sort of thing happens!

Expressing Sadness
- I just don't know what to do...
- I can't take much more of this...
- It's just been one of those days...

Expressing Comfort
- Take it easy! / Cheer up!
- Don't you think you're over-reacting a bit?
- There is no need to get so upset.
- It's not as bad as all that.
- I'm sorry to hear that.
- There must have been some good...

- Come on! It can't be all that bad.
- Try and look on the bright side.

 Two students are talking about moving to California. Complete the following dialogue with the expressions provided.

▶ I'm really upset.
▶ I've always wanted to go to California.
▶ You don't understand.
▶ You won't believe what's happening.
▶ Don't be silly.
▶ I'm so glad for you!
▶ I didn't think of it that way.

A: Lisa! What's the matter? You look so sad.
B: Oh hi Jenny. _____(1)_____
A: What is it? Is someone sick? Was there an accident?
B: Oh, no, nothing like that. My dad got transferred to California, and we'll have to move there. _____(2)_____
A: California? But that's a wonderful place. _____(3)_____
B: _____(4)_____ I'll have to go to a new school where I won't know anyone, and I won't see my friends ever again.
A: _____(5)_____ Of course you'll see us. And just think-California! You'll be in the sun, you'll make new friends, and you'll get a new house and everything.
B: _____(6)_____ Well, I guess you're right. And I could always come back here for a visit.
A: _____(7)_____ Now that you'll be there, maybe my parents will let me go.

D *Work in pairs and make conversations with the following information as reference.*

Words Describing Feelings	Situation
scared, tight muscles, wide eyes, beating heart, screaming aloud	watching horror movies
upset, feel a knot in the stomach, no energy, sick, under the weather, unwell	seeing the doctor
calm, relaxed, comfortable	listening to light music
moody, grouchy, frustrated, sad, silly	failing an examination
on top of the world, excited, wonderful, fabulous, terrific, incredible, amazing	winning a football match

Unit 12 Memories

Overview

- **Listening**
    - Part I   Dialogue
    - Part II   Sporting Memory—Jordan Hits "The Shot"
    - Part III   Five Ways to Improve Your Memory
    - Part IV   How to Improve News Listening
    - Part V   News

- **Speaking**
    - Part I   Pronunciation Practice
    - Part II   Speaking Activities
    - Part III   Situational Dialogue: Interrupting

- **Skills**
    Listening and Talking About Sporting Memories
    Improving News Listening
    Practising Short-term Memory

- **Language Focus**
    NBA Team Names

Listening

Part I Dialogue

Word List

countdown	as a rule	ailing	ignite	flourish
sportscaster	humanity	co-exist	take	
first and foremost	strut one's stuff	oft-times	creed	prototype
the upper hand	parade	solidarity	protocol	

A *Look at the following pictures. What were the most memorable moments in the opening ceremony of the Beijing Olympics?*

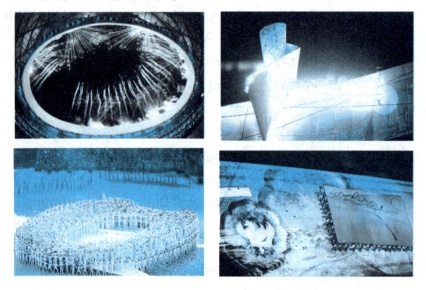

B *You are going to hear an interview on unforgettable moments of the Olympics. Listen to the interview and choose the best answer.*

1. Which of the following statements is NOT true?
   A. Antonio Todeschini is a researcher on Olympic history.
   B. Antonio Todeschini has been working for the International Olympic Committee for 10 years.
   C. Lussina Liu is a five-time Olympic medallist.
   D. Lussina Liu has competed in the Olympics twice.

Unit 12 Memories

2. What does Lussina think is the most memorable part of an opening ceremony?
   A. The countdown.
   B. The performance.
   C. The parade of athletes.
   D. The lighting of the Olympic flame.
3. Which of the following statements is NOT true?
   A. Muhammad Ali was suffering from a disease when he lit the Olympic flame.
   B. Muhammad Ali lit the flame with his trembling hands because he was very nervous and excited.
   C. Cathy Freeman lit the flame in the water.
   D. Cathy Freeman lit the flame at the 2000 Olympic Games.
4. The number of TV viewers watching the opening ceremony increased by _____ at the 2004 Olympics.
   A. 300 million   B. 30 million
   C. 3.9 million   D. 3 million
5. The Olympics are a great treasure of humanity NOT because _____.
   A. the opening ceremonies have more TV viewers than any other events
   B. people from more than 200 nations can share great joys and sorrows
   C. the Games are the largest peacetime gathering in world history
   D. young people can meet each other and learn about different cultures

C Now listen again and fill in the blanks with no more than FIVE words.

1. The opening ceremony of the Beijing Olympics was a _____ of the arts and _____ of the Chinese people. It was also an amazing spectacle in terms of _____.
2. The most exciting part is _____. The _____ Muhammad Ali _____ with his trembling hands at the _____ Atlanta Games. Cathy Freeman _____ in a splash of _____ when she _____ the torch to light it in Sydney.
3. The Olympic Games are the largest _____ in the history of the world. There is no other time or place in which _____ nations of the world meet together peacefully and _____, sharing _____ _____. Young men and women, who seemingly _____ except sport, are allowed to meet each other and often realize that they are _____ _____ than they are different.

D As the interview continues, listen and answer the following questions by filling in the blanks.

1. How are the Olympics different from the World Championships?
   The Olympics take place _____(1)_____, while the World Championships

183

take place _____(2)_____.
2. What are the two Olympic mottos? Explain with examples.
   a. _____(3)_____: More than _____(4)_____ of the more than _____(5)_____ athletes know that they will probably not win a medal, and one-third know that they will _____(6)_____.
   b. _____(7)_____: Every nation of the world wants to _____(8)_____ and wants to send athletes to the Games.
3. What does Antonio think is the greatest strength of the Games?
   The greatest strength of the Olympic Games is that it _____(9)_____ all the peoples of the world, especially _____(10)_____, and allows them to _____(11)_____ each other peacefully for _____(12)_____.
4. What are people's strongest memories of the Games?
   The strongest memories are of the _____(13)_____ between peoples of varying _____(14)_____.
5. What were Lussina's experiences in her first Olympics?
   a. They lived in the Olympic Village as _____(15)_____.
   b. They talked to athletes from different countries participating in different sports, including _____(16)_____.
   c. They would _____(17)_____ in the evenings.
6. Who helped facilitate an Olympic protocol change and how did it happen?
   In 1956, _____(18)_____ who lived in Melbourne proposed to change the _____(19)_____. Instead of having the competitors parade into the stadium as _____(20)_____, like during the opening ceremonies, he proposed to have them walk into the stadium as _____(21)_____, symbolising the _____(22)_____ of the athletes without looking at _____(23)_____.

Part II Sporting Memory—Jordan Hits "The Shot"

Word List

indelible	linger	agony	ecstasy	integral
franchise	nucleus	mesh	playoff	home-court
opener	on the line	dribble	key	jumper
hang in the air	nestle through	jubilation	Central Division	

Unit 12 Memories

A *You are going to hear a passage about Michael Jordan. Listen to the passage and write T (true), F (false) or NG (not given) beside the following statements.*

(   ) 1. "The Shot" played an integral role in the destiny of one team, the Chicago Bulls.
(   ) 2. The Cleveland Cavaliers won 42 games in the 1987–1988 regular season.
(   ) 3. The Cavaliers' dream to reach the NBA title was smashed twice by the Chicago Bulls during the playoffs.
(   ) 4. The Bulls ranked fifth both in the Central Division and in the playoffs.
(   ) 5. The Cavs won Game 4 on home-court.
(   ) 6. The Bulls won seven consecutive NBA titles from 1991 through 1997.

B *Listen again and answer the following question by filling in the blanks.*

What was "The Shot"? Describe the scene when Jordan hit "The Shot".

The Shot was a _____(1)_____ made by Michael Jordan of the _____(2)_____ in the fifth game of the first round of the _____(3)_____ against the _____(4)_____.

It came down to the _____(5)_____, and as he would so many times in his career, Jordan had the ball with the game _____(6)_____. Starting from the right side, Jordan dribbled toward _____(7)_____ and rose up for _____(8)_____ from inside the circle. Craig Ehlo, one of Cleveland's _____(9)_____, leaped out to _____(10)_____ the shot, but Jordan seemed to _____(11)_____ until Ehlo was out of his way, and then _____(12)_____ his shot. As the ball nestled through the net, Jordan _____(13)_____ in jubilation, completing a video highlight for the ages.

C *"The Shot" is one of Jordan's best performances and the memories have lingered for years.*

In groups, discuss the following questions, giving examples where possible.
1. What do you think is the most unforgettable moment in the 2008 Olympics?
2. What are some amazing, surprising or even disappointing moments in sports? Share them with your partner.

D Language Focus: NBA Team Names

Basketball was born in a school gym in Springfield, Massachusetts. The weather was bad, children were bored, and a schoolteacher hung two peach baskets on either side of a room and invited the children to shoot a ball into it. How far we've come since then!

By the 1920s, there were hundreds of men's professional basketball teams in cities and towns. Leagues came and went, and players switched loyalties like the wind. Early teams included the Original Celtics, New York Renaissance Five, and the Harlem Globetrotters.

In 1946 the Basketball Association of America was formed, and that same year the first game was played in Toronto between the Toronto Huskies and the New York Knickerbockers. In 1949 the organization officially became the National Basketball Association (NBA), which today is still the top professional league in the world.

Today the NBA has a total of 30 teams separated into six divisions—Atlantic, Central, Southeast, Southwest, Northwest, and Pacific.

Can you name all the NBA Teams? Fill in the chart below and translate all the team names into Chinese.

Eastern Conference	Western Conference
Atlantic Division	Southwest Division
Boston Celtics	Dallas Mavericks
_____ Nets	Houston _____
New York Knicks	Memphis Grizzlies
Philadelphia _____	New Orleans Hornets
Toronto Raptors	San Antonio Spurs
Central Division	Northwest Division
Chicago _____	Denver Nuggets
Cleveland Cavaliers	Minnesota Timberwolves
Detroit Pistons	Portland Trailblazers
Indiana _____	_____ Supersonics
Milwaukee Bucks	Utah _____
Southeast Division	Pacific Division
Atlanta Hawks	Golden State Warriors
Charlotte Bobcats	Los Angeles Clippers
_____ Heat	_____ Lakers
Orlando Magic	Phoenix Suns
Washington Wizards	Sacramento _____

Unit 12 Memories

Part III Five Ways to Improve Your Memory

Word List

retain	retrieve	boost	razor-sharp	reel	finalist
adaptable	antioxidant	coincidentally	artery	clog	saturated
potent	ward off	come up with	gymnastics	acrostic	

A Dictation. *Listen to the following short passage and write down what you hear.*

B *You are going to hear a passage on how to improve your memory. Before listening, discuss the following questions with your partner.*

> How do you define a good memory?
> What are some ways to boost your memory?

C *Now listen to the passage and answer the two questions with key words. Compare your answers in this section with the answers you gave in section B.*

1. Why is it important to have a good memory?
   _____

2. What are the five ways to boost your memory?
   a. _____
   b. _____
   c. _____
   d. _____
   e. _____

D *Listen to the passage again and write T (true), F (false) or NG (not given) beside the following statements.*

(   ) 1. Taking a picture of the place where you keep important things can help you find those items again later on.

(   ) 2. In order to remember important things more clearly, we should avoid overloading our precious memory with unnecessary trivia.

(   ) 3. Fruits and vegetables are believed to be good for your memory.

(   ) 4. Getting enough sleep is very important to your memory.

(   ) 5. Doing mental exercises not only protects your memory but also helps you keep alert.

E *Let's try out your memory! Answer the following questions with key words according to your memory. Then listen to the passage again and check your answers.*

1. What examples are given as ways of practising your memory?
   a. _____
   b. _____
   c. _____

2. What was the age range of the people tested in the study on the relationship between diet and memory?
   _____

3. At what age do people begin to experience the problem of recalling names or numbers?
   _____

4. What examples are given as ways of exercising your brain?
   a. _____
   b. _____
   c. _____

Part IV How to Improve News Listening

A *Listen to the following passage and fill in the missing words.*

News reports are _____(1)_____ material because they are easily accessible (易使用的, 易得到的) and there is a directed purpose in listening—people typically want

Unit 12   Memories

to know what's happening in the world. However, listening to the news can be difficult for English learners. News reports have their own _____(2)_____ when broadcasted on the radio, television or the Internet, such as their style, structure, vocabulary, and the _____(3)_____, etc.

_____(4)_____ can be a big problem when you're trying to understand the news. It pays to make extra efforts to learn words _____(5)_____ in the news. These include names of people and places and media jargon. Pay attention to names in the news; find out the English _____(6)_____ to the names that you know well in Chinese. Use a dictionary or ask a native speaker how they are _____(7)_____. Special words or phrases used by particular groups of people in their profession or workplace is known as _____(8)_____. The media uses its own jargon or special words. For instance, *regime, junta* and *hardliner* are common jargon used in political news. Try to build up your knowledge of these usages.

A news report is often packed with information or _____(9)_____, which often include _____(10)_____ the event, timeliness, _____(11)_____, proximity(接近，邻近), entertainment, oddity, or celebrity. To be considered "news", an event must contain one or more of the news values and have _____(12)_____. And so, news may contain the answers to questions like "How many people were, are or will be _____(13)_____? Did the event occur _____(14)_____? Is there significant new information _____(15)_____ _____? Was the event _____(16)_____? Does it make for _____(17)_____? Was the event highly _____(18)_____? Was anyone famous _____(19)_____?" Be sure to direct your listening to the relevant news values.

Journalists use many different kinds of _____(20)_____ _____ for organizing stories. The simplest and most common story structure is called the "inverted pyramid". The inverted pyramid is a _____(21)_____ used to illustrate how information should be arranged or presented within a text, in particular within a news story.

important stuff
↓
fluff

The "pyramid" can be drawn as a _____(22)_____ with its broad base at the top of the figure representing the most _____(23)_____, interesting, and important information the writer wants to convey. The triangle's orientation illustrates that this kind of material should head the article, while the tapered(锥形的，渐细的) lower portion illustrates that other material should follow in order of diminishing(逐渐减弱的) importance. The format is valued because readers or listeners can leave the story _____(24)_____ and understand it, even if they don't have all the details.

So remember, when listening to the news, there is no need to agonize(极度痛苦、焦虑) and try to understand everything. All the important information will most likely be given at the beginning of the report in the _____(25)_____, which in itself is a condensed form of the complete news story.

B Discussion. *What makes news listening difficult? Summarise the above-mentioned factors. Are there any other factors? What strategies can be used to overcome the difficulties?*

Part V   News

Word List

delegation	press conference	all walks of life	equestrian
wheelchair rugby	goalball	boccia	football 5-a-side
football 7-a-side	arduous	tally	under the auspices of
state-of-the-art	venue	Paralympic Games	Bordeaux, France
International Cycling Union (UCI)		UCI Paracycling World Championships	
Handisport French Federation		International Paralympic Committee (IPC)	
IPC Shooting World Championships		Andrey Lebendinsky	
Jonas Jacobsson			

A Listen to the news report and fill in the blanks with the correct numbers.

There will be altogether ____(1)____ representatives in the Chinese delegation to the Beijing 2008 Paralympic Games, including ____(2)____ athletes who will take part in all ____(3)____ events.

Among the Chinese athletes, ____(4)____ are male and ____(5)____ are female, the oldest one being ____(6)____ years old and the youngest being ____(7)____ years old. ____(8)____ of them are competing in the Paralympics for the first time.

Compared to the Athens Paralympic Games, the Chinese delegation has increased by ____(9)____ people, including ____(10)____ more athletes.

B Listen to the news report and answer the following questions.

1. Where was the 2007 UCI Paracycling World Championships held? How long did it last?

2. Which country won the most medals? How many did they win?

3. When was the Paracycling World Championships governance transferred from the IPC to the UCI?

_____

C Listen to the news report and write T (true), F (false) or NG (not given) beside the following statements.

( ) 1. Both China and Russia won six gold medals in the 2006 IPC Shooting World Championships.
( ) 2. Thirteen world records were broken at the Championships.
( ) 3. The Championships received positive reviews from the reporters.
( ) 4. Two representatives from BOCOG went to help organize the Championships.

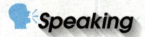

Speaking

Part I Pronunciation Practice

Listen to the following poem and imitate the recording. Pay attention to your pronunciation and intonation.

Saying Good-bye to Cambridge Again
By Xu Zhimo

Very quietly I take my leave
As quietly as I came here;
Quietly I wave good-bye
To the rosy clouds in the western sky.

The golden willows by the riverside
Are young brides in the setting sun;
Their reflections on the shimmering waves
Always linger in the depth of my heart.

The floating heart growing in the sludge
Sways leisurely under the water;
In the gentle waves of Cambridge
I would be a water plant!
That pool under the shade of elm trees

Holds not water but the rainbow from the sky;
Shattered to pieces among the duckweeds
Is the sediment of a rainbow-like dream?

To seek a dream? Just to pole a boat upstream
To where the green grass is more verdant;
Or to have the boat fully loaded with starlight
And sing aloud in the splendor of starlight.

But I cannot sing aloud
Quietness is my farewell music;
Even summer insects heap silence for me
Silent is Cambridge tonight!

Very quietly I take my leave
As quietly as I came here;
Gently I flick my sleeves
Not even a wisp of cloud will I bring away.

Part II Speaking Activities

 Key Sentence Patterns

Read aloud and memorize the following sentences.

1. Memory can be unreliable, it is a tricky thing.
2. You won't be able to remember anything if you don't pay attention to it.
3. The more you work out your brain, the better you'll be able to process and remember information.
4. Having a strong memory will pave the way for knowledge, confidence and understanding in the classroom.
5. It seems that some of my classmates can memorize things effortlessly, but I struggle and never seem to remember enough to feel at ease.
6. By turning a word or concept into an image, we instantly make it easier to remember it.
7. Organizing information can significantly improve your memory.
8. When things are memorized through association, thinking of one helps bring the other to mind.

9. Childhood is the most colorful time in life for it is a precious memory, a charming mystery and a valuable gift.
10. I did many "foolish" things in my childhood. The most foolish one was that I took a whole bottle of tablets as candies.
11. These sweet memories will always be with me for the rest of my life because they are significant, and more importantly, can encourage me when I run into obstacles.
12. It is reported that thinking of good memories for just 20 minutes a day can make people more cheerful than they were the week before, and happier than if they think of their current lives.
13. The ravages of World War II have left unforgettable memories for all people around the world.
14. Hong Kong's return to China will be a decisive righting of historical wrongs—the return of a piece of the motherland sundered after Britain forced China to buy its opium.
15. The memories, whether sweet or bitter, can help people reflect on the past, accumulate experiences, and look forward to a bright future.

B Presentation and Discussion

1. Memory is defined as the ability to retain and recall information, experiences and procedures such as skills and habits. It can be divided into short-term (also known as working or recent memory) and long-term memory. How strong is your short-term memory? Take the two tests below.

(1) Word List Recall

Verbal working memory span is very important in remembering what you have heard or read. Read the 20 words below and try to remember them without taking notes.

software	boycott	insurance	arson	terrorism
recovery	stock	virus	demand	economy
media	service	advertise	health	criminal
market	attack	supply	report	afford

Optional Activity: Pick some phrases or even sentences and do the same test.

(2) Number List Recall

You will be presented with a series of numbers. As your partner reads each group of numbers, repeat the group at once. See how many groups you can remember without any mistakes.

G1: 972   641   183
G2: 3485   2730   3750
G3: 91406   85943   79625
G4: 516927   706294   523647
G5: 3067285   1538796   3865241
G6: 58391024   29081357   27593869
G7: 2164089573   4790386251   08642671903
G8: 45382170369   4790386215   0846271903
G9: 987032614280   541960836702   726149258031
...

Optional Activity: One partner reads 10 cell phone numbers while the other one tries to recall them. Switch roles using 10 different numbers.

2. What do you think of your short-term memory capacity, as reflected in the above tests? How accurate and reliable is it? Are there any techniques to improve it? In groups, discuss the problems and ways of improving memory. Give some real-life examples.

Problems	Techniques	Examples

C Talk. Prepare a 2-minute talk about a childhood memory. You may talk about your first attempt at something or an unforgettable, pleasant or sweet moment. You can also recall your memories about some interesting, amusing or even foolish stories when you were little. You can jot down some ideas before speaking.

D *Reflection. Though bitter memories cannot change history, it can inspire a person or even an entire country to strive and become better and stronger. Have you experienced being bitter because of a painful memory? How did you deal with it? How can past memories affect a country, either positively or negatively?*

Part III Situational Dialogue: Interrupting

A *Listen to the following dialogues and repeat each sentence out loud.*

Dialogue 1

(Freddy stops at Dr. Andrews' open office door and knocks.)

Freddy: Dr. Andrews?
Dr. Andrews: Yes?
Freddy: Excuse me, I don't want to interrupt you but...
Dr. Andrews: No, no. It's quite all right. How can I help you?
Freddy: Well, I'd just like to ask you to sign a permission slip for me to take that course on American Literature you're teaching next semester. Would that be all right?
Dr. Andrews: Of course, Freddy. Actually, I'm glad you decided to take it. I think you'll like it, and I'm glad to have you in the class.
Freddy: Thank you. It sounds like an interesting course.
Dr. Andrews: I'm glad you think so. There you are. *(She gives the slip back to Freddy.)*
Freddy: Thank you very much. Good-bye, Dr. Andrews.
Dr. Andrews: Good-bye, Freddy.

Dialogue 2

(The telephone rings.)

Susan: English Department.
Ralph: Yes, I'd like to speak with Dr. Charlotte, please.
Susan: Who's calling, please?
Ralph: Ralph Davidson.
Susan: One moment, please. *(buzz)*
Dr. Charlotte: Yes?
Susan: Excuse me, but there's a Ralph Davidson on the line. Do you want to talk to him?

Dr. Charlotte: No, have him call back later. I'm in a meeting now until twelve o'clock. Please hold my calls.

Susan: Of course, Dr. Charlotte. (*click*) I'm sorry, sir, but Dr. Charlotte is in a meeting right now. May I take a message?

Ralph: Could you tell me what time he'll be free?

Susan: Well, the meeting's scheduled to last till twelve.

Ralph: OK. I'll call back then. Thank you very much.

Susan: You're welcome.

B *Practise the following expressions and sentence patterns used for interrupting politely.*

- I'm sorry to interrupt (you).
- Excuse / Forgive me for interrupting, but...
- Excuse / Pardon me, but...
- Pardon the interruption, but...
- I hate / don't want to interrupt you, but...
- May I interrupt (you)?
- Can I butt in here?
- Sorry to butt in, but...
- May I make a point here?
- Could I interrupt for a quick second?
- Just a quick interruption, if that's okay.
- I'd like to say something, if you don't mind.
- Were you in the middle of something?
- Before you go on, I'd like to / I need to ask you something.
- If I might just make a point / come in here...
- By the way, ...
- That reminds me...

C *Complete the following dialogue with the sentences provided.*

▶ Sorry, we'll have to continue this some other time.
▶ Sorry to butt in, but it's time for the production meeting.
▶ Pardon the interruption, but there's a Mr. Walters waiting to see you.
▶ Thanks for reminding me.
▶ Excuse me, but could I ask a quick question?

Unit 12 Memories

Dialogue 1

Mary and Bob are discussing a project they are working on.

Bob: Mary, we can't possibly finish by Tuesday!
Mary: But that's our deadline. You'll have to find a way!
Ann: _____(1)_____ He says he has a two o'clock appointment.
Mary: It's two o'clock already? _____(2)_____

Dialogue 2

Jean and Sue are talking.

Jean: ...and then she told me that he didn't even say he was sorry!
Sue: No kidding.
Max: _____(3)_____
Sue: Sure. What is it?
Max: When is the lecture?
Sue: Two-thirty.
Max: Thanks.
Sue: No problem. (*to Jean*) Then what did she say?

Dialogue 3

Joseph is talking about his vacation in Los Angeles.

Joseph: And then I flew to Los Angeles and stayed with my wife's sister. She took us around the city. We went shopping in...
Tara: _____(4)_____
Joseph: I thought it was tomorrow.
Tara: No, it's today.
Joseph: _____(5)_____

D *A is a student in a technical program, and B is A's adviser. A goes to see B in B's office. When A gets there, B is talking on the phone.*

B: [excuses self (to the caller), greets A]
A: [greets B and apologizes for interrupting]
B: [accepts apology, closes the phone conversation]
A: [asks for appointment]
B: [suggests a time]
A: [rejects the time because it's too close to the deadline]
B: [suggests another time]
B: [accepts the time, thanks B]

Keys

Unit 1 Family

Listening

Part I Dialogue

B

	China	America
Society based on	collectivism	individualism
Families in general	close	still close
Parents' role	meddle in their children's lives	play less of a role once they grow up
When children become adults	they live with their parents	they move out
Parents are proud of	/	their children's independence

C 1. T 2. F 3. NG 4. T 5. NG

Part II Remember, We're Raising Children, Not Flowers!

A (1) lawn mower (2) flowerbed (3) edge (4) lose control
(5) time (6) effort (7) envy (8) raise his voice
(9) priorities (10) self-esteem (11) destruction (12) deadening
(13) liveliness

B 1. B 2. C 3. C 4. A 5. B

D 1. I was woken up by a bell ringing.
2. We saw trees laden with fruits.
3. The child sitting in that corner is John.
4. Most of the people invited to the party didn't turn up.
5. The road repairs carried out on the motorway might delay traffic.
6. The decisions made at today's meeting will affect all of us.
7. At the end of the street there is a path leading to the river.

Part III Stay-at-Home Dads

A Traditionally the mother has been the one to take on the responsibility of taking care of the kids, while the father provides for the family financially. However, in recent years, there has been an increase of stay-at-home dads. In the past, the husband was the one with the career. As a matter of fact, a woman would sometimes leave work as soon as she got married. Now both partners usually work prior to having children and the wife usually has as much vested in her career as does her husband. While some people feel that a woman can better take care of a child, there are real life examples that blow this theory right out of the water. Fathers can certainly be as nurturing as mothers.

C 1. F   2. F   3. NG   4. F   5. T

D (1) equal partners   (2) parenting   (3) childcare   (4) traditional roles
   (5) out of necessity (6) of practicality (7) a better fit (8) greater benefits
   (9) career potential (10) amazing   (11) powerful bond (12) at daycare
   (13) subcontract out (14) two out of three (15) juggle (16) compromise with

Part V News

A 1. C   2. B

B 1. The news item is about the greatest Wimbledon final where Nadal competed against Federer.
   2. a. (Rafael) Nadal.
      b. Wimbledon and the French Open.
      c. Sixty-five.
      d. Four hours 48 minutes.

C (1) semi-final   (2) 18th seed   (3) showcase   (4) tenacity
   (5) triumph   (6) dazzling   (7) ankle injury (8) 133
   (9) wild card   (10) day five   (11) overcome
   (12) in blistering form (13) quarterfinals

Speaking

Part III Situational Dialogue: Making Invitations

C (1) Want to pop over after work?
   (2) Sure, why not.
   (3) OK. Want me to bring something?
   (4) No. Just bring yourself.
   (5) Tonight's no good.
   (6) Can I take a rain check?
   (7) My husband and I were just wondering if you would like to come over for dinner this evening.
   (8) Oh, thank you! I'd be delighted to.
   (9) Sure. Do I need to bring anything?
   (10) No, but thanks for asking.

D Reference answer

A: Hi Ann. Would you like to eat dinner with me tonight?

B: Sure, I'd love to. Just tell me when and where!

A: How about let's meet at the Pizza Hut in Wudaokou, say around 6:00?

B: Oooh, can we meet later? My class doesn't end until 5:40 and I'm afraid I won't be able to make it on time. How about 6:30?

A: Sure, no problem. You know where it is right? It's just across the subway station and above KFC on the second floor.

B: I know where it is, but thanks for reminding me. So, see you tonight at 6:30 then!

A: Looking forward to it. See you!

Unit 2 Jobs

Listening

Part I Dialogue

A

Name	Work Place	Job Description	Working Hours/Pay
Dan	reception desk, at the students' union on campus	answering students' questions and answering telephones	10 hours per week
Indian student	on campus	distributing leaflets	7 pounds per hour
John	radio station	working as a host, presenting a children's show "Back to Basics"	/

B 1. a mass media major / freshman / international student in a London university

2. many on campus / students' union office

3. earn extra money / London / expensive to live / enrich experience

4. answer phones / editing / host a programme, etc.

Part II Job Interviews—Selling Yourself

A 1. A   2. C   3. B   4. C   5. A

B (1) prospective employers; expertise; contacts; over your career

(2) Maintain an open attitude; openness; refreshing characteristic

(3) Be prepared; key points; jot them down; review

(4) Ask questions; persuasive; you are prepared; you care

Dos	Don'ts
b c e f i j l	a d g h k

Keys

E 1. 显然,在婚姻问题上,婚前同居并不能令婚姻生活趋于完美。

2. 做还是不做?人生答案网中来。

3. In economics, all roads lead to socialism.

4. Not all cars are born equal.

5. Where there's a will, there's a lawsuit.

Part III Sports Manager

A   Sports managers spend their time behind the scenes coordinating all business-related activities for the team that employs them. During the playing season they may work seven days a week. When they work for college or professional teams they stay behind in their offices while the team travels to away games. A few who have been in the business for many years may travel with the team from city to city, but they are the exception. During the off-season, the manager is busy negotiating trades and signing free agents. The sports manager or general manager, as he or she is sometimes called, signs all players to the professional team.

B 1. B   2. C   3. C   4. A   5. B

C

Responsibilities of Sports Managers	1. make deals 2. draft players 3. keep an eye on the team's budget, take charge of salary, make financial arrangements 4. participate in press conferences; explain reasons for decisions; ignore complimentary and critical press reports

D 1. Two years out: 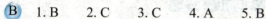 a   d   f   i

2. Five years out: a   b   e   f   i

3. Ten years out: c   f   g   h

Part V News

A 1. reduce energy costs and commuters' gasoline expenses

2. Thank goodness it's Thursday

3. 10 hours; same pay

4. prison guards; employees of the courts; public universities

B 1. About 700,000 graduates who could not find work last year will compete with them for employment.

2. About 20,000 graduates.

3. For those who have worked in rural areas for two years:

   (1) They enjoy favorable treatment in recruitment for government organs and state enterprises.

   (2) They get bonus points if they take the civil service exams.

4. (1) They can enjoy a 20 percent income tax cut for start-ups.

   (2) The government also offers small loans to them to start a business.

C 1. A   2. D   3. B   4. C

Speaking

Part III Situational Dialogue: Job Interviews

C (1) apply for the position as a salesperson
(2) thanks to those experiences
(3) help people through this job
(4) you're full of passion
(5) compensate for lack of experience
(6) starting your life all over again
(7) change the condition pretty soon
(8) Thank you for your time

Unit 3 Business

Listening

Part I Dialogue

A 1. C   2. C   3. B   4. A   5. B

B 1. (1) They don't want to alert competitors that they might be doing something that is going well.
(2) People's impression of the DPRK is coloured by the issues that tend to come along in the media.
2. If there's one shot fired across the demilitarized zone, then it's a headline straight away.
3. The population of 23 million people makes it a market the same size as Malaysia or Turkey. All those people need clothing, food and jobs.

Part II Students Carve Out Early Careers in Business

B

Name	Age	Gender	Products	Company/Brand Name	Business Expansion	Business Record
Kim	12	Female	Hawaiian backpacks	Northshore Creations	☐ Yes ■ No	sold 12 backpacks at a local garage sale; snowballed into an enterprise selling more than 600 backpacks

Alexis	8	Female	purses, jewelry, headbands and nail polish	/	☐ Yes ■ No	$650 sales record
Marisol	18	Female	clothing, T-shirts	Bassix	☐ Yes ■ No	almost 40 T-shirts
Melissa	17	Female	Pet-sitting service	/	☐ Yes ■ No	/

C

1. Kim — C. runs a company with his/her twin brother
2. Alexis — D. plans more than one way of sales channel
3. Marisol — A. is influenced by his/her parents in doing business
4. Melissa — B. started business by tending to animals/pets

A. is influenced by his/her parents in doing business
B. started business by tending to animals/pets
C. runs a company with his/her twin brother
D. plans more than one way of sales channel
E. mother gave a helping hand more than economically

Part III Seven Principles of Admirable Business Ethics

A   One of the most important attributes for small business success is the distinguishing quality of practicing admirable business ethics. Business ethics, practiced throughout the deepest layers of a company, become the heart and soul of the company's culture and can mean the difference between success and failure. A research study found that companies displaying a clear commitment to ethical conduct consistently outperform companies that do not display ethical conduct. A director of a big company stated: "Not only is ethical behaviour in business life the right thing to do in principle, but we have shown that it pays off in financial returns." These findings deserve to be considered as an important insight for companies striving for long-term success and growth.

B 1. assured reliance   2. Keep an open mind/Open to new ideas
   3. commitments and obligations   4. clear, precise and professional
   5. community-related issues and activities   6. Maintain accounting control
   7. respect; differences, positions, titles, ages or other types of distinctions

C 1. He must be open to new ideas. He should ask for opinions and feedback from both customers and team members.
   2. Re-evaluate all print materials making sure they are clear, precise and professional. Most importantly, make sure they do not misrepresent or misinterpret the wrong information.

3. Recognizing the significance of business ethics as a tool.

  4. Instill a deep-seated theme of business ethics within its strategies and policies.

E 1. You should stop smoking—it's bad for you.

  2. Correct.

  3. Don't forget to write to Aunt Mary. She misses you very much.

  4. I don't remember having said that I would never speak to Marsha.

  5. Correct.

Part IV   Listening for Numbers

A (1) digits   (2) fall into two major categories
  (3) comparatively more complicated   (4) distinguish between "-teen" and "-ty"
  (5) a comma as a separator   (6) the remaining minutes
  (7) currency units   (8) respectively
  (9) addition and subtraction   (10) multiplication and division

B 1. (1) 21–25; 758   (2) about 258; about 17%   (3) 10; 151   (4) about 45; 3; 1,510

  2.

Beijing's nominal GDP	(900.62 billion) RMB	(12.3)%
GDP per capita	(56,044) RMB	8.9%
Primary industry	10.13 billion RMB	/
Secondary industry	(247.93 billion) RMB	/
Tertiary industry	(642.56 billion) RMB	/
Urban disposable income per capita	(21,989) RMB	11.2%
Pure income of rural residents per capita	9,559 RMB	(8.2)%
Disposable income of the 20% low-income residents per capita	/	(16.7)%
The growth rate of the 20% high-income residents	/	(5.3) %

Part V   News

A 1. Pakistan handed over its role/ G-77 chair/ Antigua and Barbuda

  2. 1964; provides means for southern countries to articulate and promote collective economic interests/ enhance joint negotiating capacities

  3. At the end of the first session of the United Nations Conference on Trade and Development in Geneva; Joint Declaration of the Seventy-Seven Countries

B 1. C   2. D   3. C

C (1) counterparts   (2) Japan   (3) deployed about 20,000
  (4) UN Millennium Development Goals   (5) food safety   (6) rising prices
  (7) credit crunch   (8) predict and avoid
  (9) alleviate the food crisis

Speaking

Part III   Situational Dialogue: Making Offers

C (1) Is there anything I can do to help?

(2) ran into a problem with my computer.

(3) cannot log on to Windows.

(4) What did you do after you turned on your computer?

(5) began searching for some papers and articles

(6) Did you use an anti-virus software to kill them?

(7) you will have to reinstall Windows.

(8) I'll help you out with this problem.

Unit 4   Music

Listening

Part I   Dialogue

A 1. R&B.

2. Full of energy; exciting; having a strong beat.

3. It originated from American black music.

4. Exciting, with a fast beat and strong rhythm.

5. Classical music.

B 1. Elvis Presley—helped the rock music industry take off—called "the King"

Jimi Hendrix—a very famous guitar player

Bruce Springsteen—an all-round rock singer and songwriter—called "the Boss"

2. rock—jeans and T's

punk—tight clothing, weird hairdos and make-up

country—cowboy hats, plaid shirts, jeans and boots

rap—baggy pants and loose clothes

3. jazz—New Orleans

country—Nashville, Southern U.S.

rock'n' roll—Cleveland, Ohio

C 1. (1) travesty   (2) over-commercialization   (3) attitude

(4) creative   (5) Unfortunately   (6) comparison

2. (1) cute   (2) sexy   (3) a great voice   (4) energy and rhythm

(5) crazy over   (6) goes beyond   (7) American legend

3. (1) comes to (2) pioneers
4. (1) rocker (2) awesome (3) all-round
5. (1) was invented (2) is mainly based (3) has a Hall of Fame

Part II Fighting Music Piracy on College Campuses

B 1. A 2. B 3. C 4. A 5. B

C

	Opinions	Actions
the R.I.A.A. (the industry group)	college, big problem; more than half, download illegally	effort to catch music pirates; software, illegal sharing; civil actions; pushed Congress to take action
Educause	80% students, not linked to school networks	works for "intelligent use" of information technology
the House of Representatives	/	a bill, anti-piracy requirements, schools in federal financial-aid programs
the Senate	/	a bill, schools to inform
the schools	oppose using software to identify	already inform, fines, lose use of the school's network

E motel (motor + hotel)   smog (smoke + fog)   sitcom (situation + comedy)
brunch (breakfast + lunch)   travelogue (travel + monologue)
docutainment (documentary + entertainment)

Part III Music at Sporting Events

A   The use of music at sporting events is a practice that is thousands of years old, but has recently had a resurgence as a noted phenomenon. Some sports have specific traditions with respect to pieces of music played at particular intervals. Others have made the presentation of music very specific to the team—even to particular players. Music may be used to build the energy of the fans, and music may also be introduced in ways that are less directly connected with the action in a sporting event.

B 1. B 2. B 3. C 4. B 5. D
C 1. F 2. NG 3. T 4. T 5. F

Part IV The Symphony: A Microcosm of Life

A (1) tuning   (2) harmonize   (3) unique   (4) complement
(5) composed   (6) on their own   (7) talent   (8) similarity
(9) accompany   (10) glory   (11) eventually   (12) separately

Keys

Part V News

A 1. A   2. C   3. C
B 1. F   2. T   3. T
C 1. July 24
   2. Fans, players, officials and the media.
   3. 3 / three.

Speaking

Part II Speaking Activities

B 2. Category 1: a, f
   Category 2: c
   Category 3: b, d, e, g

Unit 5 Disasters

Listening

Part I Dialogue

A 1. C   2. B   3. D   4. C   5. D

B

Disaster	Place	Damage	Solutions
Forest fire	Australia	Covering several square kilometers; destroying the land	/
Drought	Africa	Causing starvation; millions of people having migrated to try to find food	1. EU: sending planes with relief supplies; 2. Several countries: sending soldiers to distribute food and medical supplies; 3. Setting up refugee camps
Earthquake	Iran	Casualties: less than 20 people dead; over 100 people in hospital	1. Iranians dealing with it independently 2. purchasing some special equipment to find people under the rubble

C 1. deputy bureau chief
   2. (1) oil exploration and production
      (2) importing oil and other energy materials
   3. that the oil supply will be disrupted; to increase (sharply)
   4. release oil stock; raw materials

207

5. 1 / 5 of all the nation's imports and exports; take a while to reopen; go beyond the energy ones
6. Imports and exports of energy; national implications

Part II Tsunami Wounds Still Fresh in Indonesia One Year Later

A 1. C   2. D   3. B   4. A   5. C   6. A

B 1. More than $6 billion / tens of millions of dollars

2. strong winds / no electricity / rain comes in / puddles of mud / dark / lonely

3. rivalries / aid agencies / who builds what where / government red tape / land ownership / shortages of building materials

4. most homes destroyed/ two-thirds population killed/ about 50 survivors

5. tens of thousands living in tents and barracks/ 300,000 people lost homes living with friends and relatives

6. the U.N. coordinator in Indonesia / getting people into temporary homes / making the economy work again

Part III The Nature of Disasters

A   Until recently, disaster scholars and practitioners have hardly engaged in climate change debates. Scientific assessments on climate change have mainly involved atmospheric scientists and experts in the area of environment and energy. Key questions in the scientific discourse include: If observed climate change was accidental or systematic, what role could be attributed to the human-caused emissions of greenhouse gases? Which models can tell us about future developments? How much reduction in emissions is needed to mitigate the risks of climate change? Climate change scenarios are typically expressed in terms of time scales of 50–100 years, for areas as large as northwest Europe. Such projections about significant global changes in the decades to come are difficult to comprehend or translate into real life today.

B | | |
|---|---|
| Hurricanes: | cause large waves, heavy rain, and high winds, disrupting international shipping and, at times, causing shipwrecks. On land, strong winds can damage or destroy vehicles, buildings, bridges, and other outside objects, turning loose debris into deadly flying projectiles. |
| Volcano eruption: | can cause disastrous loss of life and property, especially in densely populated regions of the world. People can be burnt to death by volcanic lava. It can harm the environment. The lava, rocks, gasses, and magma can flood towns. Lava can kill animals, destroy crops, and ruin homes. A volcano can also create an earthquake, which becomes twice as dangerous to people. |
| Floods: | They can damage anywhere from bridges, cars, buildings, sewer systems, roadways, canals and any other type of structure. People and livestock die due to drowning. It can also lead to epidemics and diseases. Clean drinking water becomes scarce. Shortage of food crops due to loss of entire harvests. |

Drought: Periods of drought can have significant environmental, agricultural, health, economic and social consequences. Examples include death of livestock, reduced crop yields, wildfires, shortages of water, dust storms in deforested areas, famine due to lack of water for irrigation, etc.

Tornados: They can generate sufficient force to destroy massive buildings. Injuries from tornados occur due to flying debris or people being thrown by the high winds (i.e., head injuries, soft tissue injuries, secondary wound infections). Stress-related disorders are more common, as is disease related to loss of utilities, potable water, or shelter.

Earthquakes: result in more or less severe damage to buildings or other rigid structures. Earthquakes may result in disease, lack of basic necessities, loss of life, higher insurance premiums, general property damage, road and bridge damage, and collapsing of buildings or destabilization of the base of buildings which may lead to collapses in future earthquakes. Earthquakes can also lead to volcanic eruptions, which cause further damages such as substantial crop damage. Most of civilization agrees that human death is the most significant human impact of earthquakes.

C) 1. D 2. C 3. B 4. C 5. D

D) 1. F 2. T 3. F 4. NG 5. T 6. F 7. F 8. NG 9. F 10. T

E)

Names	Definition	Characteristics	Damages/ Causes	Places at Risk
Hurricanes	tropical storm	Speed:74 mph; Eye: 20-30 miles wide; Extension: 400 miles	Bring torrential rains, high winds and storm surges; Cause damage and loss of lives	/
Tornadoes	Storms: twisting, funnel-shaped clouds	Short duration: less than 20 minutes; Speed: 300 mph; Touch ground several times in different areas	Cause: when cool air overrides a layer of warm air; High wind velocity and wind-blown debris can cause damages	Collapsed buildings; Flying objects; In a car
Floods	/	/	Cause: natural disasters such as heavy rains, hurricanes, or tsunamis that may follow earthquakes; human factors or technological factors such as dam failures; Property damage: over $1 billion each year in the US	/
Earthquakes	Sudden, rapid shaking of the earth	/	Cause: the breaking and shifting of rock Damage: buildings and bridges to collapse; disrupt gas, electric and phone services; trigger many other disasters	Buildings with foundations on unconsolidated landfill, or other unstable soil; buildings or trailers not tied to a reinforced foundation

Part IV Chinese Find Strength and Hope in Earthquake Rubble

C 1. 我无法喝住雷声。

2. 发现了错误一定要改正。

3. 你可以把他最喜欢的专辑作为礼物送给他。

4. Women have an equal say in everything.

5. In 2007, domestic box office receipts (ticket sales) in China totaled 3.3 billion RMB.

Part V News

A 1. 5 million; more than 22,000

2. the epicenter of the quake; has allowed foreign professionals to help

3. rescuing people from the rubble

4. Four; diminishing

5. dealing with the five million homeless people who are living in makeshift shelters outside the ruins of their homes

B

Numbers	Relevant Information
53 million	Population of Myanmar
4000	The number of people who died in the cyclone
190	Wind speed
46	The number of years that the military has ruled Myanmar
2879	The number of people missing within the Yangon and Irrawaddy divisions in a storm 3 days after Cyclone Nargis
2/5	Two of the five disaster zones that the death toll covered
351	Death toll from official reports
3934	The number of people who died within the Yangon and Irrawaddy divisions in a storm 3 days after Cyclone Nargis
41	The number of people injured within the Yangon and Irrawaddy divisions in a storm 3 days after Cyclone Nargis

C 1. A   2. A   3. B

Speaking

Part III Situational Dialogue: Disappointment and Encouragement

C (1) I'm so disappointed.

(2) I was supposed to have finished my thesis today.

(3) spend at least one more day revising the format.

(4) There's no reason to feel discouraged.

(5) There are still lots of mistakes.

(6) You always do a very good job!

(7) Finding a job is another headache for me.

(8) You're halfway there.
(9) You have my moral support.

Unit 6 Legends and Myths

Listening

Part I Dialogue

A

	Definition	Examples
Fairy Tale	A fairy tale is a type of folktale.	/
Folktale	A folktale is a story that has been passed down from generation to generation by word of mouth.	/
Legend	A legend is a type of folktale that is regarded as historical, but now they are unverifiable.	The legend of Robin Hood, and the legend of King Arthur and the Knights of the Round Table
Myth	A myth is also a story that is passed down through culture. But most of the time a myth is considered fiction, not fact.	Greek gods and goddesses

B 1. C 2. A 3. D 4. D 5. B 6. C

Part II Noah and Nü Wa

B 1. D 2. C 3. C 4. C 5. B

C order; mythology; came to earth; loneliness; by hand; too long to; dipped; in all directions; by hand; poor and weak; recounts; destruction; overthrow; failed; rammed; supported; tearing a hole; give way; restored the order; slew; tortoise

Part III Great American Myths

A   Stereotypes are impressions that people form about people whom they have never seen. They are powerful and omnipresent, usually influencing people's judgments of others. Many of the stereotypes formed are derived from the media, especially movies. There are many kinds of movies which give the perfect picture of an American stereotype—movies about families, a big house surrounded by a white fence, two cars, and three children. America is a big country and these conventional images are by no means representative of the "typical" American. Ignorance also plays a big part in forming stereotypes.

B 1. T   2. NG   3. F   4. T   5. F
   6. F   7. T   8. T   9. NG   10. T

C   **Great American Myths**

Myth 1:   Americans have blond hair and blue eyes.

Myth 2:   Americans do not take care of their parents.

Myth 3:   Americans live in big houses with big yards.

Myth 4:   All Americans are open and direct.

1. Because the U.S. is a land of immigrants and their descendants. Americans are as different as the nations from which they come.

2. Forget the stereotypes and look at the person as an individual.

3. Open question.

Part IV   Athena, Arachne, and the Weaving Contest

C huddled; discussing; approaching; wanted; requesting

Part V   News

A 1. F   2. F   3. T

B 1. D   2. C   3. C

C 1. A   2. B   3. C

Speaking

Part II   Speaking Activities

B 1.

Greek Name	Roman Name	Identity	Symbols
No.3	Venus	Goddess of <u>love and beauty</u>	<u>cupids</u>
No.1	Mars	God of <u>war</u>	<u>sword</u>; spear; <u>helmet</u>
No.2	Apollo	God of <u>music and truth</u>; son of Zeus	<u>lyre</u>; lighted torch
No.4	Diana	Goddess of hunting; Goddess of <u>the moon</u>.	forest; <u>bear</u>; <u>deer</u>

2.

(1) Pandora's box was the large box carried by Pandora that contained all the evils of mankind—greed, vanity, slander, lying, envy, pining and hope.

    E.g. *Never be exalted over a premature success, as it always turns out to be a Pandora's box.*

(2) Under the rose refers to something done in secret, privately, or confidentially.

    E.g. *The matter was finally settled under the rose.*

(3) Penelope's web refers to the tactics of delaying sth. on purpose; the task that can never be finished.

    E.g. *Mr. Jones made a long speech at the meeting. Everyone else thought it a Penelope's web.*

(4) An apple of discord indicates any subject of disagreement and contention; the root of the

trouble; dispute.

E.g. *This problem seems to be an apple of discord between Russia and the USA.*

(5) Helen of Troy refers to a beautiful girl or woman; a beauty who ruins her country; a terrible disaster brought by sb. or sth. you like best.

E.g. *It is unfair that historians always attribute the fall of the kingdom to Helen of Troy.*

(6) The Achilles' heel means a weak point in something that is otherwise without fault; the weakest spot.

E.g. *His Achilles' heel was his pride—he would get very angry if anyone criticized his work.*

(7) Swan song refers to a last or farewell appearance; the last work before death.

E.g. *All the tickets have been sold for the singer's performance in London this week—the public clearly believes that this will be her swan song.*

Part III Situational Dialogue: Possibility and Impossibility

C (1) I heard it may rain.

(2) I thought that we might go hiking in the hills.

(3) Maybe we'll meet some of the artists too.

(4) It's going to rain, isn't it?

(5) It might rain in the afternoon.

(6) I could play but I may be seeing Jill tomorrow.

Unit 7   Shopping

Listening

Part I   Dialogue

B 1. C   2. B   3. D   4. B   5. D   6. C

C 1. Next Tuesday.

2. It is too crowded. (Saturdays are a nightmare.)

3. Shopaholics.

Part II   Ten Steps to Smarter Food Shopping

A 1. list   2. Limit   3. empty   4. walls   5. portions

6. pictures   7. Grade   8. the language 9. some spice   10. the cashier

B 1. saw   2. unloading 3. fell back into 4. dietary   5. lead you astray

C 1. F   2. T   3. T   4. F   5. T   6. F

E 1a. Trade   1b. a trade   2a. a lot of time   2b. a good time; a wonderful time

3a. lights   3b. light   4a. a noise   4b. noise

5a. hair   5b. hairs

213

Part III Online Shopping—An Increasing Trend

A One third of people that shop online use a search engine to find what they are looking for and about one fourth of people find websites by word of mouth. Word of mouth has increased as a leading way for people to find websites to shop from. When an online shopper has a good first experience with a certain website, sixty percent of the time they will return to that website to buy more.

Books are one of the things bought most online. However, clothes, shoes and accessories are also very popular things to buy online. Cosmetics, nutrition products and groceries are increasingly being purchased online too. About one fourth of travelers are buying their plane tickets online because it is a quick and easy way to compare airline travel and make a purchase. Online shopping provides more freedom and control than shopping in a store.

B 1. B

2. (1) 240   (2) 233   (3) 197   (4) 70   (5) 45   (6) 60

C 1. always open; numerous bargains; lower prices; no queuing up; any product imaginable

2. average spending online; higher than; average spending on the high street

3. special offers; sales before Christmas

Part IV Listening for Signal Words

A (1) thread   (2) hints   (3) recognize   (4) indicate
     (5) signal   (6) previously   (7) ultimately   (8) additional information
     (9) warning   (10) nevertheless (11) contrasting   (12) cause-and-effect
     (13) facilitate   (14) beneficial

Part V News

A 1. B   2. C   3. A

B 1. Mark Spitz and Janet Evans.

2. They were there to film some public service announcements promoting water safety.

3. The World Water Park Association.

C 1. B   2. A   3. C   4. C

Speaking

Part III Situational Dialogue: Shopping

C 1-d; 2-a; 3-f; 4-e; 5-h; 6-g; 7-c; 8-b

Unit 8 Women Around the World

Listening

Part I Dialogue

 Women are laid-off due to the economic restructuring that China is undergoing.
The problems laid-off women face are: ① losing basic livelihood
② losing heavily subsidized housing
③ losing payment of medical bills
The current situation of women's re-employment is: the market adjustments hit women harder than men.
  Supporting statistics:
  Women's re-employment rate is less than 40%.
  Men's re-employment rate is almost 64%.
To change the status quo of women's re-employment,
  (1) the All-China Women's Federation has been conducting a pilot project:
    ① offering micro-credit loans for starting businesses
    ② giving preferential policies, such as tax waivers, for companies re-employing a substantial number of laid-off women
  (2) the laid-off women are:
    ① taking the initiative to conduct their own comprehensive job searches
    ② not relying on the state-owned companies' employment agencies

B 1. C   2. D   3. A   4. C

Part II Meet the Power Sisters

A 1. 1984   2. weight-lifting and pole vault   3. 17
   4. 40-yd. / NFL-like 5 seconds   5. clean and jerk   6. 15 ft. $1\frac{3}{4}$ in.

 1. F   2. T   3. T   4. F   5. NG   6. T

 1. Goat roping at rodeos and the heptathlon.

2. Women have brought a lot of life back into the sport, and have removed people's doubts about women's capabilities. They also fascinate the audience because of the risk involved in the sport.

3. Childhood experiences with boys made her tough physically and mentally, aggressive and competitive. Her success is also due to her male coach, who first suggested she try this sport.

4. They are opening the opportunity to other women to compete by being the first. They have prepared the way for others to follow them.

D 1. couch potato

我的朋友乔是个电视迷,他每天做的就是看电视和吃比萨。

2. hot potato

在本年度选举中,失业真是个棘手的问题。

3. mouse potato

电脑迷把大量的时间花在电脑面前。

4. mall rat

我过去爱逛购物中心,喜欢在那里看来来往往的人,特别是女孩子。但是现在我加入了足球俱乐部就没时间了。

Part III Women Struggle for Their Rights

A In the past few years, women have been elected the leaders of Germany, Liberia and Chile. Throughout the world, women are taking steps to improve their rights and increase their freedom. Yet, they have also suffered problems in their struggle for equality. In many parts of the world, women have almost no voice in politics and government. Their human rights are also denied. Sexual attacks, violence in the home, even murder are crimes that women in many parts of the world face daily.

B

Inequality	Country	Phenomenon	
Domestic Violence	Russia	9,000 women killed each year by a husband, partner or other family member	
	Pakistan	hundreds murdered every year by their families	
Social Aspects	Pakistan	Marriage	unwillingness
		Education	limited
		Family life	completely controlled by men
Political Aspects	Arab nations	few women elected	
Financial Aspects	The United States	own property, but generally lower paid than men and cannot afford health insurance	

C enforce; Elimination; 1979; bill of rights; 180; unequal citizens; equality; Half a million; are infected with; forced; human trafficking

D 1. F   2. T   3. NG   4. F   5. T

Part IV All Women Are Born for Loving

A (1) All women cry for no reason

(2) carry the weight of the world

(3) when everyone else gives up

(4) wisdom

(5) a tear to shed

Part V News

A 1. C   2. B   3. C

B 1. legal issues; techniques of conflict resolution / conflict resolution techniques; promote peaceful change in their communities
2. expression and association; own property regardless of gender
3. Islamic jurisprudence; violence

C 1. A   2. B   3. D

Speaking

Part III Situational Dialogue: Making Comparisons

C (1) The modern one's really nice, but the older one's a lot bigger.
(2) I like the furniture in the modern one though.
(3) But the older apartment's cheaper.
(4) The modern one is nicer looking.
(5) That wouldn't be so good if we're doing a lot of studying.
(6) I could live in either one.
(7) Maybe I am more interested in luxury.

D A: Which sports are popular in your country?
B: Most people like football. More boys like football than girls. A few girls play it really well. Some people like playing basketball.
A: Do many people like tennis?
B: More and more people like it now. Fewer people play table tennis than before. Many people like swimming, because it is fun and keeps you fit.
A: In my country, many people enjoy golf, but it is too expensive for some people. A few people like extreme sports, but I think the vast majority of people are afraid to try them.
B: Extreme sports are only for a small minority of people. Several people from my university enjoy them, but most of us just watch. No one I know plays golf.
A: I know loads of people who play it regularly. There are plenty of golf courses around the country. In the past, only a tiny number of people played.
B: A great number of people follow rugby in my country.
A: There are plenty of rugby fans in my country too.

Unit 9 Travel

Listening

Part I Dialogue

B 1. F   2. F   3. T   4. F   5. NG   6. T   7. T   8. F   9. NG

C 1. go away / break the cycle / wake up / work / alive / feel / the world / wonderful
2. travel / Kenya and Uganda / beaches / wildlife sightings / motivate / the rest of the semester
3. many factors / feel most comfortable / best enjoy your trips
4. create own unique itinerary / not rely on set schedules / more opportunity / communicate with local residents / tourists all over the world
5. history / architecture / a flowing continuity / shopping adventures
6. ships / gondola ride / sleek / ebony-colored / luxurious / craft
7. home of Marco Polo / original Don Juan / boats of every size and description / bridges

Part II Travel Smart: Dollars and Sense

A Travel in general:
1. ☑ off-season   ☐ peak season   ☐ shoulder season
   colder weather or the start of school makes vacationers scarce
2. Summer airfares during peak season:
   (1) ☐ popular mountain areas   ☑ warm-weather destinations
   (2) ☐ Galapagos Islands   ☑ the Caribbean   ☐ Europe
3. Staying at resorts:
   (1) ☑ midweek   ☐ weekends
   (2) for business travellers
       ☐ midweek   ☑ weekends
       Saturday night stay; local hop
   (3) domestic airfares
       ☑ in the middle of the week   ☐ at the beginning or in the end of the week
       ☐ working hours on weekdays   ☑ off-hours on weekdays
       either pay or vacation time
4. Shoulder season:
   (1) ☑ early in the season   ☐ in the middle of the season
       ☐ late in the season
       the same weather; opportunities; programs
   (2) at guest ranches
       ☐ June and July   ☐ July and August
       ☐ June and August   ☑ June and September
       adults-only; travelling during the off-season

B 1. F   2. F   3. T   4. NG   5. T   6. F   7. T
C 1. B   2. B   3. A   4. C

Part III The Experience of Travelling and Learning

A
  There are many reasons for travelling. The most common reason is probably tourism. People have always been curious about far-away places and cultures, and travelling is the only

way to experience these different environments. Travelling for tourism is not limited to any particular age group. Even small children can travel with their parents on a family vacation to see another city, region, or even another country. If you travel abroad, be sure to have all the necessary documents like a passport and a visa to travel to a specific country. You may also need to arrange tickets to travel to a foreign country and exchange some money to the local currency of the country you are travelling in.

B 1. C   2. A   3. B   4. A   5. B

C 1. We expect to meet different people, see different sights and do different things.
2. Are they going to like me? Are we going to be able to communicate? Do they have a sense of humour? Will I feel comfortable in their company?
3. The host families also feel nervous and ask themselves the same questions like the student.
4. A student can learn about another culture as well as his own culture. He might push his personal barriers, or realize his capability of achieving or succeeding. "Homestay" experiences can introduce a whole new element into his learning programme which might challenge the student's stereotypes and his preconceptions about people from a variety of backgrounds.

Part IV   Life Is a Journey

B 1. money/ a river/a traveller/a versatile performer   2. hidden treasures
3. the apple of her parents' eye   4. a lion/ a bomber/ a fighter plane
5. a discharged battery/ a broken fan belt/ a burst radiator hose/ a stripped wing nut

Part V   News

A (1) play exhibition games   (2) the baseball venue   (3) crack the market
(4) a swelling consumer class   (5) invisible on playgrounds
(6) absent from TV coverage   (7) show its appeal
(8) dropped from the 2012 London Olympics   (9) enthusiastic

B 1. It is the Yankees' qualification game for the postseason.
2. The Baltimore Orioles; At 8:05 p.m. on Sept.21.
3. ESPN
4. From the lowest price at $265 up to $65,000.

C 1. F   2. F   3. T   4. F   5. T

Speaking

Part III   Situational Dialogue: Buying Tickets

C 1. (1) What flights do you have from New York to London tomorrow?
(2) Do you want to fly first-class or economy?
(3) We have a non-stop flight leaving Kennedy at 9:25.
(4) When should I get to the airport?

2. (1) I'd like to have a Pullman ticket to Los Angeles.

(2) The 18:05 express train.

(3) When is the next day's express to Los Angeles?

(4) Thirty-two dollars for a hard sleeper.

Unit 10   Famous People

Listening

Part I   Dialogue

A 1. F   2. F   3. F   4. NG

B 1. No.

2. A national figure is a famous man or woman either now or in the past, who is or was celebrated in his or her field and recognized by the whole nation.

3. Modern media can help make national figures become "international figures".

C

Those who want to be famous:	Amy
Those who do not want to be famous:	John, Lori and David
Reasons why they want to be famous:	No job is perfect; being famous opens up a lot of doors—influencing more people on important topics
Reasons why they don't want to be famous:	No privacy (creeps; stalkers; fan pages); no personal/ordinary life; criticism

D 1. He was probably a reporter or something similar to that.

2. About a month.

3. They would like to be famous.

4. No.

5. Elton John (and others).

Part II   The Greatest Individual Athletic Achievements

A (1) diverting crowds   (2) the limits of   (3) Shakespearean tragedy

(4) In homage to   (5) greatest athletic accomplishments   (6) a panel of

B 1. Lance Armstrong—cycling—seven consecutive Tour de France victories

Jesse Owens—track and field—four world records in 70 minutes

Muhammad Ali—boxing—three heavyweight titles

2. (1) 21-stage; 3,500; 2,175; professional; summer

(2) long jump; 220-yard dash; 200-yard low hurdles; 100-yard dash; 1935; four

(3) 1964; 1974; 1978

C 1. Babe Ruth—baseball—60 home runs in a season
    Michael Jordan—basketball—ten seasons at the top
    Wayne Gretzky—hockey—2,857 career points
    Mark Spitz—swimming—seven gold medals
   2. (1) 1927; 155 games; 14%; American League
    (2) defender; scorer; dunks; Most Valuable Player; consecutive; championship; scoring average
    (3) 61 NHL; goals; assists; goals; hat tricks
    (4) seven; 1972

Part III A Great Scientist

A   Albert Einstein was born in Ulm, Germany on the 14th of March, 1879. Five years later, in 1884, he and his family moved to Munich because of his father's new job. In 1901, he became a Swiss citizen through naturalization. Eight years later as a Swiss, Einstein became professor of theoretical physics at the University of Zurich. From 1911 to 1912 he had the same job as a professor in Prague. In 1913 he was chosen to join the Academy of Science in Berlin. Einstein received his German nationality back in 1914. He worked for 19 years as a professor in Berlin. Because of the Nazis, Einstein renounced his German citizenship in 1933 and moved to the United States and worked as a professor in Princeton, New Jersey until 1945. He officially became an American in 1941. Albert Einstein died on the 18th of April, 1955.

B 1. D   2. C   3. B   4. C   5. C   6. A   7. D

D 1. The customer paid for his groceries when passing through the checkout stand.
   2. Richard got a thorn in his finger when pruning the roses.
   3. After hearing the terrible noise, they ran for their lives.
   4. He didn't see the dandelions until after watering the lawn in the morning.
   5. Will measured the board again before making his final cut.
   6. The necklace, even though staggeringly expensive, would match the dress perfectly.

Part IV Guessing Vocabulary from Context

A (1) unknown   (2) strategies   (3) strategies   (4) general   (5) related
   (6) illegal   (7) approximate   (8) regarding   (9) sacrifice   (10) comfortable
   (11) explanation (12) standard   (13) common   (14) infinitive (15) grammatical
   (16) clarifies   (17) broadly   (18) course

Part V News

A 1. World Player of the Year.
   2. No.
   3. Fitness problems. Too much football.
   4. Players should be under 23. But three over-age players for each team are allowed.
   5. Brazil.

B 1. F 2. T 3. F
C 1. C 2. C 3. B

Speaking

Part III Situational Dialogue: Getting Information

C (1) Could you tell me how to get to Carnegie Library from here?
(2) On 10th?
(3) I'm new in town.
(4) But I do know where Sears is.
(5) Let me see...
(6) Let me get this straight...
(7) That's right.
(8) You've been very helpful.
(9) That's quite all right.

D **Situation 1**

A: Excuse me officer, can you help me please?

B: My pleasure, what can I do for you?

A: Well, I am new here and I am looking for the Chinese Consulate. I wonder if you could tell me how to get there from here?

B: Well, let me see... it's about four blocks from here on the next street over. Go right at the traffic light and turn left at the next block which is Virginia Street. Go straight down Virginia Street until you reach State Street. The Consulate is the big white marble building on the right. You can't miss it.

A: Let me get this straight. So I turn right at this traffic light and turn left at Virginia Street. Is that right?

B: Yes that's right. Then go about 4 blocks down to State Street and it's on the right.

A: Let me see, do I turn right at State Street?

B: No, the Consulate is on Virginia Street right after the State Street intersection.

A: Ok great! Thanks so much, you've been very helpful.

B: That's quite alright, and welcome to Chicago!

Situation 2

Airline Rep: American Airlines, Bess speaking. How may I help you?

A:　　　I'd like some information on a ticket from San Francisco to Seattle please.

Airline Rep: I'd be happy to help you with that. When do you want to travel?

A:　　　I'd like a flight this Friday in the afternoon.

Airline Rep: There are two flights in the afternoon, one at 3:25 and the other at 5:30 p.m.

A:　　　Could you tell me how much that would be please?

Airline Rep: Sure, is it round-trip or one-way?

A: That would be round-trip returning two weeks later Sunday evening.
Airline Rep: That will be $275 round-trip including tax.
A: Okay, I'd like to book the 5:30 flight. And what time does it return on Sunday evening?
Airline Rep: There is a 7:45 flight arriving in San Francisco at 9:05. How does that sound?
A: That sounds perfect. My name is Trevor McGuire and I'll pay with a credit card.
Airline Rep: Okay Mr. McGuire, you're all set. Your ticket will be waiting at the ticket counter at the airport. Thanks for choosing American Airlines.

Unit 11 Health

Listening

Part I Dialogue

A

Health Rules	Follow	Break	Reason
A vigorous cardio workout is good for weight loss and for getting in better shape.		√	If you work out too hard or tire too quickly, there may not be any weight loss.
A moderate workout is good for losing weight.	√		It is more beneficial than a high-intensity workout.
Swimming is an ideal low-impact exercise for all people.		√	Not for somebody with asthma.
Cycling or walking is better for people with asthma.	√		People can do it everywhere and can still burn up to about 170 calories.
Drinking eight glasses of water a day is good for your health.		√	Not for some people who shouldn't have a lot of water.
All nutrients can be obtained from whole foods.		√	Some people who have food allergies (i.e. cannot drink milk or eat eggs) will need to take supplements.
Low blood pressure is better than high blood pressure.		√	Not for people who have coronary artery disease.

  1. People should set a pace that can be maintained for about 30 to 40 minutes easily without gasping for breath.

2. (1) People with asthma, because the chlorine in the pool can actually trigger an asthma attack.

   (2) Cycling or walking would be a more appropriate low-impact workout.

C liquids; fruit; soft drinks; just shouldn't have; body type; rule of thumb; urine; monitor; food allergy; eating eggs; energy; bone health; nutrients; supplements

Part II Vitamin D

A 1. T 2. T 3. F 4. F 5. F 6. T 7. T 8. F 9. NG

B 1. bones and muscles; prevent many diseases

2. rickets; osteoporosis; heart attacks; some cancers

3. sunlight; foods; dietary supplements

4. getting or taking too much vitamin D; skin cancer; damage; a poison; cover their skin; sunblock; stay out of

Part III Health Issues for College Students

A Balance in life seems to result in greater mental health. We all need to balance time spent socially with time spent alone, for example. Those who spend all of their time alone may be labeled as "loners", and they may lose many of their social skills. Extreme social isolation may even result in a split with reality. Those who ignore the need for some solitary time also risk such a split. Balancing the two needs seems to be the key, although we all balance them differently. Other areas where balance seems to be important include the balance between work and play, sleep and wakefulness, rest and exercise, and even the balance between time spent indoors and time spent outdoors.

B

Health Issues	Subcategory
1. <u>Sexual</u> health	1) sexually <u>transmitted</u> diseases 2) unintended <u>pregnancies</u> 3) sexually <u>assault</u> esp. acquaintance or date <u>rape</u>
2. Substance abuse	1) <u>alcohol</u> abuse 2) <u>drug</u> abuse 3) <u>tobacco</u> abuse 4) food abuse
3. <u>Mental</u> health	<u>emotional</u> problems, esp. <u>anxiety</u> and <u>depression</u> For example, competitive academic environments can create feelings of <u>inferiority</u>, insecurity and emotional <u>distress</u>.
4. Food and <u>weight</u>	1) malnourished 2) eating <u>disorders</u>, such as bulimia and anorexia
5. Health care	/
6. Accidents and <u>injuries</u>	<u>automobile</u> accidents and sports <u>injuries</u>

C 1. B 2. C 3. B 4. B 5. C 6. B

D (1) illegal (2) impossible (3) unsuccessful (4) irresponsible (5) inappropriate
(6) impolite (7) irreligious (8) dishonest (9) imperfect (10) discontented

Part IV Color Affects Your Moods and Health

A (1) magical powers (2) commonly assume (3) excited and nervous
(4) concentrate on our studies (5) breathing rate (6) stimulate
(7) hot or restless

Part V News

A 1. B   2. B   3. C   4. B
B 1. C   2. A   3. C
C has welcomed; independence; mayor; closer relations; sincerely; compatriots; peaceful and steady; join hands

Speaking

Part II Speaking Activities

B 3. A short walk after a meal is good for long life.
   A good breakfast makes you healthy.
   A vegetarian diet keeps the doctor away.
   开怀而笑和充足的睡眠就是医生的良方。
   一天一苹果,医生远离我。

Part III Situational Dialogue: Describing Moods and Feelings

C (1) You won't believe what's happening.
   (2) I'm really upset.
   (3) I'm so glad for you!
   (4) You don't understand.
   (5) Don't be silly.
   (6) I didn't think of it that way.
   (7) I've always wanted to go to California.

Unit 12 Memories

Listening

Part I Dialogue

B 1. B   2. D   3. B   4. A   5. A
C 1. representation; a powerful display; technology and human performance
   2. when the flame is lit; ailing; ignited the flame; 1996; was enclosed; water and fire; approached
   3. peacetime gathering of humanity; 200 or more; co-exist; great joys and sorrows; have nothing in common; far more alike

D (1) every four years (2) every year (3) Taking part is everything
 (4) two-thirds (5) 10,000 (6) drop out in the preliminaries
 (7) All games, all nations (8) become recognised (9) brings together
 (10) the world's youth (11) interact and compete against
 (12) two full weeks (13) friendly interactions
 (14) races, faiths and creeds (15) one big family
 (16) footballers, swimmers and boxers (17) sing and dance in the club
 (18) a boy of Chinese origin (19) structure of the closing ceremony
 (20) nations (21) one Olympic family
 (22) solidarity (23) race, colour or creed

Part II Sporting Memory—Jordan Hits "The Shot"

A 1. F 2. T 3. T 4. NG 5. F 6. F

B (1) game-winning basket (2) Chicago Bulls (3) 1989 NBA playoffs
 (4) Cleveland Cavaliers (5) closing seconds (6) on the line
 (7) the key (8) a jumper (9) top defenders
 (10) block (11) hang in the air (12) released
 (13) pumped his fists

D **Language Focus: NBA Team Names**

Eastern Conference 东部联盟球队	**Western Conference** 西部联盟球队
Atlantic Division	Southwest Division
Boston Celtics 波士顿凯尔特人	Dallas Mavericks 达拉斯小牛
New Jersey Nets 新泽西网	Houston Rockets 休斯敦火箭
New York Knicks 纽约尼克斯	Memphis Grizzlies 孟菲斯灰熊
Philadelphia 76ers 费城76人	New Orleans Hornets 新奥尔良黄蜂
Toronto Raptors 多伦多猛龙	San Antonio Spurs 圣安东尼奥马刺
Central Division	Northwest Division
Chicago Bulls 芝加哥公牛	Denver Nuggets 丹佛掘金
Cleveland Cavaliers 克里夫兰骑士	Minnesota Timberwolves 明尼苏达森林狼
Detroit Pistons 底特律活塞	Portland Trailblazers 波特兰开拓者
Indiana Pacers 印第安纳步行者	Seattle Supersonics 西雅图超音速
Milwaukee Bucks 密尔沃基雄鹿	Utah Jazz 犹他爵士
Southeast Division	Pacific Division
Atlanta Hawks 亚特兰大老鹰	Golden State Warriors 金州勇士
Charlotte Bobcats 夏洛特山猫	Los Angeles Clippers 洛杉矶快船
Miami Heat 迈阿密热火	Los Angeles Lakers 洛杉矶湖人
Orlando Magic 奥兰多魔术	Phoenix Suns 菲尼克斯太阳
Washington Wizards 华盛顿奇才	Sacramento Kings 萨克拉门托国王

Part III Five Ways to Improve Your Memory

A. As we get older, our ability to create new memories may be affected, making it more difficult to learn new things. It's not that we forget more easily; we may simply take longer to learn information in the first place.

In practical terms, this means that as we get older, we may have to pay closer attention to new information that we want to retain. We may also need to try different strategies to improve learning and trigger memories.

Continuing to learn new things throughout life can help keep our brains healthy. Also, as we age, we gain more knowledge and understand how to use it more efficiently. In other words, we get wiser as we get older!

C. 1. powerful advantage/ essential/ personal/ professional success
2. a. Use your imagination.
   b. Practice.
   c. Eat healthy.
   d. Do physical exercise.
   e. Exercise your brain.

D. 1. F   2. F   3. T   4. NG   5. F

E. 1. a. To try to remember which day of the week your last birthday was on, and the birthdays of all your family members.
   b. To try to remember all the Grand Slam finalists and the winner, and their scores.
   c. To try to remember the names of all 50 states.
2. Between the ages of 65 and 90.
3. Between the ages of 25 and 55.
4. a. Taking up word games like crossword puzzles and acrostics.
   b. Using your non-dominant side.
   c. Activities that require you to think and concentrate: keeping a journal, learning a new language, or taking music lessons.

Part IV How to Improve News Listening

A. (1) ideal listening practice   (2) unique characteristics
(3) logical order of presentation   (4) Vocabulary   (5) that occur frequently
(6) equivalent   (7) pronounced   (8) jargon
(9) news values   (10) the impact of   (11) revelation
(12) broad interests   (13) affected   (14) recently
(15) previously unknown   (16) nearby   (17) a fun story
(18) unusual   (19) involved   (20) leads and frameworks
(21) metaphor   (22) triangle   (23) substantial
(24) at any point   (25) news lead

Part V News

A (1) 547 (2) 332 (3) 20 (4) 197 (5) 135
(6) 51 (7) 15 (8) 226 (9) 261 (10) 132

B 1. France; Eight days. 2. Australia; 27 medals. 3. In 2006.

C 1. T 2. T 3. NG 4. F

Speaking

Part III Situational Dialogue: Interrupting

C (1) Pardon the interruption, but there's a Mr. Walters waiting to see you.

(2) Sorry, we'll have to continue this some other time.

(3) Excuse me, but could I ask a quick question?

(4) Sorry to butt in, but it's time for the production meeting.

(5) Thanks for reminding me.

D Reference answer:

B: [to person on phone]... Could you hold on for just a second? [to A] Have a seat. I'll be right with you.

A: Sorry. Take your time. I can wait outsite.

B: That's okay. [to caller on phone] I'm sorry. Can I call you back in a few minute? ... Thanks, talk to you later.

A: I'm sorry I interrupted your call. I just wanted to make an appointment with you to go through my project.

B: Of course. How about next Tuesday?

A: Could we meet earlier? Since the project's due on Wednesday, I would like to have a few more days to make any necessary changes.

B: Well, I suppose we could meet Friday later in the afternoon, say 5:00?

A: That would be great. Thank you so much. See you then!

Transcript

Unit 1 Family

Part I Dialogue

A is an American student while B is from China. They are both studying at MIT. They attend a lecture about the different ways of life. The following dialogue is their discussion after the lecture.

A: I've noticed a lot of differences between Chinese society and American society, but I think they're all based on one core difference: China is a society based on collectivism while America is a society of individualism.

B: For the most part I agree with you, but China and America are both changing, and I wouldn't say that either country is purely collectivistic or individualistic. Neither Chinese nor Americans completely rely on other people or do things one hundred percent on their own.

A: It seems that in China, families are very close and friends seem to go out of their way to help each other all the time. But in America it's a little different. Families are still close, but parents play less of a role in their children's lives once they grow up and move out.

B: Yeah, I agree. In America, when children turn 18 they usually move out—either to go to college or straight into "the real world." There aren't many kids who will let their parents tell them what to do once they're officially adults.

A: I think that's because in America more emphasis is placed on independence, individualism, and self-reliance. Most American parents expect their children to become independent adults, make their own decisions, and lead their own lives. Even though you may care about someone a lot, in order to show respect you have to let them go their own way.

B: But to me that seems kind of cruel. In China, children tend to live with their parents even after they graduate and start working. Sure, parents might meddle in their children's lives more, but families are closer and everyone can rely on one another.

A: Well of course Americans love their families too, they just express it differently. Parents in the U.S. take pride in their children's independence. It's hard to let go, but it's also rewarding to see that your children are strong enough to make it on their own. In China, people say, "If you don't listen to your elders, you'll wish you had." There really isn't an American saying with exactly that meaning.

B: Yeah, the closest thing I can think of in English would be "those who cannot learn from history are doomed to repeat it," but even that doesn't quite mean the same thing as the Chinese saying. I guess these two cultures are very different, but each has its own good points and bad points, strengths and weaknesses.

A: I agree. The fact that we're all different means that we can all learn from each other. As Confucius said, "When three men are walking together, there is one who can be my teacher."

Part II Remember, We're Raising Children, Not Flowers!

Ⓐ

David, my next-door neighbor, has two young kids aged five and seven. One day he was teaching his seven-year-old son Kelly how to push the lawn mower around the yard. As he was teaching him how to turn the mower around at the end of the lawn, his wife, Jan, called to him to ask a question. As David turned to answer the question, Kelly pushed the lawn mower right through the flowerbed at the edge of the lawn, leaving a two-foot wide path leveled to the ground!

When David turned back around and saw what had happened, he began to lose control. David had put a lot of time and effort into making those flowerbeds the envy of the neighborhood. As he began to raise his voice to his son, Jan walked quickly over to him, put her hand on his shoulder and said, "David, please remember... we're raising children, not flowers!"

Jan reminded me how important it is as a parent to remember our priorities. Kids and their self-esteem are more important than any physical object they might break or destroy. The window pane shattered by a baseball, a lamp knocked over by a careless child, or a plate dropped in the kitchen are already broken. The flowers are already dead. We must remember not to add to the destruction by breaking a child's spirit and deadening his sense of liveliness.

Ⓑ

I recently heard a story about a famous research scientist who had made several very important medical breakthroughs. He was being interviewed by a newspaper reporter who asked him why he thought he was able to be so much more creative than the average person.

He responded that, in his opinion, it all came from an experience with his mother that occurred when he was about two years old. He had been trying to remove a bottle of milk from the refrigerator when he lost his grip on the slippery bottle and it fell, spilling its contents all over the kitchen floor—a veritable sea of milk!

When his mother came into the kitchen, instead of yelling at him, giving him a lecture or punishing him, she said, "Robert, what a great and wonderful mess you have made! I have rarely seen such a huge puddle of milk. Well, the damage has already been done. Would you like to get down and play in the milk for a few minutes before we clean it up?"

Indeed, he did. After a few minutes, his mother said, "You know, Robert, whenever you make a mess like this, eventually you have to clean it up and restore everything to its proper order. So, how would you like to do that? We could use a sponge, a towel or a mop. Which do you prefer?" He chose the sponge and together they cleaned up the spilled milk.

His mother then said, "What we have here is a failed experiment in how to effectively carry a big milk bottle with two tiny hands. Let's go out in the back yard and fill the bottle with water and see if you can discover a way to carry it without dropping it." The little boy learned that if he grasped the bottle at the top near the lip with both hands, he could carry it without dropping it. What a wonderful lesson!

This renowned scientist then remarked that it was at that moment that he knew he didn't need to be afraid to make mistakes. Instead, he learned that mistakes were just opportunities for learning something new, which is, after all, what scientific experiments are all about. Even if the experiment "doesn't work," we usually learn something valuable from it.

Let's remember that our children's spirits are more important than any material things. When we do, self-esteem and love blossoms will grow more beautifully than any bed of flowers ever could.

Part III Stay-at-Home Dads

C

When Eric and Jody courted during graduate school, they assumed that when the time came to raise a family, Eric would work and Jody would stay home with the kids. Six years later, things looked different. "I liked my job, but Jody loved hers," says Eric. "Jody made a lot more money than I ever could have. It became clear to each of us that she should work and I should stay at home. We came to this decision through a lot of prayer and by discussing it with our church friends."

Three children later, Eric is passionate about being a stay-at-home dad. "My staying home and Jody engaged in her career work well for us. We each think we have the better end of the deal. I love kids, and she loves her job and our kids. I haven't traded away a bright future so my wife can work; I traded up. I worked for 12 years as an engineer; it was a good experience and I miss my colleagues. But I will have a more significant impact on the world by being home."

Eric and Jody aren't unusual. Estimates today place the number of stay-at-home dads in the United States at nearly two million—a number that has quadrupled since 1986 and is now the fastest growing family type. The exact number is difficult to determine because many fathers who devote themselves full-time to the job of parenting also have part-time jobs, work from home, or are between jobs.

Part V News

A

Total prize money at the U.S. Open will top $20 million for the first time this year, with the men's and women's singles champions each earning a tournament-record of $1.5 million.

The overall payout of $20.6 million is $1 million more than in 2007, matching the largest single-year jump in the hard-court Grand Slam tournament's history, the U.S. Tennis Association announced Tuesday.

There also was a $1 million jump in total prize money from 2006 to 2007, when the singles champions' take rose from $1.2 million to $1.4 million.

Adding in the bonuses available to the leading finishers in the summer circuit U.S. Open Series, the overall prize money could eventually be more than $23 million.

The No. 1 performers in the U.S. Open Series will earn a total of $2.5 million if they win the Grand Slam tournament, which begins August 25.

Last year, Roger Federer won both the summer series and the U.S. Open title, giving him a total payout of $2.4 million—the largest paycheck in tennis history.

B

Back and forth they went in the Wimbledon final. Rafael Nadal and Roger Federer, the two greatest tennis players of their generation, produced one of the greatest matches of any generation on the sport's grandest stage.

For five sets, through rain, wind and descending darkness, the two men swapped spectacular shots, until, against a slate sky, Nadal earned the right to fling his racket aside and collapse on his back, champion of the All England Club at last.

The No. 2-ranked Nadal ended No. 1 Federer's five-title run at the grass-court Grand Slam tournament by the slimmest of margins, 6-4, 6-4, 6-7 (5), 6-7 (8), 9-7, last night. Nadal is the first man since Bjorn Borg in 1980 to win Wimbledon and the French Open in the same season.

Nadal stopped Federer's streak of 40 victories in a row at Wimbledon, and a record 65 in a row on grass, thereby stamping his supremacy in their rivalry, no matter what the rankings say.

And that tremendous play lasted a record 4 hours, 48 minutes, longer than any of the classic Wimbledon men's finals, including Borg's five-set victory over John McEnroe in 1980.

Questions:

    a. Who was the champion of this year's Wimbledon final?

    b. What matches did Bjorn Borg win in 1980?

    c. How many victories did Federer have in a row on grass?

    d. How long did the match last?

Unit 2 Jobs

Part I Dialogue

Feifei:	Hi John! May I ask you some questions about part-time jobs?
John:	Of course, Feifei. What kind of job are you looking for?
Feifei:	I have no idea. You know, I just got accustomed to life on campus, but now I want to do something to earn extra money. What kind of jobs do British students usually do?
John:	It depends. Many students prefer working in their universities. I've got a friend named Dan who is working for the students' union at his university. He works at the reception desk.
Feifei:	What does he do there?
John:	He answers questions from students who come in to the office. He answers the telephone as well.
Feifei:	Sounds good. How many hours does he have to work every day?
John:	He probably works about 10 hours a week. Most people's hours vary. You know, some students work in the bar, some work in the housing office...
Feifei:	Oh, there seems to be many opportunities to find a part-time job on campus. John, can international students get a part-time job as well?
John:	Yes, they certainly can. An Indian student distributed leaflets on campus and she got 7 pounds per hour. It was just for a month that she did that job.
Feifei:	That's a different kind of experience, and it helped her earn money too! You need money since living in London is so expensive. So John, did you have any part-time jobs when you were a student?
John:	Well, yes I did. I worked at a radio station, and I used to be a television host to present a children's show called "Back to Basics".

Feifei: Really? That sounds like a very glamorous job!

John: Well, I was just very lucky, and I wasn't the only one. Feifei, I think you can also try to find a job at a radio or TV station since you are a mass media major.

Feifei: But I don't know what I can do exactly. I'm only a freshman and have no experience.

John: You can do a lot of things like answering phones, editing, hosting a programme... Learning by doing, remember? You can apply to be an intern during the summer vacation. It will surely do you some good not only in earning extra money but also in enriching your experience.

Feifei: OK. I will give it a shot.

John: Good luck!

Part II Job Interviews—Selling Yourself

You'll never sell any product that is as important as yourself, so you want to do it right. Selling yourself is your most basic selling job. You can sell yourself in job interviews or in your performance on the job so you can get a job or earn a promotion. You can also sell yourself in working with outsiders to make yourself attractive to other companies and thus enhance your career and your earning power. Almost everybody in business must go through the process several times throughout his or her career.

Having been through the same experience myself several times, I have my own four cardinal rules to follow which can help you in the job interview to sell yourself better.

1. Show prospective employers what you can do for them. What do you bring that's unique? To paraphrase President Kennedy, ask not what your employer can do for you, but what you can do for your employer. Don't tell the interviewers what's on your resume, which they have already read. Instead, tell them how you are going to do this job better than anyone else. In other words, sell your advantages, not your features. You do that by talking about your knowledge and your skills—the expertise and contacts you have developed in your field and the abilities you have developed over your career.

2. Maintain an open attitude. Openness is the quality that is essential in virtually every kind of social and business talk if you are to be successful. Don't be so business-like in your demeanor that you stifle your openness. Communicate your enthusiasm for the job. This is a refreshing characteristic that employers don't always find in job interviews. This quality is the one that can make the difference for the applicant who displays it.

3. Be prepared. Go over the key points you want to make about yourself. Even jot them down on a yellow pad and review them several times before the interview. And don't duck the hard questions—put them down and then figure out how you are going to answer them. If

you've changed jobs three times in the past seven years, expect to be asked why. And if you want to go that extra mile, put yourself through a dress rehearsal by having someone play the role of your prospective employer and "interview" you. It's an extremely effective technique that will give you a much better shot at getting that job.

4. Ask questions. Asking questions is how you learn, and in a job interview you definitely want to learn about the company just as much as the company wants to learn about you. You'll never have a better opportunity to get a feel for your prospective company or boss. Besides, employers respect someone who displays the initiative to ask intelligent questions about the company. It shows you possess two of the most persuasive qualities that we just talked about: you are prepared, and you care.

Part III Sports Manager

According to one successful manager, it is more important to know which deals not to make than which deals you should make. This is often the most delicate aspect of the job since a manager must make deals that satisfy the owners without alienating any of the players. Managers who work for a professional sports team are involved in the yearly ritual of drafting college players. They work closely with the coach and scouts to determine which players are the most talented, which players are economically feasible, and which player positions the team needs. Managers must do this while keeping an eye on the team's budget. They are in charge of everyone's salary, from the coach and players down to the assistants. They also make financial arrangements for travel, equipment, and uniform purchases. They must factor player injury into their budgets. Besides, they have to consider the possible team success that leads to additional playing and travel costs. Sports managers have to participate in press conferences and explain the reasons for their decisions to the media, without giving away their intentions for the future. They may be the subject of both complimentary and critical press reports which they must be able to ignore. When they sign a great player, they are considered heroes. When a respected player leaves the team or slides into a losing streak, managers are often seen as contributing to the team's downfall. Managers should expect to be fired and forced to relocate a number of times during their careers. For all of these reasons, this is a highly stressful job.

Quality of Life
Two Years Out

Satisfaction is high in this field. The manager receives a very large paycheck, and is participating in one of his/her favorite pastimes. Working in the glamorous field of professional and college sports has been a lifetime dream for many.

Five Years Out

Most managers are still involved with the sport, although they may no longer be working with their first team. Many make lateral moves to other teams, which often brings them new challenges and greater financial rewards. Satisfaction remains high.

Ten Years Out

Some managers make huge amounts of money at this point, as they have earned the trust of the team owners and coaches, if not always the general public. A few have their eye on the presidency of the club, or a partial ownership, which are the only advancements open to them at this point.

Part V News

A

Starting next month, thousands of government employees will only work 4 days per week, in an effort aimed at reducing energy costs and commuters' gasoline expenses.

It will be "TGIT" for Utah state employees, as in, "Thank goodness it's Thursday."

In a yearlong experiment aimed at reducing the state's energy costs and commuters' gasoline expenses, Utah is about to become the first state to switch to a four-day workweek for thousands of government employees.

They will put in 10-hour days, Monday through Thursday, and have Fridays off, freeing them to golf, shop, spend time with the kids or do anything else that strikes their fancy. They will get paid the same as before.

The order issued by Republican Gov. Jon Huntsman will affect about 17,000 out of 24,000 executive-branch employees. It will not cover state police officers, prison guards or employees of the courts or Utah's public universities. Also, state-run liquor stores will stay open on Fridays.

At least 5.59 million students will graduate from colleges this year, 13 percent more than last year, the Ministry of Education has said.

They face unprecedented pressure in the job market as about 700,000 graduates who could not find work last year will compete with them for employment.

But this could mean a windfall of graduates in rural areas and small towns.

About 20,000 graduates have signed up to work in the countryside. And many others, including 200 from Tsinghua University, have opted to work in the regions hit by the May 12 quake.

College graduates are encouraged to work in western and rural areas where many jobs are available. Those who have worked in rural areas for two years enjoy favorable treatment in recruitment for government organs and state enterprises, and get bonus points if they take the civil service exams.

College graduates are encouraged to start their own business too. Such graduates enjoy a 20 percent income tax cut for start-ups. The government also offers small loans to them to start a business.

Public institutions in Beijing will soon start work an hour later than normal in a plan to ease traffic congestion during the Olympic Games, state media said Monday.

Working hours in Beijing will change from July 20th in a bid to spread out morning traffic by staggering office openings and to reduce pollution.

The government also is encouraging people to work flexible hours or work from home if possible.

Working hours for companies will be set from 9 a.m to 5 p.m. Public institutions will begin work at 9:30 a.m., one hour later than normal. Shopping malls will open no earlier than 10 a.m. and stay open longer, until 10 p.m. or even later.

Schools, administrative bodies and essential service sectors are exempt from the changes.

Also on July 20th, cars with odd and even number plates will only be allowed on the roads on alternate days. Drivers violating the rule will be fined $15.

Beijing has spent more than $15 billion on anti-pollution measures for the Olympics, such as relocating factories and expanding its subway network.

Unit 3 Business

Y—Mabel Young
B—Roger Barrett

Y: What is it like doing business in the DPRK?
B: Well, it's not as difficult as people imagine. People have a preconception that it must be a very difficult place to do business only based on what they hear. But actually the Korean people that we deal with are very sincere. So if you've got something that you think is suitable for the DPRK market, then it's a good time to go into business there.

Y: Some big corporations do not want it to be known that they are actually doing business in the DPRK. Why is that?

B: When you are doing business, either you are developing the business or you have already set it up and the business is going quite well. In this case, you don't want to alert your competitors that you might be doing something that is going well. So it's best to be discreet as a businessman. But the second reason is a difficult issue to deal with and to talk about, because it's so complex. The DPRK is portrayed in the media just by the issues that tend to come along with it, and normal business itself doesn't make the news. The impression people get of the DPRK is colored by the media and they don't even think about business when it comes to that country. The overwhelming media impression is negative because all that's portrayed in the media tends to be just negative stories. For example, last year the first commercial charter flights took place between South Korea and North Korea, between Seoul and Pyongyang, but it didn't get to the international media. But if there's one shot fired across the demilitarized zone, then it's a headline straight away.

Y: What do you think the foreign companies expect from their current businesses in the DPRK? Do they expect to make a lot of money or to establish a stronghold in the DPRK market for future benefits?

B: Going into a new market, a developing market, sometimes you've got to give a little, and spend a little to gain a little. But I think most of the companies that have gone in there just to test the market have been very pleasantly surprised. There are twenty-three million people in North Korea, so it's actually a market the same size as Malaysia or Turkey. There's a real market there. All those people need clothing, food and of course they all need jobs.

Y: I was told a few years ago that the North Koreans were only able to eat eggs and meat on the birthday of their great leader and on the national day of the DPRK. Is that still the case?

B: I don't think that was ever the case. Rumors prevail. There will always be people who say different things or who "view the cup half empty", whereas we believe the cup is now much more than half full. What I mean is, people are doing more and achieving more than they did before because they are motivated. The incentives that are introduced by our joint-venture partners and those that we have introduced all have to do with increasing productivity and profitability. Everybody, every department, every unit is motivated to be not just working harder but working smarter.

Y: Can people talk openly about capitalism or the market economy?

B: Yes, absolutely. Just like in China, you can freely talk about capitalism or even communism. It's much easier, and people are much more confident now to talk more openly than before. I've seen these changes not just gradually and steadily in the past ten years but especially in the last two years. And this is a general feeling among my colleagues and friends in Pyongyang.

Part II Students Carve Out Early Careers in Business

The dream of being your own boss and making money has triggered entrepreneurship at an early age. More and more children these days are able to transform their hobbies into businesses, creating a substantial amount of pocket money.

"It's fun to make money," said 12-year-old Kim Ohlwiler, whose Hawaiian backpacks sent her on the road to success. With some help from her mom, the Lake Forest resident started out last fall by designing and sewing 12 backpacks to display at a local garage sale. She quickly sold them all and orders for more started to come in.

The company, Northshore Creations, which she now runs together with her twin brother Kyle, has snowballed into a flourishing enterprise with more than 600 backpacks sold. Even though the youngsters are being home schooled and have flexible hours, they have more sales than they can handle.

"Half of our production is done by a sewing company," said Kim. The twins' mother, Marilyn, added that their sewing manufacturers probably would take over most of the process in the future, especially since the Ohlwilers plan to expand into making Hawaiian clothing and sheets.

Eight-year-old Alexis Trudell has already discovered the taste of success. During a Christmas bazaar at La Madena Elementary School, the young Lake Forest resident sold purses, jewelry, headbands and nail polish for more than $650.

"I want to sell stuff and make money," said Trudell, whose parents are both entrepreneurs. Trudell hand-picked her products when her mom brought her to the wholesale district in Los Angeles.

Eighteen-year-old Marisol Baltierra of Laguna Hills is in the process of starting a clothing company. She created her own logo and website, and then she borrowed money from her mom to print up her own T-shirts.

"I have sold almost 40 T-shirts," Baltierra said. "So far I've only sold them to people personally, but soon I will put something on my website so they can buy them online," she added. She hopes to raise enough money to add a variety of products to her Bassix clothing collection.

"I want to be my own boss and have my own giant company," she said.

To learn more about making it in the competitive business world, the local teen enrolled in an entrepreneur class at Laguna Hills High School.

"I took this class because I thought it would help me out and it really has," Baltierra said.

Melissa Halliday, 17, of Laguna Hills is another student who participates in the class. She has taken her love for animals and turned it into a pet-sitting business.

"I take care of people's cats and dogs when people go on vacation," she said. "I feed them, play with them and give them their medication," she said. Halliday pointed out that she had never taken a business class before but wanted to learn more about entrepreneurship.

"There are a lot of opportunities out there," she said.

Part III   Seven Principles of Admirable Business Ethics

"If you have integrity, nothing else matters. If you don't have integrity, nothing else matters." —Alan K. Simpson

Seven Principles of Admirable Business Ethics

1. Be Trustful: Recognize customers want to do business with a company they can trust; when trust is at the core of a company, it's easy to recognize. Trust defined is, assured reliance on the character, ability, strength, and truth of a business.

2. Keep an Open Mind: For continuous improvement of a company, the leader of an organization must be open to new ideas. Ask for opinions and feedback from both customers and team members and your company will continue to grow.

3. Meet Obligations: Regardless of the circumstances, do everything in your power to gain the trust of past customers and clients, particularly if something has gone awry. Reclaim any lost business by honoring all commitments and obligations.

4. Have Clear Documents: Re-evaluate all print materials including small business advertising, brochures, and other business documents, making sure they are clear, precise and professional. Most importantly, make sure they do not misrepresent or misinterpret the wrong information.

5. Become Community Involved: Remain involved in community-related issues and activities, thereby demonstrating that your business is a responsible community contributor. In other words, stay involved.

6. Maintain Accounting Control: Take a hands-on approach to accounting and record keeping, not only as a means of gaining a better feel for the progress of your company, but as a resource for any "questionable" activities. Gaining control of accounting and record keeping allows you to end any dubious activities promptly.

7. Be Respectful: Treat others with the utmost respect. Regardless of differences, positions, titles, ages, or other types of distinctions, always treat others with professional respect and courtesy.

Recognizing the significance of business ethics as a tool for achieving your desired outcome is only the beginning. A small business that instills a deep-seated theme of business ethics within its strategies and policies will be evident among customers. Its overall influence will lead to a profitable, successful company. By recognizing the value of practicing admirable business ethics, and following each of the seven principles, your success will not be far away.

Part IV Listening for Numbers

1. A total of 1,510 people said they watched soap operas. Just over half of these people were in the 21–25 age group which comprised a total of 758 viewers. This was the largest age group. Seventeen percent of the viewers were in the second-largest age group (26–30), which had a total of 258 people. There was a similar number of viewers aged below 20. After the age of 30, the number of viewers fell significantly. The 31–35 age group made up only 10 percent of the viewers and there were 76 people in the 36–40 age group who said they watched the programme. Only three percent of the viewers were over 40. Obviously the genre appeals to young people most.

2. In 2007, Beijing's nominal GDP was 900.62 billion RMB (118.4 billion USD), a year-on-year growth of 12.3% from the previous year. Its GDP per capita was 56,044 RMB, an increase of 8.9% from the previous year. In 2007, Beijing's primary, secondary, and tertiary industries were worth 10.13 billion RMB, 247.93 billion RMB, and 642.52 billion RMB. In 2007, urban disposable income per capita was 21,989 yuan, an increase of 11.2% from the previous year. Per capita, pure income of rural residents was 9,559 RMB, a real increase of 8.2%. Per capita, disposable income of the 20% low-income residents increased 16.7%, 11.4 percentage points higher than the growth rate of the 20% high-income residents.

Part V News

UN Secretary-General Ban Ki-moon addressed the Group of 77 at a ceremony during which Pakistan handed over its role as G-77 chair to Antigua and Barbuda.

In his statement, Ban said the UN attaches great importance to the roles played by the G-77 and China, and is willing to make joint efforts to achieve common development of humankind.

The G-77 was established in 1964 with the signing of the Joint Declaration of the Seventy-Seven Countries. The declaration was issued at the end of the first session of the United Nations Conference on Trade and Development in Geneva.

The Group of 77 is the largest intergovernmental organization of developing states in the United Nations. It provides the means for southern countries to articulate and promote their collective economic interests and enhance their joint negotiating capacities on all major international economic issues within the United Nations system.

B

World oil prices will not come down and oil producers have done what they can to ensure supply, the Organization of Petroleum Exporting Countries (OPEC) president said Tuesday.

"OPEC has already done what OPEC can do and prices will not come down," OPEC president Chakib Khelil told reporters as he arrived for a high-level dialogue with European Union (EU) officials in Brussels.

As the world oil prices reached 140 U.S. dollars per barrel, a once unimaginable record level, producing countries have been under rising pressure from consuming countries, including the EU, to increase production.

Slovenia, which currently holds the EU's rotating presidency, said prior to the dialogue that the 27-nation bloc would particularly highlight its concerns about high oil prices.

Before hosting a summit between producers and consumers in Jeddah last weekend, Saudi Arabia, a leading member of OPEC and the world's top oil exporter, promised last Thursday to increase oil output by 200,000 barrels per day.

Unit 4 Music

Part I Dialogue

A

Dad: Janice, turn down the stereo a bit. I'm trying to read and I can't hear myself think!

Janice: This is Jay Chou's new record. It's so popular now. Don't you like it, Dad?

Dad: Not really. I can't stand that pounding noise, and I can't understand a word he's saying.

Janice: Oh, come on Dad. Jay Chou's songs are beautiful and they're typical R&B. Just feel the energy in it. It's so exciting!

Dad: What is R&B?

Janice: R&B is short for rhythm & blues. It is a very popular form of modern music that comes from American black music. It is also the basis of some other black music such as hip-hop and rap. In fact, besides jazz and blues, all black music belongs to R&B.

Dad: You confuse me with so many types of music! Does all modern music have such a strong beat?

Janice: More or less. Most modern music is exciting and makes you feel like dancing because the beat is fast and the rhythm is strong. It just helps you keep pace with the fast speed of modern life, I guess.

Dad: Maybe you're right. But modern music is really not my thing. I still prefer classical music. It helps me relax after a long day at work. Anyway, you are playing the CD too loud.

Janice: Okay, Dad, I'll turn it down.

C —A Chinese Student
M—Maggie, an American

C: Hi Maggie, can you tell us something about today's music in America?

M: Well, frankly I think much of today's music in America is a travesty of real music. MTV has destroyed the quality of music with over-commercialization. Now, any sexy, pretty face or anyone with a weird attitude can be a star. Today's musicians are not as creative as before. Many of them sound the same and act the same. Unfortunately, today's young people haven't experienced early rock music so they don't know how pitiful today's musicians are by comparison.

C: I hear Elvis Presley was a great rock'n'roll singer.

M: Yeah. Elvis is "The King" of rock'n'roll. He was cute, sexy, and had a great voice. His music was full of energy and rhythm and young girls went crazy over him. He helped the rock music industry take off, but his influence goes beyond music. He has become an American legend.

C: Did he also play the guitar?

M: Yes, he did. But when it comes to playing the electric guitar, Jimi Hendrix is considered one of the pioneers and maybe the greatest ever. I think Bruce Springsteen, "the Boss", is the greatest rocker of all time. He has a great voice, writes awesome lyrics, is a great guitar player, and is an all-round nice person.

C: How interesting! I wish I knew more about American music. What type of music is the most popular in America today?

M: Today's most popular types of music are rap and hip-hop, pop, rock, R & B, and country. Each music type comes with its own fashion. Rock goes with jeans and T's. Punk goes with tight clothing, weird hairdos and make-up. Country goes with cowboy hats, plaid shirts, jeans and boots. Rap goes with baggy pants and loose clothes. It can be quite violent and is popular with gangs.

C: It's interesting that there are so many different types of music.

M: Yeah, and they each have their own origins. Jazz was invented in New Orleans. Country music is mainly based in the south, centered in Nashville, and rock'n'roll has a Hall of Fame in Cleveland, Ohio.

Part II Fighting Music Piracy on College Campuses

When the parents of today's young people were in school, sharing music was a slow process. They had to copy songs from a vinyl record or a cassette using a tape recorder.

Today, friends can share the latest hits at the speed of light over the Internet. Peer-to-peer networks make file sharing easy—and, in many cases, illegal.

Five years ago, the Recording Industry Association of America, the R.I.A.A., launched a major effort to catch music pirates. Piracy violates copyright laws. These laws protect creative works against reproduction or sale without permission.

The industry group has brought thousands of civil actions against university students. Students caught pirating can also pay a settlement to avoid a lawsuit and possible fines.

The association uses special software to identify illegal file sharing on campus networks. But many colleges and universities oppose efforts to require schools to use similar technology. They see it as a waste of resources. They say much more illegal sharing takes place through commercial Internet providers than through campus networks.

"Educause" is a group that works for what it calls the "intelligent use" of information technology in higher education. Steve Worona from Educause says about eighty percent of college students do not live on school grounds. And their computers, he says, are generally not linked to school networks.

On its website, the R.I.A.A. says it has chosen to target college students because their music piracy remains an especially big problem. It says that some recent surveys show that more than half of the nation's college students often download music and movies illegally.

The industry group has also pushed Congress to take action. In February, the House of Representatives approved a higher education bill containing anti-piracy requirements. The measure would require all schools involved in federal financial-aid programs to develop plans to deal with unlawful downloading. Schools could invest in technology to block piracy, or they could offer legal file-sharing services.

A similar bill in the Senate would require schools to inform their students about issues related to peer-to-peer file sharing. Educause's Steve Worona says most American colleges and universities already do this with incoming students. Students who get caught often have to pay fines, or they lose their use of the school's network.

Part III Music at Sporting Events

Basketball music

At NBA games, repetitive organ music is played at key points of the game. For example, the announcers often play the "Charge" fanfare to accompany the home team entering the visitor's side of the court with possession of the ball. A different theme is used to encourage the home team in defense of their own side of the court. Many NBA teams now play a particular theme to accompany the home team when taking the court to begin the game.

Baseball music

Take Me Out to the Ball Game is often played or sung at major- or minor-league baseball games, typically during the seventh-inning stretch. Ballpark music performed by an organist debuted at Chicago's Wrigley Field in 1941, and had spread to most other Major League parks by the 1960s. Beginning in the mid-1970s, prerecorded pop and rock music began to supplement the organ music (or replace it entirely) at many ball parks. A very popular theme song is "Meet the Mets" from 1962 when the Mets joined the MLB. The Mets also had a theme song for their World Series run in 1986; it was "Let's Go Mets".

Association football music

In the many countries where football (soccer) is popular, and in the UK in particular, football music is a varied and popular subgenre of popular music. Songs are often released to coincide with specific events, such as the World Cup, or to become anthems for particular teams. Since football has a huge spectator base, such songs are often very popular on the charts. Examples of music created to be football songs include New Order's "World in Motion", and "Three Lions" by The Lightning Seeds in collaboration with comedian football fans, David Baddiel and Frank Skinner. A subset of football music is novelty football music, which typically includes humorous lyrics. Examples of novelty football songs include "Vindaloo" by Fat Les, "Meat Pie, Sausage Roll", and numerous Frank Sidebottom songs.

Theme music in other sports

Entire teams will occasionally adopt a theme song (such as the Chicago Bears with their *1985 Super Bowl Shuffle*, sung by the members of the team). *Monday Night Football* has its own theme, sung by Hank Williams, Jr.; the Hockey Night in Canada theme has sometimes been referred to as Canada's second national anthem; and the Olympic Games have long had powerful theme music composed to accompany ceremonies opening and closing the games.

Perhaps the most extreme example of this can be found in professional wrestling, where almost every wrestler has an entry theme written to suit their particular character.

An album entitled "ESPN Presents Stadium Anthems" has been released that includes many songs that are played over the public address system at North American sporting events. Similar albums, such as Jock Jams have also been released in the past.

Part V News

AC Milan has announced that they have reached an agreement with FC Barcelona for the transfer of Ronaldinho to the Rossoneri's club. Ronaldinho will arrive in Milan on Wednesday for a medical exam and sign a contract through June 2011.

Manchester City had also bid for the 28-year-old Brazilian, but media reports said Milan won the race despite offering just 18.5 million euros, almost half as much as the Premier League club.

Milan will play in the UEFA Cup this season after finishing fifth in Series A last term. They have been chasing Ronaldinho for three months and the player has consistently said a move to San Siro was appealing. He has spent five years at the Nou Camp, helping Barca win the Champions League in 2006 and their domestic title in 2005 and 2006.

The playmaker was named FIFA World Player of the Year in 2004 and 2005 but has been told he can leave Barcelona after suffering form and fitness problems last season.

There has been an increase of 4.5% in season ticket prices at the Emirates Stadium.

The new hike sees an increase in the cheapest season ticket from £885 to £925. This leaves Arsenal with the highest season ticket prices in the Barclays Premier League. Liverpool has the second highest prices, but a staggering £275 cheaper than Arsenal's.

Defending the high prices of season tickets, Arsenal director Danny Fizman was quick to point out that Arsenal's tickets include all cup and Champions League matches for which other clubs charge extra. At Arsenal they are included in the price of the season ticket.

Fizman was also quick to point out that this was the first price increase in four years.

England's David Beckham is one of five players to make the Major League Soccer All-Stars for the first time after voting results were announced by the league on Thursday.

The first-eleven will be joined by seven other players to make up the squad for the July 24 match against English Premier League club West Ham United in Toronto.

Beckham's L.A. Galaxy team-mate Landon Donovan, was top of the selection, which was based on voting by fans, players, officials and the media, with Beckham and Chicago Fire's Mexican international Cuauhtemoc Blanco.

New England Revolution's Scottish coach Steve Nicol will be in charge of the All-Star team and has three of his club's players in the All-Star eleven.

Unit 5 Disasters

Part I Dialogue

A—B

A: Are there any interesting stories in the newspaper today?

B: There are a few stories about natural disasters. There is a massive forest fire in Australia covering several square kilometers and destroying the land.

A: Was it caused accidentally or naturally? Sometimes it gets so hot that fires begin naturally in Australia and Africa.

B: Nobody knows at the moment, but it has been very hot there recently. The drought in Africa is causing starvation. Millions of people have migrated to try to find food.

A: What is the international community doing to help?

B: The European Union has sent several planes with relief supplies. Several countries have sent soldiers to distribute food and medical supplies. Refugee camps have also been set up across the region.

A: How many countries have been affected?

B: Six have been seriously affected, but the refugees are also migrating to several surrounding countries.

A: I saw on TV yesterday that there was another earthquake in Iran.

B: Yes. There have been a few there recently. They say that this one was not a big quake. The Iranians are dealing with it on their own. They purchased some special equipment to find people buried under the rubble.

A: Does the newspaper say anything about casualties?

B: So far, less than 20 people have died, but over 100 are in hospital.

A: What a pity! I hope the Iranian government can make the rescue effort more efficient.

B: Yeah, the more efficient the rescue efforts, the less people would die.

C

C—Contessa Brewer   D—David Wessel

C: Joining me to discuss how the damage from Katrina could affect the economy, from Washington is David Wessel, deputy bureau chief of the Wall Street Journal. David, nice to see you today.

D: Nice to see you.

C: So how much has Hurricane Katrina affected oil and gas production here?

D: Well, the Gulf of Mexico is a very important center of oil exploration and production, and also a port for importing oil and other energy materials into the United States. So the reason why oil prices have spiked is because there are concerns that the supply will be disrupted.

C: Yeah. We heard the President is considering releasing some oil stock from the Strategic Petroleum Reserve, but if the refineries can't handle that work, how would that help?

D: Well, it wouldn't help. What the Strategic Petroleum Reserve has is raw material that would have to be refined. It is a very delicate moment. One fifth of all the nation's imports and exports come out from the ports down there, in the areas affected by the hurricane. If it turns out that those ports are damaged, it'll take a while to reopen. The economic effects could go beyond the energy ones.

C: Ok! That's good to know. I didn't even realize it was such a big import situation.

D: Right. As a center of production in the U.S., in the overall U.S. economy, it's not very big. But our imports and exports of energy are a very important part of that region's economy, and that could have national implications.

Part II Tsunami Wounds Still Fresh in Indonesia One Year Later

Ⓐ—Ⓑ

At least 169,000 people were left dead or missing by the tsunami that swept through Aceh on December 26, 2004. Half a million were left homeless, but the unprecedented generosity of the international community pledged more than $6 billion in aid to Aceh. Tents and emergency aid were quickly brought to the area, yet a year later, more than 70,000 people still languish in tent camps.

Petria, who lost her husband and three of her four children, is one of those that live in a tent camp along the devastated west coast. Strong winds knock the tents down, there is no electricity, rain comes in, and puddles of mud are everywhere around the forlorn-looking camp. Ms. Petria says she is grateful for the food aid, but hopes there can be more of it. She says some people from an aid agency came to the camp and promised the people their homes. But that was six months ago, and no one has been there since.

Many in the camps echo her complaints. Despite promises, there are not enough new homes. People say they know what they need, but do not know where to find help.

And yet help is there. Aid agencies have budgets running into tens of millions of dollars to provide survivors with new homes. But an array of problems have slowed reconstruction, ranging from rivalries among aid agencies over who builds what where, to government red tape, land ownership issues and shortages of building materials.

Many survivors now have left the squalid tent camps and barracks and moved back to their ruined villages. They've built ramshackle huts with wood washed up by the sea, or they live under bits of plastic and canvas next to the foundations of their destroyed homes.

In a beachside area of Banda Aceh called Ulhee Lhee, where most of the homes were destroyed and two-thirds of the population killed, about 50 survivors have set up their own tent camp. Their frustration rings out with a sign at the entrance of their camp that reads, "It is better to stay here in our own village."

But camp leader Dalman says they decided to move back because they could no longer bear the conditions in the camps. An aid organization has provided sanitation, but like many of the tent camps, there is no electricity and it is dark and lonely at night. Mr. Dalman says they have been promised homes for a year, but still have not received anything, which is why they put up the banner.

In addition to the tens of thousands living in tents and barracks, more than 300,000 people who lost their homes live with friends and relatives. Those people, too, need to rebuild their homes and re-establish their lives.

Bo Asplund, the U.N. coordinator in Indonesia says getting people into temporary homes is a priority, along with getting the economy working again in Aceh. "They've got to make the economy work. As long as people have a cash wage, they will take matters into their own hands. People are masters of their own destinies. If they have a cash wage and employment, other things will be worked out. That's very, very important."

Indeed, for the people of Aceh, having their own homes will be the biggest step toward controlling their own destinies again.

Part III The Nature of Disasters

Natural disasters introduced here include hurricanes, tornadoes, floods and earthquakes.

Hurricanes—A hurricane is a tropical storm with winds that have reached a constant speed of 74 miles per hour or more. Hurricane winds blow in a large spiral around a relatively calm center known as the "eye." The "eye" is generally 20–30 miles wide, and the storm may extend outward 400 miles.

As a hurricane approaches, the skies will begin to darken and winds will grow in strength. As a hurricane nears land, it can bring torrential rains, high winds and storm surges.

Hurricanes can spawn tornadoes, which add to the destructiveness of the storm. Following a hurricane, inland streams and rivers can flood and trigger landslides. Floods and flash floods generated by torrential rains also cause damage and loss of life.

Tornadoes—Tornadoes are storms that are characterized by a twisting, funnel-shaped cloud created by thunderstorms. Sometimes tornadoes are spawned by hurricanes. A tornado is produced when cool air overrides a layer of warm air, forcing the warm air to rise rapidly. The damage from a tornado is the result of the high wind velocity and wind-blown debris.

Although short in duration, lasting no more than 20 minutes when they ground, tornadoes are most destructive when they do touch ground. Wind speeds of a tornado may approach 300 miles per hour. One tornado can touch ground several times in different areas.

Injuries or deaths related to tornadoes most often occur when buildings collapse, when people are hit by flying objects, or when they are caught trying to escape the tornado in a car.

The best protection during a tornado is an interior room, away from windows and doors on the lowest level of a building, preferably a basement. Rooms constructed with reinforced concrete or brick with no windows and a heavy concrete floor or roof system overhead are also considered safe.

Floods—Except for fires, floods are the most common and widespread of all natural disasters. In fact, more than half of all presidential disaster declarations over the past 40 years resulted from natural phenomena in which flooding was a major component. Property damage from flooding now total over $1 billion each year in the United States.

Flooding can occur after heavy rains, melting snow, tides, storm surges that follow hurricanes, or tsunamis that may follow earthquakes. Dam failures, water main breaks and sewer main breaks are some of the human factors or technological factors that contribute to flooding.

Earthquakes—An earthquake is a sudden, rapid shaking of the earth caused by the breaking and shifting of rock beneath the earth's surface. This shaking can cause buildings and bridges to collapse.

Earthquakes can disrupt gas, electric and phone service. They can sometimes trigger landslides, avalanches, flash floods, fires and tsunamis, which are huge, destructive ocean waves.

Most at risk are buildings with foundations resting on unconsolidated landfill, old waterways, or other unstable soil. Buildings or trailers that are not tied to a reinforced foundation are also at risk. These buildings can be shaken off their mountings during an earthquake. Earthquakes can occur at any time of the year.

Part V   News

A

Chinese officials say nearly 5 million people have been left homeless by the earthquake that devastated its southwestern regions four days ago. More than 22,000 people are confirmed dead, many are still missing. The first foreign rescue crews have started work near the epicenter of the quake, the first time China has allowed professionals from outside the country to help with disaster relief. Premier Wen Jiabao and President Hu Jintao both said today that the number one priority is to rescue people from the rubble. It has been four days since the earthquake, and the chances of dragging any more people out of the rubble alive are diminishing by the day. A major challenge for the government now is to deal with the five million homeless people who are living in makeshift shelters outside the ruins of their homes.

B

A devastating cyclone killed nearly 4,000 people and left thousands more missing in army-ruled Myanmar, state media said on Monday, a dramatic increase in the toll from Saturday's storm.

The death toll only covered two of the five disaster zones where U.N. officials said hundreds of thousands of people were without shelter and drinking water in the impoverished Southeast Asian country.

Three days after Cyclone Nargis, a storm with winds of 190 km/h that hit the Irrawaddy Delta, Myanmar TV reported confirmed numbers of 3,934 dead, 41 injured and 2,879 missing within the Yangon and Irrawaddy divisions.

Earlier, official reports put the death toll at 351, but the number of casualties had been expected to rise as authorities made contact with hard-hit islands and villages in the delta, the rice bowl for the nation of 53 million.

The military, which has ruled for 46 years and is shunned by the West, has not yet issued an appeal for international aid.

Its leaders, in the isolated new capital of Naypyidaw, 400 km north of Yangon, said they would go ahead with a May 10 referendum on a new army-drafted constitution that critics say will entrench the military.

C

More than 750 people have perished as a result of severe cold and heavy snowfalls this winter across Afghanistan, a government official said on Saturday.

The cold spell, the worst in decades in the impoverished and mountainous central Asian country, has also killed nearly 230,000 cattle, according to the National Disaster Management Commission.

The worst affected areas were the western provinces of Herat and Badghis where some people had to have amputations because of frostbite. Media reports said several families even sold their children recently because they were unable to care for or feed them.

Many key roads linking districts with provincial capitals have also been blocked because of snow, hindering deliveries of supplies.

The deaths of cattle are regarded as a huge loss for Afghanistan, an agricultural country that largely relies on foreign aid.

In the face of a harsh winter that has pushed food prices to record highs, the United Nations World Food Program last month appealed for extra food assistance for 2.55 million Afghans until the next harvest in June.

Unit 6 Legends and Myths

Part I Dialogue

A

Ken: Hey, Mary, is a fairy tale like a folktale?

Mary: Yes, it is. A fairy tale is a type of folktale. And a folktale is a story that has been passed down from generation to generation by word of mouth.

Ken: Word of mouth? What do you mean by that?

Mary: If something is passed by word of mouth, it is passed from person to person by verbal means rather than by mass media.

Ken: What are some other types of folktales?

Mary: Good question, Ken. A legend is a type of folktale that is regarded as historical, but now they are unverifiable. In other words, nobody can prove that it is true. Do you know any famous legends?

Ken: Sure, there's the legend of Robin Hood, and the legend of King Arthur and the Knights of the Round Table.

Mary: Oh, those are good examples. Some people believe in these legends, but other people regard them as myths.

Ken: So what's the difference between a myth and a legend?

Mary: Not much. A myth is also a story that is passed down through culture. But most of the time a myth is considered fiction, not fact. Some of the most famous myths are those of the Greek gods and goddesses.

B

Host: Our special guest today is legendary figure skater, Alexei Yagudin, the Olympic gold medalist, four-time World Champion and three-time European Champion. Hi, Alexei, welcome to the show.

Alexei: Thanks, good to be here.

Host: Alexei, what is the atmosphere like just before competition between skaters? Are friendships strained or tense?

Alexei: Before competitions we are all extremely nervous, but that doesn't affect our personal relationships. We are all just trying to skate the best that we can.

Host: Yeah, competitions are indeed really important. What is the toughest part about competing for you?

Alexei: The schedule is very demanding, and sometimes that can feel overwhelming. I still love it though.

Host: What did you do to celebrate your Olympic win?

Alexei: The night after I won the gold medal I went out to dinner with my coaches and a few close friends to celebrate. I enjoy low-key celebrations with those closest to me.

Host: Are you entertaining possible thoughts to compete at the 2006 Olympics?

Alexei: I love to compete and I love to perform. I don't know exactly what the future has in store for me. I just know that I intend to skate for a long, long time.

Host: What do you feel is the key ingredient to becoming an Olympic champion?

Alexei: First, I have always loved to skate, and I have always known that I had the ability to be the best. But the true key to my success has been the support of my coaches, friends and family. Without them I could not have achieved such great results!

Host: Thank you for sharing your story with us, it was truly magical.

Part II Noah and Nü Wa

B

Every culture on earth has their own stock of legendary figures. Their stories are passed down through countless retelling from one generation to another. Nobody truly knows what is real or not, but their sagas can stir up the imagination of both young and old, even today.

Noah

In the book of Genesis in the Bible, Noah was the hero chosen by God to survive a great flood on earth. The biblical story is similar to other accounts of flood myths from Mesopotamia.

According to the story in Genesis, the human race had become so wicked that God was sorry He ever created them. He decided to wash away all the creatures of the earth in a great flood. However, God saw that Noah was a righteous man so he decided to save him. God told Noah of His plans and instructed him to build a great ark in which he could ride out the storm with his wife and children. Then He commanded Noah to find male and female species of every type of animal on the earth and to gather plants and seeds and bring them into the ark. Noah followed God's instructions and entered the ark as the rain began to fall.

It rained for 40 days and 40 nights until the waters covered even the tops of the highest mountains. After the rain ended, Noah released a raven and a dove to find out whether there was any dry land on earth. Both birds returned, indicating that water still covered the planet. Seven days later, Noah sent the dove out again. This time it returned with an olive branch, which meant that dry land had finally appeared. The ark came to rest on the top of Mount Ararat (in what is now Turkey), and Noah and his family emerged with all the animals.

Noah built an altar and made a sacrifice to God. God then made a covenant or agreement with Noah, promising never again to destroy the earth because of the wickedness of humans. He placed a rainbow in the sky as a reminder of this covenant.

Nü Wa

In Chinese mythology, Nü Wa is the goddess of order who created humans and saved the world from destruction. According to legend, Nü Wa came to earth before there were any people.

Nü Wa became lonely and decided to make copies of herself from mud in a pool. The figures she created came to life and wandered off to populate the earth. After a while, Nü Wa realized that it would take too long to fill the earth with people if she made each one by hand. So she took a rope, dipped it into the mud, and flung the drops of mud in all directions. Each drop became a separate human being. The people Nü Wa created by hand became the rich and powerful people in the world; those she flung as drops from the rope became the poor and the weak.

Another popular story recounts how Nü Wa saved the earth. The water god Gong Gong had tried to overthrow the fire god Zhu Rong. When Gong Gong failed, he became angry and rammed Imperfect Mountain with his head. The mountain which supported the heavens crumbled, tearing a hole in the sky and causing the ends of the earth to give way. The disorder that followed included fires and floods. Selecting several stones from a river, Nü Wa shaped them to repair the hole in the sky. She also slew a giant tortoise and used its legs to support the heavens. Nü Wa's actions restored the order of the universe and saved the world from destruction.

Part III Great American Myths

Myth 1: Americans have blond hair and blue eyes.

This is perhaps the most obviously inaccurate of all American stereotypes. About 30 percent of Americans are of Asian, African or other non-white ethnic descent. Many Caucasians have brown, black or red hair, and many of them also have green or brown eyes. In fact, blond, blue-eyed Americans are actually the minority!

Myth 2: Americans do not take care of their parents.

Some Chinese people think Americans don't have strong family ties. This is because when parents get too old to take care of themselves, their kids sometimes put them in nursing homes. However, there are some children who have their elderly parents come live with them. There are people on both ends of the spectrum.

Also, some Americans truly believe that a nursing home is the best choice for their parents as they feel that they cannot adequately care for their parents at home.

Myth 3: Americans live in big houses with big yards.

The stereotype that "all Americans are rich" is contrasted by studies which show that 14 percent of Americans, and almost one-fifth of U.S. children, live in poverty. Researchers estimate that about 700,000 people are homeless.

About 68 percent of Americans live in homes. Only some of these are big, and only some have big yards. Suburban American houses often do have bigger yards than the typical Asian home. But the rest of Americans live in apartments, mobile homes or other housing.

Myth 4: All Americans are open and direct.

Americans vary greatly in general personality, as do people of any culture. To say that all Americans are open is like saying all Chinese are reserved. Neither is true.

Some topics that Chinese are open about are considered taboo in American culture. For example, Americans aren't usually open about their personal finances.

In American culture, it's rude to make unflattering comments to people about their appearance. So never tell an American, "I think you're getting fatter."

The Real Truth about Americans

You will meet some Americans who seem to match these myths. But you will also find many Americans who won't match them at all. When you meet an American, forget the stereotypes. Look at the person as an individual.

The U.S. is one of the most diverse nations in the world. It's a land of immigrants and their descendants. Americans are as different as the nations from which they come. Get to know Americans as individuals and remember that you too are more than just a stereotype.

Part V News

One of the world's best-known sportsmen, American golfer Tiger Woods, will miss the rest of the 2008 season because of injury. He will undergo reconstructive surgery on his left knee and will need time off to recover from a double stress fracture in his left leg.

Tiger Woods is widely regarded as the most talented golfer of all time. This reputation was enhanced when he battled to a narrow victory in the US Open despite grimacing with pain after many of his shots. He had undergone knee surgery just a few weeks before the tournament. Going into the final day of the US Open, Woods was asked by journalists what advice doctors had given him about his knee. He replied wryly, "Don't play golf." He ignored the advice then, but now, with the adrenaline of competition ebbing away, Tiger seems to have decided to, if not lick his wounds, at least heed the doctor's advice.

B

  SUPERSTITION MOUNTAIN, Ariz. —Angela Stanford shot a career-best 10-under 62 on Thursday to break the Prospector Course record, taking a three-stroke lead over defending champion Lorena Ochoa in the Safeway International.

  Stanford, the 2003 ShopRite LPGA Tour Classic winner, had a bogey-free round at Superstition Mountain Golf and Country Club. She had six birdies in a front-nine 30 and birdied the final two holes for a back-nine 32.

  "It all happened so quickly," Stanford said. "I'm still in a fog. It's just one of those days you can't even get in your own way."

  The 30-year-old Texan broke the course record of 63 set by Cristie Kerr in 2004, and topped her previous career best of 64 in the first round of the 2006 Canadian Open.

  Ochoa, the Mexican star who won the tournament last year for the first of her eight 2007 titles, had nine birdies and two bogeys. She won the HSBC Championships on March 2 in Singapore for her 18th LPGA Tour title.

C

  SOUTHPORT, England—Efforts to place golf in the 2016 Summer Games was publicized during a gala press conference Wednesday before the British Open at Royal Birkdale. A few of golf's big hitters declared that they are uniting as never before to enhance the 'globality' of their game.

  Using that word early and often, the group announced the appointment of Ty Votaw, executive vice president of the PGA Tour, to head up a newly formed International Golf Federation committee to negotiate with the International Olympic Committee, which has two vacancies available for 2016. In October of 2009, the IOC will decide how they shall be filled. While chairing this committee to meet with that committee, Votaw essentially will be on loan to organize the Olympic proposal and presentation.

  Peter Dawson, chief executive of the R&A, said he has received enthusiastic vibes from the IOC about golf becoming part of the Olympic fare. "But there is much work to do," said Dawson, noting that the IOC clearly would want only the best players available (i.e. professionals, not amateurs). Also, there are other sports vying for those two slots, including baseball and softball, which will be part of next month's Olympics in Beijing but are dropping out for 2012 and reapplying. The other candidates for 2016 are karate, roller sports, squash and rugby seven.

Unit 7 Shopping

Part I Dialogue

B—C

Alice: Hi, Rosa! Buy anything today? I heard that there are a lot of sales downtown.

Rosa: Ugh, I really regret going there today. Saturdays are a nightmare.

Alice: Too crowded, huh?

Rosa: I'll say! I will never go shopping on weekends again.

Alice: Did you go there alone?

Rosa: Yes. I love shopping alone. Buying things always takes me a long time because I never buy the first thing I see. You know, I can never count on my husband to go with me. Ivan is not interested in shopping at all—in fact he hates it.

Alice: So does my husband. Simon always says shopping is a pain! He gets stressed if I ask him to go shopping with me. Every time he steps into the shopping mall, he's always in a hurry, and worries about spending money.

Rosa: Seems that shopping is only for us women.

Alice: Yes, it's more than buying things. It's... it's a pleasure, an enjoyment for us. Just looking at the fancy clothes makes me forget all my worries.

Rosa: Right, right! That's why I always enjoy looking around a lot in different shops. Of course if I really want to buy something, I can compare prices and find things cheaper. I am quite good at finding a bargain.

Alice: Are you? So next time we can go shopping together since we are both kind of shopaholics.

Rosa: No problem. I'm going downtown again next Tuesday. Do you want to go together? I know that you've got good taste and always know what's in fashion.

Alice: Ok! I am thinking of buying some Levi's for my husband. He really doesn't know how to shop for jeans. He's got a collection of awful mistakes from his past attempts at shopping by himself. This time he wants me to buy some for him.

Rosa: That's good. I'm sure you'll avoid the mistakes he made. We have a better fashion sense than men. I always do the shopping for Ivan. He hates shopping, but he enjoys buying electronics from the TV shopping channels.

Alice: Men are fond of electronic stuff, aren't they! So let them enjoy their things, and we'll enjoy ours.

Rosa: Ok, so see you next Tuesday! Will you bring your kids?

Alice: Oh, of course not. No husbands, no children! See you then!

Part II Ten Steps to Smarter Food Shopping

A—C

You came, you saw, you shopped. But then you got home from the supermarket and started unloading fatty snack items and deli meats. What went wrong? You fell back into the habit of shopping like an average American rather than a person with a dietary purpose. In an enticing palace of eating designed to lead you astray, here's how to stay on track.

1. Make a list.

Before you shop, write down what you need to reduce the chances of buying what you don't need.

2. Limit your trips.

Make your shopping list long so you have to make only one or two trips to the store per week. Besides being more efficient, this provides less opportunity to make impulse purchases.

3. Avoid shopping on an empty stomach.

When you're hungry, you're more likely to grab high-fat snacks and desserts.

4. Follow the walls.

Limit browsing to the perimeter of the store where you'll find the freshest, most healthful foods: raw produce, low-fat dairy products, fresh lean meats and fish. Venture into the interior aisles only when you're after specific foods such as pasta and dried beans to avoid picking up extra items not included in your diet plan.

5. Pay attention to portions.

Those cookies look great—and hey, eating them only costs you 75 calories. But check the serving size: 1 cookie. Eating "them", say three cookies—brings your calorie count up to 225.

6. Ignore the pictures.

Golden sunshine glows on heaps of freshly harvested grains—an image of good health that signifies nothing. Look at the side of the box instead for the facts, and choose foods that are high in fiber and low in fat and calories.

7. Grade your grains.

Want high-fiber bread? Look for the words "whole grain", "100 percent whole wheat" or "stone-ground" on the label. Breads labelled simply "wheat"—even if they are brown in color—may not contain whole grains. True whole-grain bread contains at least two grams of fiber per serving.

8. Watch the language.

Beware of foods labelled "no sugar added"—the wording is carefully chosen because the product may be loaded with natural sugar. You'll find the real story on the label, under "Sugars".

9. Add some spice to your life.

Instead of creamy condiments, load up on such spices as basil, chives, cinnamon, cumin, curry, garlic, ginger, horseradish, nutmeg, oregano, paprika, parsley, and Tabasco sauce. They're very low in carbohydrates, fat, protein, and calories.

Transcript

10. Keep your eye on the cashier.

You're waiting in line, nothing to do—a captive audience. It's no accident that supermarkets pile their impulse items next to the registers. Keep a couple of items from your basket in your hands. It'll stop you from reaching for the candy bars.

Part III Online Shopping—An Increasing Trend

Shopping online offers lots of benefits that you won't find shopping in a store or by mail. The Internet is always open—seven days a week, 24 hours a day—and bargains can be numerous online. With a click of a mouse, you can buy an airline ticket, book a hotel, send flowers to a friend, or purchase your favourite fashions.

With only two weeks to go before Christmas, buying presents is a high priority for a lot of people. However, this year not so many people are leaving their homes to browse around the shops. These days lots of people can do their shopping in the comfort of their own home with the help of the Internet.

Online shopping is becoming more and more popular for a number of reasons; prices are often lower online, you don't have to queue up in busy shops and you can buy almost any product imaginable with just a few clicks of your mouse.

Computer trends are often male-dominated but this year women are expected to do more shopping on the Internet than men. It seems women are now more attracted to the convenience of online shopping than they used to be.

Average spending online this Christmas by women will rise to £240 compared to the slightly lower average of £233 for men, while the average spending per person on the high street is only £197. Seventy percent of Internet users, male and female, are now buying their Christmas gifts online.

In the past a lot of people were reluctant to shop online. Many were worried about the security of entering their card details on the Internet and the reliability of the Internet but as shopping online has become more widespread, these worries have begun to disappear. Forty-five percent of Internet users still do have security worries but it hasn't slowed down the ever-increasing numbers of online shoppers.

One victim of the online shopping boom is the UK high street. Christmas trading can represent up to 60% of turnover for some stores. Many companies are concerned that not enough shoppers are coming through their doors in the run-up to Christmas. As a result, there are lots of special offers in the shops.

Most shops traditionally have sales after Christmas, but this year the bargains have come early in an attempt to lure consumers to spend. Bad news for the high street has become good news for the bank balances of UK shoppers this Christmas!

Part V News

A

At the US Olympic swimming trials today in Omaha, Nebraska, it's more than athletes that are making a splash; it's all about what they are wearing.

The suit is Speedo's new LZR Racer that took more than 3 years and millions of dollars to develop. Tested by NASA, the suit is designed to reduce drag with bonded seams and fabric that compresses the body. Speedo claims its suit is working. So far this year, from swimmers wearing the Laser, at least 38 world records were counted.

So many athletes are wearing the Laser that Tear filed a lawsuit claiming Speedo, with help from USA Swimming, has an unfair advantage over other swimsuit makers, something the sports governing body and Speedo denies. It's a new era of swimsuits, which began with Australian Ian Thorpe, who won five medals at the Sydney Games while wearing a full body suit. He wore one again for more Olympic glory in Athens, as did Michael Phelps, who plans to wear a Laser during the trials.

Most are hoping the attention on swimsuits will not overshadow those winning in the water.

B

Two of the Summer Olympics' greatest athletes appeared at Splash Aquatic Center on Thursday to lend their names to a worthy cause—water safety.

Using the $30 million facility as a backdrop, two-time Olympic swimmer Mark Spitz and three-time Olympic swimmer Janet Evans filmed public service announcements promoting safety in and around public and private pools.

Both Spitz, 58, and Evans, 36, are now highly sought-after motivational speakers.

Spitz swam his way into Olympic history at the 1972 Munich Games, breaking seven world records on his way to seven gold medals. He still holds the record for the most medals won at a single Olympics. Evans won her first gold medal at the Seoul Games as a teenager.

They were asked by the World Water Park Association to do the public service announcements. They both talked about the importance of teaching children to swim and adhering to safety rules in and out of the water in their taped segments.

C

Shane Gould and Murray Rose, two of the biggest legends of swimming history, will swim at the fifth Fiji Swims Championships next week.

Gould, who held every freestyle world record from 100m to 1,500m simultaneously, is the only woman to have ever won five solo medals at one Olympic Games in the pool, her 1972 haul including three golds. Rose won three gold medals at a home Games in Melbourne in 1956 and backed up with victory in the 400m four years later in Rome.

Alongside the Aussie legends are Allison Wagner of the USA, a silver medallist in the

400m medley at Atlanta in 1996 and a woman who has held many world records, and Neil Rogers, the captain of the Australian swimming team at the 1976 Games in Montreal and a man returning to the Fiji fray for a third time.

Unit 8   Women Around the World

Part I   Dialogue

A: China has been undergoing economic restructuring for a decade. The process has resulted in many laid-off employees from state-owned companies. How do you view this problem from the perspective of working women?

B: My organization, the All-China Women's Federation, has been following this problem closely. The problems that laid-off women face are similar in some ways to those that laid-off men face.

A: Such as?

B: They not only lose their basic livelihood, they also lose heavily subsidized housing and payment of medical bills.

A: So their big concern is being re-employed?

B: Yes. In this aspect, women have been harder hit by the market adjustments. Less than 40% of women who lose their state-enterprise jobs find new jobs. In contrast, men's re-employment rate is almost 64%.

A: How can we encourage the private sector to re-employ more laid-off women?

B: The All-China Women's Federation has been conducting a pilot project. We offer micro-credit loans to women to help them start their own businesses. We also support preferential policies, such as tax waivers for companies that re-employ a substantial number of laid-off women.

A: How are women responding to this problem?

B: More women than men are now conducting their own comprehensive job searches. They are finding jobs on their own initiative and not relying on the employment agencies established within state-owned companies.

A: China supports women's equal right to employment. But are women and men really treated equally on the job?

B: Despite the principle of equal pay for equal work, women's pay lags behind men's. Women earn 70% of what men earn. This gap has widened since 1990.

A: Isn't this because women are mainly in non-supervisory positions? Maybe they don't pay attention to office politics as much as men.

B: In many cases, women are discouraged from voicing their concerns in the office. They are expected to be quiet and hardworking. When men make suggestions, their supervisors listen carefully, but women's suggestions are ignored or generate negative reactions. As a result, women have scarce promotion opportunities.

A: If women refuse to accept these problems, what can they do?

B: One thing they can do is to start their own business. More than 20 percent of urban women are now working in their own enterprise. This is roughly the same percentage as for men.

A: More power to them!

Part II Meet the Power Sisters

The "modern" Olympics which began in 1896 did not include women. Founder Pierre de Coubertin held the notion that a woman's "organism is not cut out to sustain certain shocks." No wonder it wasn't until 1984 before women were allowed to run the Olympics' signature event, the marathon. No organisms were shocked.

This year in Sydney there will be two more signs that these aren't the Victorian Olympics. For the first time, women will compete in weight-lifting and the pole vault, once thought of as two of the highest testosterone events of the Summer Games. Poised to make Olympic history are two American women who came to their sports via goat roping and tree-house building. Since those events aren't yet sanctioned, lifter Cheryl Haworth and vaulter Stacy Dragila will have to settle for medals in what used to be exclusively male pursuits.

Haworth busted the gender barrier a couple of years ago in her hometown of Savannah, Ga., to the amazement of the local "Y chromosomes". Men and teenage boys are, in fact, her biggest fans. At 17, this high school senior is already the world's best junior weight-lifter, and she aims to be an Olympic champion. "She's the best woman lifter I've ever seen," says her coach, Mike Cohen, a former an Olympian who now runs Team Savannah, one of the country's top weight-lifting centers.

Haworth, at 5 ft. 10 in. and 300 lbs., is an exceptional athlete in a body that screams "couch potato". As a high school softball player, she was so good that kids called her "the Arm", but Haworth wasn't satisfied with the game. Her dad, knowing she had always been interested in those bodybuilding TV shows, took her to see Cohen in 1996. When Haworth lifted a bar with more than 100 lbs. on it "like it was a loaf of bread", he knew he'd found a keeper.

And Haworth discovered a purpose. "It took me a while, but I finally found something that someone my size can be very good at," says Haworth. "It's an individual and straightforward sport: either you can lift the weight or you can't." Haworth uses her speed (she can run the 40-yd. dash in an NFL-like 5 seconds) and her power (she can jump an NBA-like 34 in.) to routinely, and repeatedly, lift a groaning bar with a couple hundred pounds on it. Buff football players pass by, not even bothering to hide their admiration. In competition she has lifted 264 lbs. in the snatch (lifting the weight overhead in one motion) and 319 lbs. in the clean and jerk (lifting the weight first to the chest, then overhead).

While Haworth discovered weight lifting, Stacey Dragila was using coordination honed by years of goat roping at rodeos in a different contortion: pole vaulting. Dragila started experimenting with vaulting in the early 1990s after enjoying only modest success as a heptathlete. She is drawn to the daredevil aspect of the sport. "I think women have brought a lot of life back into the sport—first, because a lot of people doubted women could actually do it well. Second is that odd fascination some people have in watching athletes risk injury to win." Dragila, 29, is doing something right: she holds the world record of 15 ft. $1\frac{3}{4}$ in. and is the favorite for gold.

While Dragila won't be competing against men this summer, it is men she has to thank for getting her to the vaunted position she holds. "Growing up in rural Idaho, I had to keep up—and put up—with my brother and all his friends. I got tough physically and mentally, and it's one reason why I'm so aggressive and competitive." It was also her male coach, Dave Nielsen, who first suggested she try the pole vault. "I admit the women aren't anywhere near the men in height (the men's record is 20 ft. $1\frac{3}{4}$ in.)," says Dragila, "but I've got the words 'World Record' next to my name, and that's something all athletes would like."

Neither Dragila nor Haworth promotes herself as a pioneer, in part because both realize they're just the first of what should be a long line of female athletes to follow. "We've proved women can do anything, but we're just setting the stage for younger athletes who will come after us," says Dragila, "and hoping today's young girls don't have to wait another century to compete in every sport."

Part III Women Struggle for Their Rights

B—D

In Russia about nine thousand women are killed each year by a husband, partner or other family member.

In Pakistan violence against women in their homes is a serious problem as well. Girls are forced into marriages, young women are kept out of school, and men have complete control over their families. What's more, hundreds of Pakistani women are murdered every year by their families. They are victims of so-called "honor killings".

Most women in Arab nations have a very hard time getting elected. In Bahrain, for example, thirty-nine women ran for local and national office in 2002. Not a single woman was elected. Few Arab countries have a sizeable number of women in government.

Women in the United States have an easier time owning property. They also have more educational, professional and political choices than in the past. Yet, they still face struggles in the fight for equality. American women are generally paid less than men. The average woman often cannot pay for health insurance.

The international community has taken steps to protect and enforce the rights of women. More than twenty-five years ago, the United Nations approved a treaty called the Convention on the Elimination of All Forms of Discrimination Against Women. The 1979 treaty is considered a bill of rights for women.

To date, one hundred eighty nations have approved the treaty, but, women in many of these countries are still treated as unequal citizens. Around the world, the struggle for women's rights and equality is progressing slowly. The U.N. estimates half a million women die every year while having babies. The number of women and girls in the world infected with H.I.V. and AIDS is growing. Often this is the result of a sexual attack. And, violence against women, forced labor and human trafficking of young females continue. Women are about half the population in the world, but experts wonder if they will ever have social, financial, legal, political and professional equality with men.

Part V   News

A

Susan Athey, an economics professor at Harvard University, has won the John Bates Clark Medal. The American Economics Association awards the Clark Medal to the most promising economists, and it may be even harder to win than a Nobel Prize in economics. The Clark Medal is given every two years, and the winner has to be under the age of forty.

Susan Athey is thirty-six years old and the first woman to win the Clark Medal in its sixty-year history. No woman has yet won the Nobel economics prize which has been awarded since 1969.

Past winners received the Clark Medal for a single area of research, but Susan Athey was honored for her work across several areas of economics, including government auctions. Her work has dealt with both applied theory and empirical studies. In other words, it has dealt both with the complex methods that help economists do their jobs and with economic problems in the real world.

B

A group of Muslim women from around the world is participating in a summer leadership program at the U.S Congress and George Washington University. The program is designed to educate the participants about legal issues and conflict resolution techniques with the aim of empowering Muslim women to promote peaceful change in their communities.

At the opening of the program, 25 Muslim women from various countries listened to presentations about how Islamic law provides for principles such as freedom of expression, freedom of association and the right to own property regardless of gender.

The training program focuses on traditional Islamic jurisprudence and how Muslim women around the world can deal with issues such as domestic violence and other abuses against women.

Sponsors of the program are hopeful that these Muslim women will eventually be able to articulate and defend Muslim women's rights within their own cultural and institutional contexts.

C

Is pregnancy getting safer? The answer is "yes" and "no". In Latin America, the Caribbean, North Africa, and Oceania, maternal deaths are falling. But in sub-Saharan Africa, the numbers are going up at the moment.

According to WHO estimates, 536,000 women died from pregnancy complications in 2005, the last year for which numbers were calculated. In Scandinavia the number is two, maybe three, sometimes one per 100,000 live births, whereas in sub-Saharan Africa it is 900 per 100,000 live births. And all the other regions fall somewhere in the middle.

Fifteen percent of women worldwide suffer complications with pregnancy that requires emergency care. But woefully inadequate healthcare systems in sub-Saharan African countries are further compromised by war and other social and economic circumstances. And, donor funding has been falling for maternal health.

Unsafe abortions account for 13 percent of maternal deaths globally. Making them safe, legal and accessible could resolve death from abortion almost immediately. This kind of change requires leadership that values women. Women's lives depend on it.

Unit 9 Travel

Part I Dialogue

B—C

Interviewer: Can you imagine what life would be like without travelling? Travelling is a part of people's lives. We all do it. How do you feel about travelling? Today, we're honoured to have Molly as our guest. She will share her opinion and experience of travel with us. Good evening, Molly.

Molly: Good evening, Ted.

Interviewer: Why do you think people love to travel?

Molly: I'd say most of us love travelling because the nine to five grind bores us. Going away and breaking the cycle of "waking up, going to work, going to sleep" is the only way to remind ourselves that we are alive, and most importantly to feel the world is a wonderful place. It can be as simple as going on a road trip to a different town, camping, or even going to another country.

Interviewer: What is your travel plan this spring? Travel domestically or abroad?

Molly: Well, for spring break, my friend Ronald and I plan to head off to Kenya and Uganda, hoping that some beaches and wildlife sightings may motivate us through the rest of the semester. A lot of other people are heading off to the Red Sea or to other parts of the Middle East.

Interviewer: Would you recommend doing the package tours or touring independently?

Molly: Many factors will affect your choice. The best choice is that which makes you feel most comfortable so you can best enjoy your trips. I personally prefer to travel independently and create my own unique itinerary instead of relying on set schedules. I like to be able to go from one place to another as I please. It can also get annoying when tour leaders with their megaphones herd you like sheep. Furthermore, independent travel gives me more opportunity to communicate with the local residents or other tourists from all over the world.

Interviewer: Can you share some of your travel experiences with us?

Molly: Hmm... I can tell you something about my trip to Venice...

Interviewer: When was that?

Molly: I went there with my cousin Tracy in 2004. It was a remarkable experience. I didn't know that one had to take a train over a causeway, i.e. a land bridge, to get inside the city. The only other way is by boat.

Interviewer: That's interesting.

Molly: Yeah. Once inside the ancient city, you're greeted and overwhelmed by the history, architecture, arts and crafts and a flowing continuity of shopping adventures. We took a gondola ride down the canals on a sleek ebony-colored luxurious craft and saw the home of Marco Polo and the original Don Juan who, my guide said, "had a different woman every night". As far as the eye could see, there were boats of every size and description, criss-crossing the canals, transporting people and products in every possible direction. There were no traffic lights, no screeching of tires, nor the ugly din of car horns.

Interviewer:	Did you see a lot of bridges in Venice?
Molly:	Yes. I was impressed by the enormity of Venice for I had always envisioned a rather small, quaint place, but one cannot possibly walk over 400 bridges in a few minutes!
Interviewer:	Did you visit the "drawing room of Europe"?
Molly:	Of course. The expansive Piazza San Marco was host to tourists from every place imaginable. I strained my neck to view the gigantic Campanile in the east. It's so much grander than the version at Epcot Centre in Disney World. In fact, Venice reminded me of an "ancient Disney World", because the sights and sounds of entertainment could be heard and seen everywhere. Roaming musicians, wonderful Italian food, quaint shops with glassware, porcelains, and unusual gifts were too tempting to pass by.
Interviewer:	How long did you stay in Venice?
Molly:	Only for one day. And even though it was raining a little that day, the day went by all too quickly. It was one of the highlights of my trip to Italy and I have expressed my admiration for that city time and again.

Part II Travel Smart: Dollars and Sense

Most travellers know that some of the best bargains are to be had in the off-season, when colder weather or the start of school makes vacationers scarce.

So when should you travel to get the best deals? That depends. Peak season varies from region to region. Summer airfares to popular mountain areas especially in some parts of Canada and Europe can be high. But summertime travel to warm-weather destinations— Florida, the Southwest, parts of Mexico, and the Caribbean—can be a bargain. If heat isn't a big deal to you, why not take advantage of lower costs? Summer in the United States is winter in Australia and the Galapagos Islands (as well as many other places), so travel deals are available. You can still see and do many of the same things as in the peak season.

Midweek stays at resorts are often less costly than weekends; but city hotels that cater to business travellers have high rates during the week and bargains on weekends. The best airfares often require a Saturday night stay unless it's a local hop. You'll sometimes find better domestic airfares in the middle of the week or during off-hours on weekdays (late at night, early in the morning). Weekend flights almost always cost more. Here's the catch: If you have to take off two days of work in order to get a midweek flight or book a midweek resort stay, but in doing so you lose either pay or vacation time, what have you really saved? You'll need to consider those factors as well.

Seasonal Savings

When it comes to lodging, consider the "shoulder" season—the time between peak and low travel periods. If you book a stay early in shoulder season, you can get a deal and probably still have the benefits of the same weather and opportunities available during peak season. But sometimes programs are not available in shoulder season. At many guest ranches, for example, families can cut costs in June and September, but there may not be a supervised children's program or as many children to make friends with. If you have older kids who would be out riding with you anyway, this is an excellent time to visit a guest ranch, as it's often less crowded and more relaxed than during July and August. But if you were counting on a children's program so you could get in adults-only time, the money you save by travelling during the off-season may not make up for that loss.

Year-round Bargains

Keep in mind that deals can be had at almost any time of the year and that bargaining skills are not just for use in foreign market places. At many hotels it's standard practice to quote callers the highest rate first. Reservationists are often told not to volunteer deals unless specifically asked about them. To get a better deal after a rate is quoted, ask if there's a better price available. There usually is. If you've seen a special deal in a newspaper or flyer, you should mention it. Ask about discounts for group members. You're likely to have the best luck bargaining with reservationists at the hotel itself as opposed to those at a nationwide number, but try both. If no one will offer a deal, find a different hotel. You can almost guarantee that your costs will come down if you negotiate. After booking your stay, check periodically to see if new deals have come up in newspaper travel sections. Ask your travel agent to continue checking airfares in case of special promotions. But don't obsess about it. Vacation is all about letting go and being laid-back.

Tipping

Paying gratuities is usually a voluntary gesture that's based on performance and service. Many people who work in the travel industry depend on tips as a major part of their income. Tour guides, for example, make a decent living only if they receive decent tips. If you travel with a guide in a city, on a river, or on a walking or biking tour, you should tip unless the service is notably poor.

Some tips, however, are built into the pricing structure and are included on your bill. There are ranches with mandatory tips for wranglers and other staff, and there are restaurants that automatically add a gratuity to food bills. And with some types of travel—cruise ships, for example—tipping falls just short of mandatory. Exactly what's expected will usually be spelled out in the brochures.

It's a good idea to check guidebooks and consulates about attitudes toward tipping in foreign countries; what we mean as a thank-you might be taken as an insult in some cultures. And it's important to note, too, that some resorts here and abroad have a policy of no tipping. When in doubt, always ask.

Part III The Experience of Travelling and Learning

When travelling in other countries, we expect to meet different people, see different sights and do different things. Perhaps the best way to learn about a culture is to be immersed in it. Instead of just observing it, live it. Not only will you learn about the culture, but you will also discover more of yourself.

Many of my experiences abroad have been gained by staying with families who live in the country that I am visiting. Of course, when a student first meets his host family, he will feel nervous. He asks questions such as "Are they going to like me? Are we going to be able to communicate? Do they have a sense of humour? Will I feel comfortable in their company?" Having hosted students myself, I know that host families also feel nervous and ask themselves the same questions. "Homestay" experiences can introduce a whole new element into your learning programme, even if it is for a short period before moving on to college. The learning that comes from interacting with families of the culture that one is visiting can be so much greater than the learning that is gained from just staying in hotels and hostels. Mixing the type of accommodation can bring a variety of benefits. I have often travelled with groups of young people, and it has been remarkable to see their self-confidence blossom.

Travelling to new cultures and interacting with strangers teaches one as much about oneself as it does about other people. The challenge of new experiences will push one's personal barriers. Coping with situations that have not been previously encountered can show you that you are capable of achieving or succeeding at so much more than you had previously thought. Learning about different cultures can teach you things about your own culture— things you had erstwhile neither appreciated nor understood.

Spending time with friends from another culture will challenge stereotypes that may be held by both parties. Some of the greatest joys of travel are gleaned from knowing that your preconceptions were wrong. Many of the opportunities offered through voluntary work or projects can bring you into contact with volunteers from a wide range of countries and cultures. In this circumstance, being in a different country might well allow you to meet, learn and challenge your preconceptions about people from a variety of backgrounds.

When travelling, do not expect to learn just about others, but revel in the learning that you obtain about yourself!

Part V News

B

Yankee Stadium's regular-season finale will be a night game.

The Yankees' Sept. 21 game against the Baltimore Orioles has been scheduled for 8:05 p.m. and will be televised nationally by ESPN as part of its Sunday night package.

The game was listed as TBA on the original schedule and was selected by ESPN just before the All-Star break, MLB senior vice president Katy Feeney said Wednesday.

If New York fails to qualify for the postseason, it would be the last game at the Yankees' longtime home.

Up to $65,000 was being asked for a ticket to the game on Wednesday on Stubhub.com, with the lowest price at $265.

C

Baseball's All-Stars came to say goodbye to Yankee Stadium—and what a long, long goodbye it was.

In a game that started Tuesday night and faded well into Wednesday, Justin Morneau slid home just in time on Michael Young's sacrifice fly in the 15th inning, giving the American League a 4-3 victory that extended its unbeaten streak to 12.

Young ended a 4-hour, 50-minute marathon at 1:37 a.m., with the grand old ballpark half-empty. It was a good thing, too—neither team had any pitchers left in the bullpen, but this one was not going to end in another tie.

Unit 10 Famous People

Part I Dialogue

Kathy: David, what is your understanding of the term "a great national figure"? How would you define it?

David: It's not very easy to define, but I think we all know what we mean when we talk about a national figure.

Kathy: How would you describe one?

David: Well, when we talk about "a national figure" we mean a famous man or woman, either now or in the past, who is or was celebrated in his or her field and recognized by the whole nation.

Kathy: But there must be hundreds of such figures!

David: Well, no, because to be a national figure you must be very famous—a war hero or a celebrated artist, for example.

Kathy: Would you include famous film stars and pop singers as well?

David: Oh yes, why not? Sir Laurence Olivier and The Beatles are national figures, and so are some of our great artists and thinkers, men such as Henry Moore, Benjamin Britten and Bertrand Russell.

Kathy: In this age of television, movies, and the Internet, some national figures have become world-famous, haven't they? Like The Beatles. I suppose we could call them "international figures"!

David: Yes, even great national figures of the past, such as William Shakespeare and Sir Isaac Newton, have become world-wide figures.

Kathy: Who do you think has been our greatest national figure in the last century?

David: Difficult to say. Churchill, I suppose.

David: Would you want to be famous, John?

John: At one point in my life I thought it would be cool to be famous. A lot of that had to do with the fact that in my younger days I spent a lot of time interviewing famous people.

David: And now?

John: And now, I don't particularly see why anyone sane would want it. One definitely gets the vibes from being famous, but once the shininess of fame wears off, which I figure takes about a month, it's kind of a drag not to be able to go to the grocery store without people pointing and staring and asking for autographs and stuff like

	that.
David:	Not to mention the creeps and the stalkers and the people who put up the "fan pages" on the Internet and so forth.
John:	Exactly. Fame gets you a lot, but it also takes a lot out of you. I don't imagine that for most famous people—the ones who are not actually pathologically addicted to attention—it ends up being a fair trade in the end. What do you think, Lori?
Lori:	I wouldn't want to be famous. I wouldn't be able to handle not having a personal life. I know plenty of people that thrive off of what celebrities do. I, however, don't care about whether or not Brittany gets her kids or if some person gets a divorce with their soul mate!
David:	I'm with you, Lori. Fame has never really been something I have looked forward to, especially after seeing what the ultra-famous have had to endure: criticism, loss of privacy and the worst case of all, the death of Princess Diana, being relentlessly pursued.
Amy:	I would want to be famous. It's not because I think it'd be a bed of roses or anything, because no job is perfect. But being famous, especially at the Hollywood level, opens up a lot of doors that a person might not otherwise have.
Lori:	What do you mean, Amy?
Amy:	One of the gifts of celebrity is that you can reach out to so many more people, and because people will take notice of you, you can shed some light on some very important topics, like what Nancy Reagan has done for stem cell research, Elton John and others for AIDS causes, and Princess Diana for, well, almost everything. I mean, to be able to do that is fantastic! And if you get to help others by doing something you love—acting, music, writing, whatever—why not?

Part II The Greatest Individual Athletic Achievements

B

1. Lance Armstrong

Prior to being diagnosed with testicular cancer in 1996, Lance Armstrong was a successful professional cyclist. After his recovery, he became a legend. Armstrong won the Tour de France, which many consider to be the most gruelling event in professional sports. He won the 21-stage race, covering more than 3,500 kilometers (2,175 miles) in the heat of the French summer, a record seven consecutive times. Prior to Armstrong, no one had won the race more than five times.

2. Jesse Owens

In the spring of 1935, heading into the Big Ten Conference Championships, Jesse

Owens, a 21-year-old track star from Ohio State University, was suffering from a back injury he had sustained falling down a flight of stairs. He received treatment right up to race time. Then lightning struck. In less than 70 minutes, Owens broke three world records, namely in the long jump, the 220-yard dash and the 200-yard low hurdles, and tied a fourth in the 100-yard dash. The following year, Owens won four gold medals at the 1936 Olympic Games in Berlin.

3. Muhammad Ali

On February 25, 1964, a young boxer named Cassius Clay faced off against Sonny Liston, the heavyweight champion of the world. The odds were seven-to-one against the mouthy upstart, known as "The Louisville Lip"—a boxer so brash he promised during the weigh-in to "float like a butterfly and sting like a bee". But Clay proved true to his word, pummeling Liston so badly that the champ quit before the start of the seventh round. Soon after, Clay joined the Nation of Islam, changed his name to Muhammad Ali and refused to serve in the Vietnam War, a move that got him stripped of the championship belt. But in 1974, Ali came back, pulling the "rope-a-dope" on George Foreman in "The Rumble in the Jungle" and regained the belt. In February 1978, Olympic champion Leon Spinks defeated the aging star in a 15-round decision. But only a few months later, Ali won a rematch and regained the title. The victory made him the first man in heavyweight history to win three heavyweight titles.

4. Babe Ruth

You don't get a nickname like "The Sultan of Swat" without being able to knock the ball out of the park. George Herman "Babe" Ruth was the first player to hit 30 home runs in a season, and the first to hit 40, and the first to hit 50. His 1927 record of 60 home runs in just 155 games represented 14% of all of the home runs hit in the American League that year.

5. Michael Jordan

Few athletes have ever dominated their sport as completely as basketball's Michael Jordan, a tenacious defender and outrageous scorer whose gravity-defying dunks earned him the nickname "Air" Jordan. Drafted out of North Carolina to join the Chicago Bulls in 1984, Jordan began one of the most successful runs in sports history. In his 13 seasons with the Bulls, Jordan led the league in scoring a record ten times—including seven seasons in a row. He was the NBA's Most Valuable Player five times, set the NBA record for most consecutive games scoring in double digits (842), was a member of six championship teams, and ended his career with a regular-season scoring average of 30.12 points per game—the highest in NBA history.

6. Wayne Gretzky

They call him "The Great One". Hockey seemed to be second nature to Wayne Gretzky. At age 10, he scored 378 goals and had 120 assists in a mere 85 games. He signed with his first agent at age 14. As a professional, he racked up more records than seems possible. By the time he retired in 1999, Gretzky held or shared 61 NHL records, including most career regular-season goals (894), most career regular-season assists (1,963), most goals in a season (92) and most hat tricks (10). After 20 years, Gretzky ended his reign with the most shocking record of all: 2,857 career points scored.

7. Mark Spitz

Going into the 1972 Olympic Games in Munich, Mark Spitz was a cocky 22-year-old swimmer who had failed to win a single individual gold in the 1968 Games in Mexico City, although he did get two team golds. Nonetheless, Spitz bragged he would win six gold medals in Germany. He didn't. He won seven — the most anyone has ever won in a single Olympiad—and broke seven world records in the process. Spitz's career total of 11 medals ties him with fellow swimmer Matt Biondi for the most decorated U.S. Olympic athlete.

Part III A Great Scientist

B

At an early age, Einstein revealed an independence of mind that was to become characteristic of his entire future life. On a visit to Milan, Einstein announced to his father his three final decisions: he would quit school; he would abandon the Jewish community, and he would drop his German nationality. The school did not provide him with a proper education, the Jewish community was too narrow-minded, and Germany was too chauvinistic. Einstein assumed that a small nation like Switzerland would be devoid of superpower ambitions and he eventually acquired Swiss citizenship.

Einstein entered the Polytechnic Academy in Zurich, Switzerland, where he earned a doctorate in physics in 1905. The same year he published four research papers. Each contained a great discovery: the theory of Brownian motion; the equivalence of mass and energy; the photon theory of light; and the special theory of relativity. In 1915, Einstein proposed the general theory of relativity as an extension of the special theory. Its basis was the identification of gravity with inertia, and its discovery provided the theoretical expectation that vast amounts of energy could be released from the nucleus.

In 1919, a prediction of Einstein's General Relativity was verified, and in a few years it became the basis of new cosmologies. Einstein was awarded the Nobel Prize for Physics in 1921. Although a committed pacifist, Einstein began to warn against the dangers of fascism as the Nazis denounced his work as "Jewish science". In 1933 he left Germany and took up residence at the Institute for Advanced Studies in Princeton, New Jersey, where he pursued his research towards unifying the laws of physics.

Einstein's last years were spent searching for a unified field theory, for a universal force that would link gravitation with electromagnetic and subatomic forces, a problem in which no one to date has been entirely successful.

Einstein was filled with reverence for the works of nature, and he noted that "The most incomprehensible thing about the world is that it is comprehensible." He thought of himself more as a philosopher than as a scientist. In many ways he was from the same mold as the Greek natural philosophers, such as Plato and Aristotle, in trying to understand the natural world through mental concepts instead of experimentation. His success did draw on the insights of predecessors and the powerful analytical tools of mathematics, but most of all it was the result of an unerring cosmic intuition, the likes of which have been equaled by very few.

Part V News

World Player of the Year Kaka predicted on Sunday that he would reach his peak in time for the 2010 World Cup.

In an interview with the Brazilian sports daily *Lance*, the AC Milan and Brazilian player reaffirmed his wish to play at the Olympic Games in August but admitted the matter was out of his hands.

"I think the best is yet to come," said Kaka, who has suffered a dip in form this year.

"The year 2007 was marvellous but I still think I can improve technically and physically."

"I want to reach a very high level for the 2010 World Cup. I will be 28, at my peak. It could be a great World Cup for Brazil, a new cycle and new players."

However, Kaka has had some fitness problems recently, which he blames on too much football.

"The biggest problem with injuries today is the quantity of games," he said. "There comes a time when your body can't take any more."

The 26-year-old said he wanted to help Brazil win their first Olympic gold medal in Beijing. The Olympic soccer tournament is for under-23 years of age teams but three over-aged players are allowed.

"Nobody has won the Olympic gold for Brazil yet, that's the big motivation," he said. "But, how I get to the Olympics is something which does not depend on me."

He was unsure if he would still be playing international football when Brazil hosts the World Cup in 2014.

"I don't know if I will be there," he said.

"It depends on how I am physically, if I am still in condition to play football at a high level with the right motivation to play a World Cup."

Emma Watson is to be the new face of Chanel perfume. The "Harry Potter and the Order of the Phoenix" star has won a two-year contract worth millions to promote Coco Mademoiselle.

The 18-year-old actress will take over from fellow British star Keira Knightley, 23, when her contract ends this summer. A source said: "Emma has been excitedly telling friends that she is going to be replacing Keira." Emma landed the deal with the French fashion house after signing up with top modelling agency Storm in an attempt to branch out from acting.

Chanel has been preparing Emma for her new role by dressing her for film premieres and parties. A source said: "She has been slowly integrated into the Chanel brand. Once it became clear she was growing into a beautiful young woman and wears the Chanel brand so elegantly, they had to sign her up. Chanel realises it is important to target a young audience." Bosses at Warner Bros—who made the "Harry Potter" films—have given the deal their blessing.

C

Miss Venezuela was crowned Miss Universe 2008 on Monday in a contest marked by the spectacle of Miss USA falling down during the evening gown competition for the second year in a row.

An elated Dayana Mendoza received the crown from her predecessor, Riyo Mori of Japan, and then prepared to meet a gaggle of reporters. Miss Venezuela, 22, was once kidnapped in her homeland and says the experience taught her to remain poised under pressure.

Tension got under the skin of Crystle Stewart of Texas, the second Miss USA in a row to fall down during the Miss Universe pageant. She tripped on the train of her bejewelled evening gown as she made her entrance.

During the 2007 Miss Universe contest in Mexico City, Miss USA Rachel Smith also tumbled during the evening gown competition and became an unintended star on YouTube, where the video was shown over and over again.

Like Smith, Stewart quickly stood up after her fall and continued on as if nothing had happened.

The final five contestants included four from Latin America: Miss Mexico, Miss Dominican Republic, Miss Colombia and Miss Venezuela. Rounding out the final five was Miss Russia.

Unit 11 Health

Part I Dialogue

A—C

Host: This morning on "Today's Health" we are talking about breaking health rules. We invite Liz Vaccariello, editor-in-chief of "Prevention" magazine to give us some guidelines to follow, and more importantly, some for us not to follow. Hi, Liz, good to see you.

Liz: Good morning.

Host: So one size doesn't fit all when you hear some health rules.

Liz: That's right. You should always ask your doctor, that's the bottom line because everybody's health goals and health circumstances are different.

Host: People say if you want to lose weight and get in better shape you must do a vigorous cardio workout—not true for everybody.

Liz: Right. If you work out too hard or tire too quickly, you are not going to be able to make a dent in your weight loss.

Host: So in other words, for those people, a moderate workout is much more beneficial than a high-intensity workout.

Liz: Right. You should set a pace that you can maintain for about 30 to 40 minutes easily without gasping for breath.

Host: Here's one you hear all the time, that swimming is an ideal low-impact exercise for all people.

Liz: Yeah. It's a wonderful low-impact exercise but not for somebody with asthma. Many studies have shown that the chlorine in the pool can actually trigger an asthma attack.

Host: So for people with asthma, what would be a more appropriate low-impact workout?

Liz: Low-impact workout? Cycling or walking 'cause you can do it anywhere; you can still burn up to about 170 calories.

Host: We've all heard the advice: drink eight glasses of water a day for better health. But those tried-and-true rules may not be good for everyone. Most of us get all the liquids we need in fruit, drinks and even soft drinks. But there are also some people who just shouldn't have a lot of water.

Liz: Right, it depends on your body type and body size. 20 percent of the fluids that we need we get from the foods we eat—all foods contain some water. An easy rule of thumb is to check the color of your urine. It should be the color of straw; if it's amber you are likely dehydrated. So you can monitor your own intake.

Host: All right, next one. Getting your nutrients from whole foods as opposed to pills or supplements. Why is that not appropriate for all people?

Liz: Well, it doesn't apply if you have a food allergy, or for some reason you are not drinking milk or eating eggs. In this case you may be low in vitamin B12 which is important for energy, and vitamin D which is important for bone health. Some recent studies have also shown that it can lower your risk of breast and colon cancer.

Host: All right, this next one sounds like common sense: Low blood pressure is better than high blood pressure.

Liz: And it is, except if you have coronary artery disease. You should aim for about 120 over 80 which will lower your risk of a heart attack or stroke. But if you have coronary artery disease, make sure the lower number doesn't go under 70 as it can double your risk of a heart attack.

Host: All right, that's great. Again, one size doesn't fit all. Make sure you check with your own doctor and find out what is best for you. Liz, thank you very much.

Part II Vitamin D

A—B

Vitamin D helps bones and muscles grow strong and healthy. Low levels of vitamin D can lead to problems such as rickets, a deformity mainly found in children. Osteoporosis, the thinning of bone, is a common problem as people, especially women, get older. But more and more research is suggesting that vitamin D might also help prevent many diseases.

The easiest way to get vitamin D is from sunlight. The sun's ultraviolet rays react with skin cells to produce vitamin D. But many people worry about getting skin cancer and skin damage from the sun. As a result they cover their skin, wear sunblock, or simply stay out of the sun.

Also, darker skinned people produce less vitamin D than lighter skinned people. Production also decreases in older people and those living in northern areas that get less sunlight.

Not many foods naturally contain vitamin D. Foods high in this vitamin include oily fish such as salmon, tuna and mackerel, and fish liver oils.

Boston University researchers reported last year that farmed salmon had only about one-fourth as much vitamin D as wild salmon.

Small amounts of vitamin D are found in beef liver, cheese and egg yolks. Some people take dietary supplements containing the vitamin, but most of the vitamin D in the American diet comes from foods that are D-added, like milk.

In 1997, the United States' Institute of Medicine established levels for how much vitamin D healthy people need. It set the daily amount at two hundred international units from birth through age fifty. It set the level at four hundred I.U.s through age seventy, and six hundred for age seventy-one and over.

But some groups say these amounts are not high enough. They are hoping that the new research findings will lead to new recommendations.

Research in the last several years has shown that low levels of vitamin D may increase the risk of heart attacks in men and deaths from some cancers. Other studies have shown that people with rheumatic diseases often have low levels of vitamin D.

More doctors are now having their patients tested for vitamin D levels. But as research continues, some experts worry that if people take too much vitamin D, it might act as a poison. Also, skin doctors warn people to be careful with sun exposure because of the risk of skin cancer.

Part III Health Issues for College Students

What health issues do North America's 15 million college students face? Here's what college and university health and medical professionals think:

Sexual health. More than any others, sexual issues have the potential to affect the health of college students. These include sexually transmitted diseases (7% to 10% of college students carry an undiagnosed STD), unintended pregnancies, and sexual assault, especially acquaintance or date rape.

Sexuality is also related to issues of self-esteem, peer acceptance, loneliness, and relieving academic stress with superficial sexual relationships. All of these issues have the potential to produce psychological harm and establish negative attitudes and behavior that may impair future sexual and intimate relationships.

Substance abuse. The abuse of alcohol, drugs, tobacco, and food is related to trying to gain peer acceptance, trying to cope with psychological distress, and unhealthy role modeling in families and in society at large. Students whose parents abuse substances often have a tendency for substance abuse. Alcohol abuse is related to the majority of sexual assaults, unintended pregnancies (from not using contraceptives properly or at all), and the transmission of STDs (from not practicing safe sex).

Mental health. Failure to achieve, academic stress, lack of social support, difficulty adjusting to young adulthood, and pressures to fit in socially all contribute to emotional problems (especially anxiety and depression) that may impair a student's academic performance and sense of well-being. They can also lead to stress-related physical illnesses. Competitive academic environments can create feelings of inferiority, insecurity and emotional distress.

Food and weight. Many students are highly concerned about their body size and shape and may become malnourished to meet their perceptions of social ideality. Eating disorders, such as bulimia and anorexia, affect a large number of students.

Health care. A large proportion of college students in the United States have limited access to health care because their colleges do not have comprehensive services for students or they do not have private health insurance.

Accidents and injuries. Many students are susceptible to automobile accidents (often alcohol-related) and sports injuries.

Part V News

A

84-year-old President Mugabe made it clear at a rally Tuesday that he won't refuse to negotiate with the opposition party, The Movement for Democratic Change, though he was still determined to hold the poll on Friday. He emphasized that "there is only one thing for us to accomplish... it's the legal process on the 27th of June."

The MDC on Tuesday handed a letter to the electoral commission formally withdrawing from the presidential run-off. Tsvangirai said the election was rigged and his supporters were facing too much violence for him to keep running. He won the first round of voting on March 29th, but lacked an outright majority against Mr. Mugabe.

Observers are worried that the violence will continue to spiral out of control. One ominous sign is the withdrawal of independent monitors who would be able to observe and protect voters at the polls.

As of Tuesday, 38 organizations say they have withdrawn after the Zimbabwe Election Support Network, or ZESN, said only 500 observers were able to get accreditation. There were more than 9000 observers allowed to monitor the election on March 29th.

B

The U.N. Security Council on Monday formally nominated South Korean Foreign Minister Ban Ki-Moon to succeed Kofi Annan as U.N. secretary-general.

Ban, 62, topped four informal polls in the council, and in the last one he was the only candidate not to get a veto by one of its five permanent members. After that result, the other five candidates dropped out of the race.

Under the U.N. Charter, the 15-member Security Council makes a recommendation for the next secretary-general to the 192-member General Assembly, which must give final approval. Ban will be the only name on the ballot.

The 192-member U.N. General Assembly is expected to endorse Ban later this month as the eighth secretary-general of the United Nations since 1946, replacing Kofi Annan of Ghana who ends 10 years in office on December 31st.

C

BEIJING (Reuters)—China has welcomed the election of a new leader for Taiwan's main opposition party who rules out independence for the island.

A day after the Nationalist Party chose Taipei mayor Ma Ying-jeou as its new chairman, Chinese President Hu Jintao said he looked forward to the Chinese Communist Party (CCP) and the Nationalists promoting links between the island and the mainland.

The Nationalist Party (KMT) favors closer relations across the Taiwan Strait, in contrast to the pro-independence stance of Chen Shui-bian's Democratic Progressive Party.

The KMT once ruled all of China before losing a civil war to Mao Zedong's Communists and fled to Taiwan in 1949.

Ma himself has closer connections with the mainland than many other Taiwan people. His father is a native of China's southern province of Hunan.

"I sincerely hope that the KMT and the CCP, together with compatriots on both sides of the Taiwan Strait, will continue to promote the peaceful and steady development of cross-Strait relations, and join hands to create a bright future for the Chinese nation," Hu said in a message to Ma and the KMT.

Unit 12 Memories

Part I Dialogue

B—C

T—Tim Williams (host)   A—Antonio Todeschini   L—Lussina Liu

T: Hello and welcome to "The Olympics Forum". Joining us to talk about the Olympics today are Antonio Todeschini, who has studied the history of the Olympic Games for 10 years, and Lussina Liu, an athlete who has won 5 medals in the Olympics. Nice to see you two today.

A&L: Nice to see you.

T: With the opening of the Beijing Olympics, the whole world's attention has been drawn to the Olympics again. I have to say the opening ceremony was really amazing.

A: Yes, it was a representation of the arts and a powerful display of the Chinese people. It was the most amazing thing I have seen in terms of technology and human performance.

L: Right. The 29 footprints, the countdown, the performers... It was really impressive.

T: Lussina, I know you've competed in the Olympics twice. As a rule, the most memorable moment is the opening ceremony and the lighting of the Olympic flame. What do you think is the most memorable part of an opening ceremony?

L: There are so many unforgettable moments. Each time the ceremonies are different but I think the most exciting part is when the flame is lit. I'll always remember when the ailing Muhammad Ali ignited the flame with his trembling hands at the 1996 Atlanta

Games. Just as impressive was when Cathy Freeman was enclosed in a splash of water and fire when she approached the torch to light it in Sydney four years later.

T: The opening ceremonies always set some kind of world record. No event of the Olympic Games has so many TV viewers than the opening ceremonies. There have been increasingly more viewers watching the Olympics. 3.9 billion people had access to the coverage of the Athens 2004 Games, compared with 3.6 billion for Sydney in 2000. Why does the Movement continue to flourish?

A: Well, just as American sportscaster Jim McKay once said, the Olympic Games are the largest peacetime gathering of humanity in the history of the world. There is no other time or place in which 200 or more nations of the world meet together peacefully, and co-exist, sharing great joys and often great sorrows. Young men and women, who seemingly have nothing in common except sport, are allowed to meet each other and often realize that they are far more alike than they are different.

D

T: Lussina, what's your take on it?

L: As a sportswoman, taking part in the Olympics as well as the World Championships is a treasure. The difference is, an athlete can become world champion each year, but the Olympic Games take place only every four years. As you know, the prize of an Olympic medal is the first and foremost goal of an athlete. I'm sure many multiple world champions who did not succeed at the Olympic Games would exchange their titles for an Olympic gold medal if given the chance. The tennis player Michael Stich once said that he is an Olympic victor for his whole life.

T: There are two Olympic mottos that reflect just how powerful the Olympics can be. The first one, "Taking part is everything": More than two-thirds of the more than 10,000 athletes know that they will probably not win a medal, and one-third know that they will drop out in the preliminaries. Nevertheless, they participate, having trained a lot for "only" taking part. The second motto, "All games, all nations": Every nation of the world wants to become recognised and wants to send athletes to the Games. So Antonio, what do you think is the greatest strength of the Games?

A: I think the greatest strength of the Olympic Games is that it brings together all the peoples of the world, especially the world's youth, and allows them to interact and compete against each other peacefully for two full weeks. During that time, the greatest athletes of the world strut their stuff on the world's greatest stage. We always remember the superb athletic feats, but oft-times, the strongest memories are of the friendly interactions between peoples of varying races, faiths, and creeds. This is something that is seen almost no other time except during international sporting events, and the Olympic Games are the prototype and the epitome of that ideal.

L: Absolutely. In my first Games, the experience was quite special. We lived in the

Olympic Village as one big family for the first time. We talked to athletes from different countries participating in different sports, including footballers, swimmers and boxers. And in the evenings we would sing and dance in the club. Even though the workload was demanding, the youth took the upper hand during those evenings.

T: That's really an ideal state when people from different regions can co-exist peacefully. The International Olympic Committee did do a lot to achieve it.

A: Right. There are many different moments which are significant in Olympic history but there is one historic decision that I would like to highlight. In 1956, a boy of Chinese origin by the name of John Ian Wing, who lived in Chinatown in Melbourne, proposed to the Organising Committee for the 1956 Melbourne Games to change the structure of the closing ceremony. Instead of having the competitors parade into the stadium as nations, like during the opening ceremony, he proposed to have them walk into the stadium as one Olympic family, symbolising the solidarity of the athletes, without looking at race, colour or creed. This symbolic change in the Olympic protocol has since been adopted and, in my opinion, is one of the most significant moments in Olympic history.

T: We will see that harmonious scene again in this year's Olympics. That's all for today's programme. I'm Tim Williams. Thanks for watching.

Part II Sporting Memory—Jordan Hits "The Shot"

Some things leave an indelible impression, for instance, when man first walked on the moon. People remember exactly where they were and what they were doing when it occurred. The same is true with the NBA playoffs; the memories linger for years, even decades. One in particular has older fans still talking about it as if it just happened, while the younger ones wished they were born to see it.

It is known, in Chicago and especially in Cleveland, as "The Shot". It was replayed on television hundreds of times to the agony of Cleveland fans and the ecstasy of Bulls supporters. It was only one basket, yet it played an integral role in the fortunes of not one but two NBA franchises.

The Cleveland Cavaliers were one of the NBA's best young teams in the late 1980s, with a nucleus that included Brad Daugherty, Mark Price, Ron Harper, Larry Nance and John "Hot Rod" Williams. Under the guidance of coach Lenny Wilkens, the Cavs improved by 15 games to a franchise-best 57–25 record in the 1988–89 regular season, and appeared poised to challenge for the NBA title.

In their way stood the Chicago Bulls, a young team led by Michael Jordan that was just beginning to mesh into the unit that would dominate the NBA in the 1990s. The Bulls had finished fifth in the powerful Central Division with a 47–35 record, but they had beaten the Cavs in a five-game playoff series the year before and were matched up against Cleveland once again.

Chicago stole the home-court advantage in the best-of-5 series by winning the opener 95–88 and could have closed out the set at home, but Cleveland rallied for a 108–105 overtime win in Game 4 to set up a deciding game in Cleveland.

It came down to the closing seconds, and as he would so many times in his career, Jordan had the ball with the game on the line. Starting from the right side, Jordan dribbled toward the key and rose up for a jumper from inside the circle. Craig Ehlo, one of Cleveland's top defenders, leaped out to block the shot, but Jordan seemed to hang in the air until Ehlo was out of his way, and then released his shot. As the ball nestled through the net, Jordan pumped his fists in jubilation, completing a video highlight for the ages.

Two years later, the Bulls won the first of five NBA titles they would win from 1991 through 1997. Cleveland, meanwhile, has yet to reach the NBA Finals.

The lasting image of Jordan's leap into the air, his wild and emphatic celebration, his fist pumping and his shouting at the visiting crowd, all while Ehlo fell to the floor in defeat and agony a short distance away, has become part of many fans' recollection of The Shot. This scene will undoubtedly be remembered by basketball fans for many years to come.

Part III Five Ways to Improve Your Memory

C—E

Have you ever considered the benefits of having a good memory?

Being able to remember important pieces of information like names, facts and figures, directions, procedures, quotations, etc. can give you a powerful advantage in life. In fact, the ability to retain and retrieve information is essential to your personal and professional success. Here are five ways to boost your memory and keep it razor-sharp.

1. Use Your Imagination

An easy way to remember something is to "take a picture". For example, to remember where you've left your car keys, pretend to hold a camera to your eyes, focus on the scene, and click the image into your memory when you are leaving. Then, when you want to find your keys again, try to develop the negative film and you'll be able to draw out a clear picture. This technique works with almost everything you want to remember, as the film reel in your mind is endless.

2. Practice

You can boost your memory with just a little regular practice. There are lots of ways of doing this:

Try to remember which day of the week your last birthday was on. Then extend this to the birthdays of all your family members.

Try to remember all the Grand Slam finalists and who the winner was. If you can try to remember the scores as well, it would be an even better exercise.

Try to remember names of all the 50 states and see if you can do it in alphabetical order too.

It won't be long before your daily practice pays off—making your mind sharper and more adaptable.

3. Eat Healthy

The best way to protect your memory is to eat plenty of antioxidants and nutrients commonly found in fruits and vegetables.

In a study published by the *American Journal of Clinical Nutrition*, researchers tested people between the ages of 65 and 90 and discovered that the people with the best ability to memorize words were those whose diets included the most fruits and vegetables. Coincidentally, the same group of people ate the least artery-clogging saturated fat. Of all the fruits and vegetables studied, blueberries and blackberries contain the most potent antioxidants.

4. Do Physical Exercise

Physical exercise not only boosts memory but also helps you think faster. A combination of mental and physical activities can protect your memory and help keep you alert.

The brain's processing speed gradually slows as you age. Between the ages of 25 and 55, many people begin to experience the problem of recalling names or numbers. The memory is there, but it just takes longer to retrieve it.

Staying physically fit can ward off some of the effects of aging on the brain. In real life, that could mean coming up with a forgotten name more quickly or jumping out of danger in the face of an oncoming car.

5. Exercise Your Brain

Mental gymnastics are just as important as physical ones in preserving brainpower.

Take up word games like crossword puzzles and acrostics. Memorize favorite poems, read challenging books or articles that encourage you to expand your interests.

Practice using your non-dominant side. If you're right-handed, try brushing your teeth or writing your grocery list with your left hand.

Any activity that requires you to think and concentrate—from keeping a journal or learning a new language to taking music lessons—will challenge your brain.

And your brain will thrive on the challenge.

Part V News

(BEIJING, July 17)—The Chinese delegation to the Beijing 2008 Paralympic Games hosted a press conference on Thursday, revealing that a total of 547 representatives will be part of the group, which includes 332 athletes who will be competing in all 20 events.

197 men and 135 women will make up the competitive team, the largest in Chinese history. The oldest athlete is 51 years old and the youngest is 15 years old. Compared to the Athens Paralympic Games, the Chinese delegation this time around has increased by 261 people, which includes 132 more athletes than in 2004. The athletes come from all walks of life from all over the country: students, farmers, self-employed individuals and workers will be representing China in September. For 226 of these athletes, 2008 will be their Olympic debut year.

For the first time in the Paralympic Games, equestrian, wheelchair rugby, wheelchair basketball, rowing, sailing, boccia, goalball, football 5-a-side and football 7-a-side events will be held.

B

After eight days of top-level international competition in Bordeaux, France, the 2007 UCI Paracycling World Championships came to an end. The Championships, organized by the International Cycling Union (UCI) and the Handisport French Federation (FFH), saw some of the world's best cyclists take on the challenge of arduous track and road races.

A total of 400 athletes, many of whom will be competing at the 2008 Paralympic Games in Beijing, battled it out for World Champion titles. Australia topped the medal tally with 27, closely followed by Germany with 25 and Spain with 21 medals.

Races in the different sport classes were strongly contested with millisecond differences between first, second and third place.

This was the first World Championships to be held under the auspices of the UCI, after transfer of governance from the International Paralympic Committee took place in 2006.

C

On July 22, the 2006 IPC Shooting World Championships came to a close in Sargans, Switzerland. At the completion of the Championships, China came away as leaders of the medal tally with six gold medals, five silvers and one bronze. They were closely followed by Russia who captured six gold, four silver and two bronze medals.

In the final days of competition, individual world records were set by Andrey Lebendinsky (RUS, P3) and Jonas Jacobsson (SWE, R7). Three more team records were also set by Korea (P1 and R7) and Russia (P3). This made a total of six individual and seven team world records broken at the Championships.

The Championships received positive reports from athletes, staff and IPC representatives, who were particularly impressed by the use of state-of-the-art technology and equipment in the competition venues.

Two representatives from the organizing committee for the Beijing 2008 Olympic and Paralympic Games were also present, observing the Championships to assist them with preparations for the Beijing 2008 Paralympics.